MAKING THE CLASSICS IN JUDAISM
The Three Stages of Literary Formation

Program in Judaic Studies
Brown University
BROWN JUDAIC STUDIES
Edited by
Jacob Neusner
Wendell S. Dietrich, Ernest S. Frerichs, William Scott Green,
Calvin Goldscheider, David Hirsch, Alan Zuckerman

Project Editors (Projects)

David Blumenthal, Emory University (Approaches to Medieval Judaism)
William Brinner (Studies in Judaism and Islam)
Ernest S. Frerichs, Brown University (Dissertations and Monographs)
Lenn Evan Goodman, University of Hawaii (Studies in Medieval Judaism)
'illiam Scott Green, University of Rochester (Approaches to Ancient Judaism)
Norbert Samuelson, Temple University, (Jewish Philosophy)
Jonathan Z. Smith, University of Chicago (Studia Philonica)

Number 180
MAKING THE CLASSICS IN JUDAISM
The Three Stages of Literary Formation

by
Jacob Neusner

MAKING THE CLASSICS IN JUDAISM

The Three Stages of Literary Formation

by

Jacob Neusner

Scholars Press
Atlanta, Georgia

MAKING THE CLASSICS IN JUDAISM
The Three Stages of Literary Formation

Library of Congress Cataloging in Publication Data

Neusner, Jacob, 1932-
  Making the classics in Judaism : the three stages of literary
formation / by Jacob Neusner.
    p. cm. -- (Brown Judaic studies ; no. 180)
  Includes index.
  ISBN 1-55540-377-8
  1. Rabbinical literature--History and criticism--Theory, etc.
2. Halakhic Midrashim--History and criticism--Theory, etc.
3. Midrash rabbah--Criticism, Redaction. I. Title. II. Series.
BM496.5.N4814 1989
296.1'2066--dc20   89-35719
                                                       CIP

Printed in the United States of America
on acid-free paper

In memory of

Pearl Elman

neé Kagan

Born in Shpola 1910

Died in New York 1989

A tribute to her through her son,
who is also my friend, teacher, disciple,
and, as to Tosefta, heir
Rabbi and Doctor Yaakov Elman

Her children bless her memory
through their work in Torah

Table of Contents

Preface

A research report on an experiment in method, this book runs parallel to *The Philosophical Mishnah* (Atlanta, 1989: Scholars Press for Brown Judaic Studies) I-IV, and so forms a further chapter in an on-going intellectual experiment in the analysis of the paramount traits of classics of Judaism. As a working paper, the book therefore reports an experiment that, I am confident, others may replicate with the same results and also with no other results but these. It seems to me that only when a variety of investigators working on their own reach the same conclusions – and when they do so only after undertaking the work, not merely passing their opinions or ignoring the work of others – we shall frame a viable hypothesis for more substantive and detailed results in the literary history of formative Judaism. Then, when the work proceeds apace, we shall have a clearer conception of the literary history of the several documents of the canon of the Judaism of the Dual Torah than is presently in mind. Accordingly, the introduction spells out the issues, method, and program of inquiry. This book consists of sizable reviews of arguments set forth in a primitive context of thought (Chapters Two, Three, and Four), on the one side, and long samples of sources meant to exemplify taxic processes, on the other (Chapters Five, Six, Seven). It is therefore a rethinking of ideas I originally framed in a more limited setting, together with a research report.

Prior writings of mine that form the foundation of this book are of two kinds. First, I have described as autonomous documents all of the components of the canon of Judaism in late antiquity. Each description then permits us to identify the purposes and traits of form and intellect of the authorship of that document. Second, I have compared document to document and so proven that documents possess integrity and are not merely scrapbooks, compilations made with no clear purpose or aesthetic plan. The earlier books of mine that describe documents in their own terms are these:

The Tosefta: Its Structure and its Sources. Atlanta, 1986: Scholars Press for Brown Judaic Studies.

Form Analysis and Exegesis: A Fresh Approach to the Interpretation of Mishnah. Minneapolis, 1980: University of Minnesota Press.

Torah from Our Sages: Pirke Avot. A New American Translation and Explanation. Chappaqua, 1983: Rossel. Paperback edition: 1987.

Pesiqta deRab Kahana. An Analytical Translation and Explanation. II. *15-28. With an Introduction to Pesiqta deRab Kahana.* Atlanta, 1987: Scholars Press for Brown Judaic Studies.

Sifré to Deuteronomy. An Introduction to the Rhetorical, Logical, and Topical Program. Atlanta, 1987: Scholars Press for Brown Judaic Studies.

Sifra in Perspective: The Documentary Comparison of the Midrashim of Ancient Judaism Atlanta, 1988: Scholars Press for Brown Judaic Studies.

Mekhilta Attributed to R. Ishmael. An Introduction to Judaism's First Scriptural Encyclopaedia. Atlanta, 1988: Scholars Press for Brown Judaic Studies.

A History of the Mishnaic Law of Purities. Leiden, 1977: Brill. XXI. *The Redaction and Formulation of the Order of Purities in the Mishnah and Tosefta.*

A History of the Mishnaic Law of Purities. Leiden, 1977: Brill. XXII. *The Mishnaic System of Uncleanness. Its Context and History.*

A History of the Mishnaic Law of Holy Things. Leiden, 1979: Brill. VI. *The Mishnaic System of Sacrifice and Sanctuary.*

A History of the Mishnaic Law of Women. Leiden, 1980: Brill. V. *The Mishnaic System of Women.*

A History of the Mishnaic Law of Appointed Times. Leiden, 1981: Brill. V. *The Mishnaic System of Appointed Times.*

A History of the Mishnaic Law of Damages. Leiden, 1985: Brill. V. *The Mishnaic System of Damages.*

The Talmud of the Land of Israel. A Preliminary Translation and Explanation. Chicago: University of Chicago Press: 1983. XXXV. *Introduction. Taxonomy.*

Judaism. The Evidence of the Mishnah. Chicago, 1981: University of Chicago Press. Second edition, augmented: Atlanta, 1987: Scholars Press for Brown Judaic Studies.

Judaism in Society: The Evidence of the Yerushalmi. Toward the Natural History of a Religion. Chicago, 1983: University of Chicago Press.

Judaism and Scripture: The Evidence of Leviticus Rabbah. Chicago, 1986: University of Chicago Press. *Judaism: The Classical Statement. The Evidence of the Bavli.* Chicago, 1986: University of Chicago Press. *Choice,* "Outstanding Academic Book List, 1987."

Judaism and Story: The Evidence of The Fathers According to Rabbi Nathan. Chicago, 1990: University of Chicago Press.

Editor: *The Formation of the Babylonian Talmud. Studies on the Achievements of Late Nineteenth and Twentieth Century Historical and Literary-Critical Research.* Leiden, 1970: Brill.

Editor: *The Modern Study of the Mishnah.* Leiden, 1973: Brill.

The books of mine that compare one document to another and therefore demonstrate that each of the documents possesses its own textual integrity are these:

The Integrity of Leviticus Rabbah. The Problem of the Autonomy of a Rabbinic Document. Chico, 1985: Scholars Press for Brown Judaic Studies.

Comparative Midrash: The Plan and Program of Genesis Rabbah and Leviticus Rabbah. Atlanta, 1986: Scholars Press for Brown Judaic Studies.

From Tradition to Imitation. The Plan and Program of Pesiqta deRab Kahana and Pesiqta Rabbati. Atlanta, 1987: Scholars Press for Brown Judaic Studies. [With a fresh translation of Pesiqta Rabbati Pisqaot 1-5, 15.]

Canon and Connection: Intertextuality in Judaism. Lanham, 1986: University Press of America. *Studies in Judaism* Series.

Midrash as Literature: The Primacy of Documentary Discourse. Lanham, 1987: University Press of America. *Studies in Judaism* Series.

The Bavli and its Sources: The Question of Tradition in the Case of Tractate Sukkah. Atlanta, 1987: Scholars Press for Brown Judaic Studies.

Writing with Scripture: The Authority and Uses of the Hebrew Bible in the Torah of Formative Judaism. Philadelphia, 1989: Fortress Press.

The Formation of the Jewish Intellect. Making Connections and Drawing Conclusions in the Traditional System of Judaism. Atlanta, 1988: Scholars Press for Brown Judaic Studies.

The Making of the Mind of Judaism. Atlanta, 1987: Scholars Press for Brown Judaic Studies.

From Mishnah to Scripture. The Problem of the Unattributed Saying. Chico, 1984: Scholars Press for Brown Judaic Studies. Reprise and reworking of materials in *A History of the Mishnaic Law of Purities.*

The Peripatetic Saying: The Problem of the Thrice-Told Tale in Talmudic Literature. Chico, 1985: Scholars Press for Brown Judaic Studies.

The Memorized Torah. The Mnemonic System of the Mishnah. Chico, 1985: Scholars Press for Brown Judaic Studies.

Oral Tradition in Judaism: The Case of the Mishnah. New York, 1987: Garland Publishing. *Albert Bates Lord Monograph Series* of the journal, *Oral Tradition.*

Why No Gospels in Talmudic Judaism? Atlanta, 1988: Scholars Press for Brown Judaic Studies.

Formative Judaism. Religious, Historical, and Literary Studies. Fourth Series. Problems of Classification and Composition. Chico, 1984: Scholars Press for Brown Judaic Studies.

Formative Judaism. Religious, Historical, and Literary Studies. Fifth Series. Revising the Written Records of a Nascent Religion. Chico, 1985: Scholars Press for Brown Judaic Studies.

JACOB NEUSNER

September 1, 1989

The Institute for Advanced Study
Princeton, New Jersey

Introduction

Two questions in the framing of a theory of the history of the anonymous literature of formative Judaism form the program of this book. The first is, what is the correct starting point of analysis of a document and its formative history? The second is, what are the principal results of starting from that designated point of entry? Part One addresses the two possibilities for starting the analysis of a given document: the document as a whole or the smallest whole units of thought, treated autonomous of documentary location? In Part One I test the hypothesis that the discrete sayings (lemmas) form the correct point of entry and show, through the formation and testing of a null hypothesis, that that hypothesis is false.[1] We cannot begin work in the assumption that the building block of documents is the smallest whole unit of thought, the lemma, nor can we proceed in the premise that a lemma traverses the boundaries of various documents and is unaffected by the journey. The opposite premise is that we start our work with the traits of documents as a whole, rather than with the traits of the lemmas of which documents are (supposedly) composed.

Since, in a variety of books, particularly *From Tradition to Imitation. The Plan and Program of Pesiqta deRab Kahana and Pesiqta Rabbati, Canon and Connection: Intertextuality in Judaism, Midrash as Literature: The Primacy of Documentary Discourse,* and *The Bavli and its Sources: The Question of Tradition in the Case of Tractate Sukkah,* as well as *The Talmud of the Land of Israel. 35. Introduction. Taxonomy,* and *Judaism. The Classic Statement. The Evidence of the Bavli,* I have set forth the documentary hypothesis for the analysis of the rabbinic literature of late antiquity, I proceed immediately to the exploration of the second of the two possibilities in Part Two. How

---

[1]As a matter of fact, the identification of the lemma as the primary unit of inquiry rests upon the premise that the person to whom a saying is assigned really said that saying. That premise is untenable. But for the sake of argument, I bypass that still more fundamental flaw in the methodology at hand.

shall we proceed, if we take as our point of entry the character and conditions of the document, seen whole? And what are the results of doing so? Part Two shows the first steps dictated by the entry into documents as a whole. That same part provides rich exemplary materials on the workings of the taxonomic hypothesis yielded by the documentary point of entry. That, sum and substance, is the program of this book.

The upshot is not uninteresting. Once I have demonstrated beyond any doubt that a rabbinic text is a document, a well-crafted text and not merely a compilation of this and that, and further specified in acute detail precisely the aesthetic, formal, and logical program followed by each of those texts, I am able to move to the logical next step, which is to show that in the background of the documents we have is writing shaped not by documentary requirements, writing that is not shaped by the documentary requirements of the compilations we now have, and also writing that is entirely formed within the rules of the documents that now present that writing. These then are the three kinds of writing that form, also, the three stages in the formation of the classics of Judaism. As work proceeds, we may form a plausible theory of how some writings were formed independent of the plan of using them in a given compilation, while other writings were formed in response to the program of the authorship of a given compilation.

Then we shall have a firm grasp of the requirements of a theory to explain the characteristics and even origin of those floating materials that progress from one document to another – some bearing names of authorities, some anonymous – and we shall come to grips with the corpus of writings autonomous of all documents and conceivably prior to them all. These – and as a matter of fact, by definition! – will guide us to that prior ("a priori") system that underlay all of the discrete documents of the canon of the Judaism of the Dual Torah. But this speculation, moving from literary history to theological history, lies somewhat beyond the limits of a research report.

What is at stake in this work? The answer is simple. We have at present no theory of the formation of the various documents of the rabbinic literature that derives from an inductive sifting of the evidence. Nor do we have even a theory as to the correct method for the framing of a hypothesis for testing against the evidence. In this book I set forth the fundamental alternatives on how we may approach the history of the making of classics in Judaism. On the basis of the methodological hypothesis proposed at the beginning, I lay out data to test the hypothesis that seems to me best to account for the evidence examined in a very preliminary and primitive probe. Much more work, of course, remains to be done even for the framing of a viable hypothesis, let alone a theory that sets forth what I conceive to be the three stages of literary formation in the making of those classics. But when others test the methods and attempt to replicate the results offered here, I am confident they will attain success. In consequence, the history of the making of the rabbinic documents as we have them and also of the forming of the materials that are assembled in them will in due course become increasingly evident.

Even though, therefore, the issue is a very simple one – what we must select as the starting point for research and how we shall identify the pertinent data – the sakes are considerable. When we ask, Is the beginning point the finished document? Or should we commence analysis with the smallest components of the document? we in fact dictate the kind of information we seek to test the kind of hypotheses – documentary and encompassing, episodic and discrete – that we frame. I advocate starting with the completed document and works backward and inward. The other position – here exemplified by a principal exponent in U.S. debate – starts with the smallest whole units of thought, which are discrete and free-standing sentences, and works forward and outward. There is no compromise between these two positions on the fundamental point of departure for all literary research. And once a decision has been reached on where and how to start, all else is determined.

I insist that we begin with what we have and work back from that point, in the manner of peeling an onion or an artichoke, I owe it to readers to present my views of the opposed approach. That is the one that starts not with the documents but with the individual sentences, or at most paragraphs, of which those documents are composed. It is best represented in our generation by David Weiss Halivni, and that accounts for my including a sustained representation of a null hypothesis, meant to test his method of beginning with discrete sentences. I believe I have – alas – demonstrated that the null hypothesis is valid, and his approach therefore wrong.

Accordingly, Chapter Two attends to the approach that is diametrically opposed to mine, the one that begins with individual lemmas and ignores all questions of form and redaction. I take as the representative figure of that approach in our own day the work of David Weiss Halivni, and here reproduce my test of his results and demonstration that his results are not only not to be replicated but in fact wrong. When we compose a null hypothesis to test his approach, we find that the null hypothesis is correct, and, it must follow, Halivni's entry into the problem is precisely the opposite of the right one, which I have defined and which in these pages I explore still further. Halivni, like others in his school, completely ignores the

work of all other scholars,[2] but that does not free us from the obligation
to adhere to the normal canons of scholarship in the academy. That is
why I have read his work with care, both on my own and in successive
seminars, and now contrast my approach to the history of the rabbinic
literature with the approach outlined in his exegetical writings.

After Chapter Two, Chapters Three and Four contribute to the
formation of a theory of method that accords with the point of entry
advocated by me – starting at the outside of the document and working
our way in. Here I explain the distinctions that seem to me important
and also objective and accessible of evidentiary testing and
demonstration. Then Chapters Five, Six, and Seven turn to the
detailed development of a hypothesis on the classification of the
writing in the classics of Judaism. That hypothesis rests upon a
taxonomic theory, which I set forth through a sustained
exemplification of precisely what I mean. Then Chapter Eight
broadens the discussion to set forth a theory of literary history that
derives from that classification.

This book therefore carries forward, upon a much expanded front, a
line of questioning on why we have what we have and do not have
what we do not have that I began in *Why No Gospels in Talmudic
Judaism?* (Atlanta, 1988: Scholars Press for Brown Judaic Studies).[3] In
Why No Gospels in Talmudic Judaism? I pointed out that while we
have ample raw materials for the writing of gospels – sustained and
well-composed accounts of the lives of holy men and their teachings
and wonders – in fact in the canon of Judaism we have no such books as
lives of saints or gospels. The stories were told, but not then compiled
into books; they were preserved in compilations to the purposes of the
redactors or compilers of which they were simply irrelevant. I further
claimed to explain why there were stories about sages but no gospels of
sages. What this means is that there is no clear relationship between
the writing of the stories and the formation of the classics. The two

---

[2]Or, as in his *Midrash, Mishnah, and Gemara. The Jewish Predilection for
Justified Law* (Cambridge, 1986: Harvard University Press), he alludes to other
peoples' results without actually reckoning with them in the composition of his
own, which is worse since it is deceiving. In fact he has understood nothing of
the critical program of the present century, and his work in literary history and
history of religion (Judaism) is essentially idiosyncratic and fabricated. He
simply is not engaged in discourse with academic learning. In his defense I
have to say that his act of *Todschweigen* committed against nearly all other
scholars who have worked on the same questions and texts is perfectly routine
and regarded as ethical in Jewish studies; he in no way diverges from the norm
of his academic subject.

[3]Chapter Four reviews the problem and thesis of that book.

processes – framing completed units of thought, collecting and organizing into documents completed units of thought – went on essentially in isolation from one another.

That same distinction between the writing of materials in response to a redactional program and the writing of materials autonomous of all redactional stimulus generates Chapters Five, Six, and Seven. In these chapters, in rich exemplary detail, I show how some writings were made for documents we now have, the very documents in which they occur; some writings were made for documents we do not have but can readily envisage; and some writings fall outside of all known or imaginable redactional requirements. This third kind of writing corresponds to the biographical materials that never yielded gospels or lives of holy men, such as, in *Why No Gospels?* I have analyzed. In Chapters Six and Seven, therefore, I point out that the canonical writings of Judaism contain materials that can have yielded other kinds of compilations than the ones we now have. Through ample instances I demonstrate what some of these other kinds of writings should have contained.

Then I make the distinction between writings we can, on the basis of the documents we have, readily imagine people to have written (Chapter Six), and those that lie beyond the imaginative powers of our canonical authors (Chapter Seven). I spell out the criterion for what can, and cannot, be imagined, since – so I insist – the judgment is utterly objective and derives from the evidence in our hand. In Chapters Six and Seven, therefore, the question broadens beyond why no gospels (or: why no treatises of philology or theology, such as can have been compiled out of materials now collected in rabbinic books). It is now, precisely how did the sages of Judaism go about making the classics in Judaism? Specifically, I claim to discern three types of literary formation, which, for the moment, I call "three stages." But these are merely classifications of writing, and "stages" should not be endowed with a heavy burden of temporal significance.

In the chapters of taxic exemplification, I pursue a single question, covering a variety of midrash-compilations. At hand are all of the midrash-compilations generally assumed to have reached closure in late antiquity. In Part One, moreover, I attend to the Mishnah and the Talmud of the Land of Israel, as well as with The Fathers According to Rabbi Nathan, thirteen documents in all. I have covered nearly the whole of the classics of Judaism, excluding only the Bavli, which presents a separate set of problems, different from those deriving from all other compilations in the canonical corpus.

The generative question that underlies the whole concerns the relationship between the components of a composite document (and the classics of Judaism in important aspects all form composite documents) and the purposes of the compilers of that document. On the basis of perfectly objective traits, defined in Chapter One I propose to classify pericopes of a variety of compilations of the canon of the Judaism of the Dual Torah. Specifically, I shall show that by the criteria defined here, these fall into four classes, which yield, as to sequence of ordinal formation, three distinct classifications, that is, last, penultimate, and antepenultimate.

My contribution then is to demonstrate that a given document draws upon three classes of materials, and that these were framed in temporal order relative to their appearance in a given piece of writing. Last comes the final class that the redactors themselves defined and wrote; prior is the penultimate class that served other redactors but not these; and first of all in the order of composition (at least, from the perspective of the ultimate redaction of a document) is the antepenultimate writings, those that circulated autonomously and served no redactional purpose we can now identify. While I refer to "literary history" and speak of "the three stages of literary formation," that is only for purposes of framing a hypothesis.

There is no reason that all four types of writing described in the preface cannot have proceeded at exactly the same time. I do not base my argument on temporal order, even though I frame the hypothesis in ordinal terms. It seems at this stage in the work simpler to admit to the work of classification a theory of the order in which different classes of writing can have been carried out. That is so even though I readily concede, without argument, that there is no ineluctable connection between types of writing and the order in which these types of writing are accomplished; that is, after all, proven every day of every year of every century in the history of literature. When we recognize these classifications, we may frame a viable theory of the formation of the components of the documents of the rabbinic corpus of late antiquity. We may further begin to cope with the problem of analyzing the formation of writing that occurs in two or more documents and framing a theory on how that writing took shape and moved from one compilation to another.

Part One
THE STARTING POINT

1

Making the Classics in Judaism

I. The Starting Point

We do not now know how the various classics of the Judaism of the Dual Torah that reached closure in late antiquity, by the seventh century, took shape. The reason is that all the books are anonymous. We not only do not know who wrote or compiled them, we also do not know when any one of them reached closure. The sole evidence in hand is inductive: the characteristic traits, as to rhetoric, logic of cogent discourse, and topic, of the writings themselves. The manner in which that evidence is to be interpreted has to be carefully considered. But, short of believing that all sayings assigned to named authorities were really said by those to whom said sayings are attributed – and such an act of utter gullibility is inconceivable – we have no clear notion of the history of the canonical writings of Judaism from the Mishnah, ca. 200, through the Bavli, ca. 600. Nor do we even know where to begin the work of framing a hypothesis for rigorous testing.

But two starting points present themselves: the whole or the smallest part. That is to say, do we start from the document as a whole and examine its indicative traits? Then the reading of the parts will be in the light of the program of the whole. We shall define the norm on the base line of the whole and ask where, how, and why the parts diverge from the norm. That is the mode of comparison and contrast that will generate our hypotheses of literary history and purpose – and also, therefore our hermeneutics. The manner of analysis dictated by the entry from the outermost layer is simple. We commence our analytical inquiry from a completed document and unpeel its layers, from the ultimate one of closure and redaction, to the penultimate, and onward into the innermost formation of the smallest whole units of thought of which a document is comprised. In so doing, we treat the

9

writing as a document that has come to closure at some fixed point and through the intellection of purposeful framers or redactor. We start the analytical process by asking what those framers – that authorship – have wanted their document to accomplish and by pointing to the means by which that authorship achieved its purposes. Issues of prevailing rhetoric and logic, as well as the topical program of the whole, guide us in our definition of the document as a whole. The parts then come under study under the aspect of the whole. Knowing the intent of the framers, we ask whether, and how, materials they have used have been shaped in response to the program of the document's authorship.

The alternative point of entry is to begin with the smallest building block of any and all documents, which is the lemma or irreducible minimum of completed thought, and working upward and outward from the innermost layer of the writing. That point of entry ignores the boundaries of discrete documents and asks what we find common within and among all documents. There is the starting point, and the norm is defined by the traits of the saying or lemma as it moves from here to there. Within this theory of the history of the literature, the boundary-lines of documents do not demarcate important classifications of data; all data are uniform, wherever they occur. The stress then lies not on the differentiating traits of documents, but the points shared in common among them; these points are sayings that occur in two or more places. Literary history consists in the inquiry into the fate of sayings as they move from one place to another. The hermeneutics of course will focus upon the saying and its history rather than on the program and plan of documents that encompass, also, the discrete saying. The advantage of this approach, of course, is that it takes account of what is shared among documents, on the one side, and also of what exhibits none of the characteristic traits definitive of given documents, on the other.

II. The Issue of Method in Literary Analysis

As in all rigorous inquiry, one important methodological initiative requires the formation of a null hypothesis and the testing of that hypothesis. That is to say, can we frame the results that a given hypothesis should yield and then test those hypothetical results against the facts of a given body of data? If the correct point of entry is the individual lemma or saying, then what traits should characterize the writing in hand? That somewhat opaque framing of matters takes on concreteness when we come to the case at hand.

It involves, specifically, the theory on "sources and traditions" set forth by David Weiss Halivni in a variety of his works (cited in Chapter Two). He maintains that the indicative and definitive building block of a document is its smallest whole unit of thought or saying (lemma). That is where matters start, and that is, therefore, the point at which we should commence our analysis. As is already self-evident, I maintain the opposite. For the document defines the traits of a sizable proportion of its contents, and that means the authorship bears responsibility for the composition of much, though not all, that that authorship has compiled. Some materials, to be sure, exhibit traits of composition that in no way respond to the program of any authorship known to us (Chapter Six) or even imaginable by us[1] (Chapter Seven). But even here, the differentiating criteria *to begin with* derive from the traits of the document as a whole, and not from the character of the sayings or lemmas of which a document is – also, as a matter of fact, in a sizable proportion of the contents – comprised. Now to the matter of the null hypothesis, what it is, how it may be tested.

If Halivni were right that documents begin from "the beginning," that is, the individual sentences of which they are composed, then principles of [1] composition and [2] conglomeration would prove contradictory, so that a discourse or sustained discussion of a problem would appear jerrybuilt, episodic, rough-hewn, and ad hoc. But any analysis of whole units of discourse, as distinct from the sentences that define the arena for Halivni's analysis, shows the opposite. Analysis of any passage beginning to end demonstrates that the whole is the work of the one who decided to make up the discussion on the atemporal logic of the point at issue. Otherwise – again the null hypothesis, that would favor Halivni's position – the discussion would be not the way it is: continuous. Rather, discourse would prove disjointed, full of seams and margins, marks of the existence of prior conglomerations of materials that have now been sewn together. What we have are not patchwork quilts, but woven fabric. Along these same lines, we may find discussions in which opinions of Palestinians, such as Yohanan and Simon b. Laqish, will be joined together side by side with opinions of Babylonians, such as Rab and Samuel. The whole, once again, will unfold in a smooth way, so that the issues at hand define the sole focus of discourse. The logic of those issues will be fully exposed. Considerations of the origin of a saying in one country or the

---

[1]This obviously subjective criterion is shown to be objective and subject to replication; I explain in due course what I mean by what can, and cannot, be imagined by a systematic authorship.

other will play no role whatsoever in the rhetoric or literary forms of argument. There will be no possibility of differentiation among opinions on the basis of where, when, by whom, or how they are formulated, only on the basis of what, in fact, is said.

In my view – it hardly bears repetition by now! – it follows that the whole, the unit of discourse as we know it, was put together at the end. At that point everything was in hand, so available for arrangement in accordance with a principle other than chronology, and in a rhetoric common to all sayings. That other principle will then have determined the arrangement, drawing in its wake resort to a single monotonous voice: "the Talmud Yerushalmi." The principle is logical exposition, that is to say, the analysis and dissection of a problem into its conceptual components. The dialectic of argument is framed not by considerations of the chronological sequence in which sayings were said but by attention to the requirements of reasonable exposition of the problem. That is what governs.

The upshot is simple. In these two traits the Yerushalmi's character utterly refutes the hermeneutical premises of Halivni's reading of the Talmud. First, the Yerushalmi speaks with a single, fixedly modulated voice. Second, the Yerushalmi exposes the logic of ideas in a dialectical argument framed without regard to the time and place of the participants. In fact, the Yerushalmi (not to mention the Bavli) is like the Mishnah in its fundamental literary traits, therefore also in its history. Both documents were made up at the end, and whatever materials are used are used to achieve the purposes of ultimate redaction. Any theory of "sources" as against "traditions" will have to explain why some things were changed and some things were not changed. But all Halivni explains is that where he finds "forced interpretations," that imputed trait, which he himself fabricates or posits, identifies the "tradition" as distinct from the "source." And then the exegesis takes on its own momentum.

But, to the contrary, the literary history of the Mishnah, and, by analogy, of the Yerushalmi and the Bavli, begins on the day it concludes. Therefore there can be no distinguishing "sources" from "traditions" on the foundation of the evidence of the document, and that is the only evidence (as distinct from premise or postulate or first principle, to which, these days, intellectual discourse rarely appeals!) that we have. Accordingly, Halivni's basic mode of thought is, in a precise sense, a recrudescence of medieval philosophy, which begins not with data and inductive analysis thereof but from postulates, premises, and first principles. In the case at hand, we know that the Mishnah was formulated in its rigid, patterned language and carefully organized and enumerated groups of formal-substantive cognitive units, in the very processes in which it also was redacted. Otherwise the correspondences between redactional program and formal and patterned mode of articulation of ideas cannot be explained, short of invoking the notion of a literary miracle. Then on what basis shall we know the difference between "sources" and "traditions," unless we know without evidence that the work is composed, indifferently, of sources and traditions. The same argument pertains to the Talmuds. The Yerushalmi evidently underwent a process of redaction, in which fixed and final units of discourse (whether as I have delineated them or in some other division) were organized and put together.

The probable antecedent work of framing and formulating these units of discourse appears to have gone on at a single period among a relatively small number of sages working within a uniform set of literary conventions, at roughly the same time, and in approximately the same way. These framers of the various units of tradition may or may not have participated in the work of closure and redaction of the whole. We do not know the answer. But among themselves they cannot have differed very much about the way in which the work was to be carried on. For the end-product, the Talmud Yerushalmi, like the Mishnah, is uniform and stylistically coherent, generally consistent in modes of thought and speech, wherever we turn. That accounts for the single voice that leads us through the dialectical and argumentative analysis of the Talmud Yerushalmi. I spell out the matter in vast detail in Chapter Two.

III. The Hypothesis: The Three Stages of Literary Formation

Now let me explain the opposite conception and its consequences. It is that, as to method, we begin with the whole and work inward, as we peel an onion. As to the parts, we classify them by their indicative traits of relationship with the plan and program of the whole. That is to say, are writings responsive to the program of the compilation in which they occur? Are they responsive to the program of some other compilation, not the one where they now are? Or are they utterly autonomous of the requirements of any redactional setting we have or can envisage?

In this book I show two things. The first is that rabbinic documents – particularly midrash compilations – in some measure draw upon a fund of completed compositions of thought that have taken shape without attention to the needs of the compilers of those documents. The second is that some of these same documents draw upon materials that have been composed with the requirements of the respective documents in mind. Within the distinction between writing that serves a redactional purpose and writing that does not, we shall see four types of completed compositions of thought. Each type may be distinguished from the others by appeal to a single criterion of differentiation, that is to say, to traits of precisely the same sort. The indicative traits concern relationship to the redactional purpose of a piece of writing, viewed overall.

[1] Some writings in a given midrash compilation clearly serve the redactional program of the framers of the document in which those writings occur.

[2] Some writings in a given midrash compilation serve not the redactional program of the document in which they occur, but some other document, now in our hands. There is no material difference, as to the taxonomy of the writing of the classics in Judaism, between the first and second types; it is a problem of transmission of documents, not their formation.

[3] Some writings in a given midrash compilation serve not the purposes of the document in which they occur but rather a redactional program of a document, or of a type of document, that we do not now have, but can readily envision. In this category we find the possibility of imagining compilations that we do not have, but that can have existed but did not survive; or that can have existed and were then recast into the kinds of writings that people clearly preferred (later on) to produce. Numerous examples of writings that clearly have been redacted in accord with a program and plan other than those of any document now in our hands will show precisely what I mean here. Not only so, but the entire appendix is devoted to showing that stories about sages were told and recorded, but not compiled into complete books, e.g., hagiographies about given authorities. In *Why No Gospels in Talmudic Judaism?* I was able to point out one kind of book that we can have received but were not given. The criterion here is not subjective. We can demonstrate that materials of a given type, capable of sustaining a large-scale compilation, were available; but no such compilation was made, so far as extant sources suggest or attest.

[4] Some writings now found in a given midrash compilation stand autonomous of any redactional program we have in an existing compilation or of any we can even imagine on the foundations of said writings.

In general I treat types one and two together; these form the first component (Chapter Five) of my sustained text-presentation. But they are to be distinguished at the outset. The first of those four kinds of completed units of thought (pericopes) as matter of hypothesis fall into the final stage of literary formation. That is to say, at the stage at which an authorship has reached the conclusion that it wishes to compile a document of a given character, that authorship will have made up pieces of writing that serve the purposes of the document it wishes to compile. The second through fourth kinds of completed units of thought come earlier than this writing in the process of the formation of the classics of Judaism represented by the compilation in which this writing now finds its place.

The second of the four kinds of completed units of thought served a purpose other than that of the authorship of the compilation in which said kind of writing now occurs. It is therefore, as a matter of hypothesis, to be assigned to a stage in the formation of classics prior to the framing of the document in which the writing now occurs; in the context of a given compilation that now contains that writing, it is in a relative sense earlier than a piece of writing that the framers have worked out to serve their own distinctive and particular purposes. It is then earlier than a writing that has been made up to serve the document in which it now occurs. But it is also later in its formation than what we find in the third kind of writing.

The third of the four kinds of completed units of thought – the kind in the second part (Chapter Six) of my catalogue of pertinent materials – clearly presupposes a location in a document of a kind we do not have. But the characteristics of a set of such writings permits us to identify and define the kind of writing that can readily have contained, and been well served by, pericopes of this kind. Compositions of this kind, as a matter of hypothesis, are to be assigned to a stage in the formation of classics prior to the framing of all available documents. For, as a matter of fact, all of our now extant writings adhere to a single program of conglomeration and agglutination, and all are served by composites of one sort, rather than some other. Hence we may suppose that at some point prior to the decision to make writings in the model that we now have but in some other model people also made up completed units of thought to serve these other kinds of writings. These persist, now, in documents that they do not serve at all well. And we can fairly easily identify the kinds of documents that they can and should have served quite nicely indeed. These, then, are the three stages of literary formation in the making of the classics of Judaism.

Type four in the list above stands outside of the three stages of literary formation, because these are kinds of writings that fall outside of any relationship with a redactional program we either have in hand or can even imagine. These free-standing units can have been written any time; the tastes as to redaction of a given set of compilers of documents make no impact upon the writing of such materials. When we find them in existing documents – and they are everywhere – they are parachuted down and bear no clear role in the accomplishment, through the writing, of the redactors' goals for their compilation. They are given, by way of rich example, in Chapter Seven.

Of the relative temporal or ordinal position of writings that stand autonomous of any redactional program we have in an existing compilation or of any we can even imagine on the foundations of said writings we can say nothing. These writings prove episodic; they are commonly singletons. They serve equally well everywhere, because they demand no traits of form and redaction in order to endow them with sense and meaning. Why not? Because they are essentially free-standing and episodic, not referential and allusive. They are stories that contain their own point and do not invoke, in the making of that point, a given verse of Scripture. They are sayings that are utterly ad hoc. A variety of materials fall into this – from a redactional perspective – unassigned, and unassignable, type of writing. They do not belong in books at all. By that I mean, whoever made up these pieces of writing did not imagine that what he was forming required a setting beyond the limits of his own piece of writing; the story is not only complete in itself but could stand entirely on its own; the saying spoke for itself and required no nurturing context; the proposition and its associated proofs in no way was meant to draw nourishment from roots penetrating nutriments outside of its own literary limits.

My analytical taxonomy of the writings now collected in various midrash compilations points to not only three stages in the formation of the classics of Judaism. It also suggests that writing went on outside of the framework of the editing of documents, and also within the limits of the formation and framing of documents. Writing of the former kind then constituted a kind of literary work on which redactional planning made no impact. But the second and the third kinds of writing responds to redactional considerations. So in the end we shall wish to distinguish between writing intended for the making of books – compositions of the first three kinds listed just now – and writing not responsive to the requirements of the making of compilations.

The distinctions upon which these analytical taxonomies rest are objective and in no way subjective since they depend upon the fixed and factual relationship between a piece of writing and a larger redactional context.

[1] We know the requirements of redactors of the several documents of the rabbinic canon because I have already shown what they are in the case of a large variety of documents. When, therefore, we judge a piece of writing to serve the program of the document in which that writing occurs, it is not because of a personal impulse or a private and incommunicable insight, but because the traits of that writing self-

evidently respond to the documentary program of the book in which the writing is located.

[2] When, further, we conclude that a piece of writing belongs in some other document than the one in which it is found, that too forms a factual judgment.

[3] A piece of writing that serves no where we now know may nonetheless conform to the rules of writing that we can readily imagine and describe in theory. For instance, a propositional composition, that runs through a wide variety of texts to make a point autonomous of all of the texts that are invoked, clearly is intended for a propositional document, one that (like the Mishnah) makes points autonomous of a given prior writing, e.g., a biblical book, but that makes points that for one reason or another cohere quite nicely on their own. Authors of propositional compilations self-evidently can imagine that kind of redaction. We have their writings, but not the books that they intended to be made up of those writings. Another example, as I have already pointed out, is a collection of stories about a given authority, or about a given kind of virtue exemplified by a variety of authorities. These and other types of compilations we can imagine but do not have are dealt with in the present rubric.

[4] And, finally, where we have utterly hermetic writing, sealed off from any broader literary context and able to define its own limits and sustain its point without regard to anything outside itself, we know that here we are in the presence of authorships that had no larger redactional plan in mind, no intent on the making of books out of their little pieces of writing. Here the judgment of what belongs and what does not is not at all subjective, as I shall show in Chapter Seven.

I shall further identify the traits that permit us to postulate the existence of such a common fund of completed writings and in a sustained experiment shall show in this book for a variety of completed documents precisely what I conceive to constitute the specific contributions of that common fund of writings. But I do not describe that common fund of writings drawn upon here and there, nor do I claim that that common fund forms a fully redacted document (or set of documents) that now has been dismantled and reconstructed for the purpose of the compilations now in our hands. That may be the fact, but we are a long way from demonstrating it. The present work – the report of an experiment, rather than the exposition of final results – therefore forms the first step in the analysis of the formation of the rabbinic documents viewed not in isolation from one another but in relationship both to one another and also to shared antecedent writings to which we have access only in the re-presentation of the now-completed documents. I have now completed the bulk of my re-presentation and analysis of the documents of the Judaism of the Dual Torah one by one. Here I begin the analysis of those documents seen not in isolation from one another, but rather in relationship to what may be a common fund of materials framed without.

The work of analysis begins with the data *in situ*: as we have them. That is why the shank of the book – out of all proportion to the beginning and ending – is made up simply of long catalogues of items, drawn from the ten midrash compilations I have translated – that fall into the three categories I have identified. In logical terms this work rests upon establishing first the genus, and only then the species. It is the genus which permits us to describe and analyze the species of that genus. When, therefore, we propose to undertake a work of analysis of the components of a document and the strata of a document, we must begin at the level of the genus, and not at any lesser layer. What that means is simple. The work of description, prior to analysis and so comparison and contrast, begins with the whole, and only then works its way down to the parts. My work of description of the documents seen whole and one by one now nearing its conclusion, I now turn to the first stages in the analysis of the writings seen as a group. The first issue is whether there are shared traits that characterize the compositions of which the various documents, respectively, are composed. The traits that seem to me visible to the naked eye, right on the surface of things, concern the relationship between a composition used within a document and the purposes of the framers of the document as a whole who have made use of that composition.

2

The Documentary Approach or the Source-Critical Approach to the Literary History of the Classics of Judaism?

I. Did the Talmud's Authorship Utilize Prior Sources and Traditions?

In his commentary to selected passages of the Talmud of Babylonia (Bavli), David Weiss Halivni has worked out not merely episodic and ad hoc remarks about diverse passages but a sustained hermeneutics, in which a theory of the whole has guided him in his identification, in many parts, of problems demanding solution. Halivni's *Sources and Traditions*,[1] Halivni sets forth the theory that the Bavli is made up of sources, "those sayings which have come down to us in their original form, as they were uttered by their author," and traditions, "those which were changed in the course of transmission." Changing these "traditions" required later generations to deal with the remains of earlier statements, and they did so by a "forced interpretation" (in Halivni's language). The premise of Halivni's exegesis is therefore precisely the opposite of the hypothesis offered here. He sees documents as composites of already preserved sayings, the sayings then conglomerated into sizable discourses, the discourses then aggregated into completed writings. As is clear in Part One and Part Two, I see the documents as prior to the formation of much of their contents, and, as is clear in Part Three, I also see the free-standing pericopes as prior to much of *their* contents. The difference is that I start from the finished

---

[1]*Mekorot umesorot* (Tel Aviv, 1968 et. seq.)

19

product, while Halivni starts from the smallest whole units of thought. Let us now test his thesis.

Halivni knows how to deal with the problem of the "forced interpretation," distinguishing it from the simple one as follows, in the account of Robert Goldenberg:[2]

> The simple interpretation of a text is defined as "the interpretation which arises from the text itself, without either adding to it or subtracting from it." "Sometimes a simple comparison with parallel sources is sufficient to show that a forced explanation has its origin in an incorrect text....In most cases, however, it is necessary to study the sugya in depth, to break it into its parts before the motivation for the forced explanation becomes clear."

Halivni's sense for the self-evidence of his position is expressed as follows: "Any divergence from the simple interpretation is a divergence from the truth."[3] The work is entirely exegetical; there is no historical inquiry whatever. He takes for granted the reliability of all attributions, the historicity of all stories.[4] Literary criticism plays no role in his identification of exegetical problems or in their solution, and everything is either a source or a tradition, so Goldenberg, "The reliability of the tradition and the manner of its formation are to a great extent simply assumed, despite the mass of evidence of a more complicated situation that Weiss's own book reveals."[5]

Part of the problem of studying Halivni's *ouevre* is his failure to deal with competing theories of the literature, on the one side, and his incapacity to compose a null hypothesis for the testing of his hermeneutic, on the other. His unwillingness to read other scholars' treatments of the same literature and problems has now become so notorious as to elicit the comments of book reviewers.[6] We really do not know, therefore, how Halivni has taken into account other approaches to the same literature, competing theories of its character, origins, and, consequently, correct hermeneutics. That fact, his failure to read and comment on the work of others and its implications for his own work, renders the critical reading of Halivni's *ouevre* exceedingly parlous.

---

[2]"Robert Goldenberg, "David Weiss Halivni, Meqorot uMesorot: Ketuvot," in J. Neusner, ed., *The Formation of the Babylonian Talmud* (Leiden, 1970: E. J. Brill), p. 136.

[3]Cited by Goldenberg, p. 137.

[4]See Goldenberg, *ibid.*, p. 146.

[5]Goldenberg, *ibid.*, p. 147.

[6]Cf. for example, David Singer in *Commentary*, April, 1988, on Halivni's disinterest in views other than his own. He apparently does not even read and take account of competing readings of the same documents.

II. Testing against a Null Hypothesis for David Weiss Halivni's Theory of Sources and Traditions

The omission of a null hypothesis can now be demonstrated to form a fatal flaw in his entire hermeneutical fabrication. Let me now show how one might compose and test a null hypothesis as to the character of the sources subjected to exegesis. On that basis we shall see that Halivni's premise of a composite text, in which materials that preserve original versions are mixed together with materials that exhibit deformations of those original versions, contradicts the character of the Talmud of the Land of Israel (Yerushalmi). Indeed, any exegesis that rests upon Halivni's premises will violate the fundamental literary traits of the Yerushalmi, and, everyone must then recognize, the Bavli as well, which in these traits does not differ in any material way. Having devoted considerable effort to the study of Halivni's ouevre,[7] I am now prepared to address its principal positions and to demonstrate that they contradict the evidence, read from an analytical and critical perspective. They form, therefore, merely another chapter in the dreary story of fundamentalist exegesis of a text not studied but merely recited. Without a null hypothesis presented

---

[7]See the articles by Goldenberg, Shamai Kanter, "David Weiss Halivni, *Meqorot uMesorot. Qiddushin,*" in *Formation of the Babylonian Talmud,* pp. 148-153, and David Goodblatt, "David Weiss Halivni, *Meqorot uMesorot. Gittin,*" in *Formation of the Babylonian Talmud,* pp. 164-173; also Jacob Neusner, ed., *The Modern Study of the Mishnah* (Leiden, 1973: E. J. Brill), in particular Joel Gereboff, "David Weiss Halivni on the Mishnah," pp. 180-196; and William Scott Green, ed., *Law as Literature = Semeia. An Experimental Journal for Biblical Criticism* 27 (Chico, 1983: Scholars Press for Society of Biblical Literature), pp. 37-116. Note in particular Louis Newman, "The Work of David Weiss Halivni: A Source Critical Commentary to b. Yebamot 87b," in which Newman compares Halivni's exegetical approach to that of Shamma Friedman, treated at length in the same collection of papers. All of these papers were prepared in my graduate seminar. From 1968 through 1983, I regularly devoted semesters to the comparative study and history of the exegesis of the rabbinic literature and paid close attention to Halivni's work in the context of the modern hermeneutics of the Talmud, broadly construed. In the context of Singer's devastating comments on Halivni, the three monographs that I have brought into being, whole or in part, should be called to mind. My impression is that Halivni has so persuaded himself of the correctness of his views that he found it unnecessary to read competing approaches just as he found it unproductive to compose a null hypothesis and to test it. In his defense, however, it should be said that what outsiders might deem to be intellectual sloth or mere self-absorption is in fact an established convention in the field of rabbinics, one that Halivni merely replicates.

and analyzed by Halivni himself, we have no alternative but to judge as a missed opportunity his entire exegetical *ouevre* and the hermeneutical theory on which it rests.

If Halivni were right, then, we should identify in the Talmuds a multiplicity of voices. But the opposite characterizes the Yerushalmi. The Talmud Yerushalmi utilizes a single, rather limited repertoire of exegetical initiatives and rhetorical choices for whatever discourse about the Mishnah the framers of the Talmud Yerushalmi propose to undertake. The Yerushalmi identifies no author or collegium of authors. When I say that the Talmud Yerushalmi speaks in a single voice, I mean to say it everywhere speaks uniformly, consistently, and predictably. The voice is the voice of a book. The ubiquitous character of this single and continuous voice of the Talmud Yerushalmi argues for one of two points of origin. First, powerful and prevailing conventions may have been formed in the earliest stages of the reception and study of the Mishnah, then carried on thereafter without variation or revision. Or, second, the framing of sayings into uniform constructions of discourse may have been accomplished only toward the end of the period marked by the formation of the Talmud Yerushalmi's units of discourse and their conglomeration into the Talmud Yerushalmi of the Land of Israel as we know it. This latter possibility is pertinent to the claim of David Weiss Halivni that the Talmud (he speaks of the Bavli, but the Yerushalmi provides a perfectly adequate extension to his position) rests upon prior writings or traditions, and that these writings or traditions are preserved in the document as we have it. Let us examine the two possibilities for explaining the Yerushalmi's authorship's uniformity of discourse.

In the former case, we posit that the mode of reasoned analysis of the Mishnah and the repertoire of issues to be addressed to any passage of the Mishnah were defined early on, then persisted for two hundred years. The consequent, conventional mode of speech yielded that nearly total uniformity of discourse characteristic of numerous units of discourse of the Yerushalmi at which the interpretation of a law of the Mishnah is subject to discussion. In the latter case we surmise that a vast corpus of sayings, some by themselves, some parts of larger conglomerates, was inherited at some point toward the end of the two hundred years under discussion. This corpus of miscellanies was then subjected to intense consideration as a whole, shaped and reworded into the single, cogent and rhetorically consistent Talmud Yerushalmi discourse before us. That would seem to me to contradict the position outlined by Halivni in his exegetical work on the Bavli. Indeed, if we see this Talmud (and the other) as a work accomplished essentially in the ultimate phase of its redaction, then there can be no strong case for the authorship's extensively using and preserving prior "traditions" and "sources," in the language of Halivni. In that case, his entire exegetical program rests upon false premises. Seeing the document whole argues strongly in favor of the second of the two possibilities and hence against Halivni's fundamental hermeneutics.

As between these two possibilities, the latter seems by far the more likely. The reason is simple. I cannot find among the Yerushalmi's units of discourse concerning the Mishnah evidence of differentiation among the generations of names or schools. But a null hypothesis, that is, evidence against my position and in favor of Halivni's, would dictate that such differentiation among the putative "sources and traditions" should be much in evidence. To the contrary, there is no interest, for instance, in the chronological sequence in which sayings took shape and in which discussions may be supposed to have been carried on. That is to say, the Talmud Yerushalmi unit of discourse approaches the explanation of a passage of the Mishnah without systematic attention to the layers in which ideas were set forth, the schools among which discussion must have been divided, the sequence in which statements about a Mishnah-law were made. That fact points to formation at the end, like igneous rock, and assuredly not agglutination in successive layers of intellectual sediment, such as Halivni's "sources and traditions" leads us to anticipate.

Once the elemental literary facts make their full impression on our understanding, everything else falls into place as well. Arguments such as the ones we shall now review did not unfold over a long period of time, as one generation made its points, to be followed by the additions and revisions of another generation, in a process of gradual increment and agglutination running on for two hundred years. That theory of the formation of literature cannot account for the unity, stunning force, and dynamism of the Talmud Yerushalmi's dialectical arguments. To the contrary, someone (or small group) at the end determined to reconstruct, so as to expose, the naked logic of a problem. For this purpose, oftentimes, it was found useful to cite sayings or positions in hand from earlier times. But these inherited materials underwent a process of reshaping, and, more aptly, refocusing. Whatever the original words – and we need not doubt that at times we have them – the point of everything in hand was defined and determined by the people who made it all up at the end. The whole shows a plan and program. Theirs are the minds behind the whole. In the nature of things, they did their work at the end, not at the outset. To be sure, the numerous examples we shall now inspect may, as I just said, yield one of two conclusions. We may see them as either the gradual and "natural" increment of a sedimentary process or as the creation of single-minded geniuses of applied logic and sustained analytical inquiry. But there is no intermediate possibility.

One qualification is required. I do not mean to say the principles of chronology were wholly ignored. Rather, they were not determinative of the structure of argument. So I do not suggest that the framers of the Talmud Yerushalmi would likely have an early authority argue with a later one about what is assigned only to the later one. That I cannot and do not expect to instantiate. I do not think we shall find such slovenly work in either our Talmud Yerushalmi Yerushalmi or the other one. Our sages were painstaking and sensible. The point is that no attention ever is devoted in particular to the sequence in which various things are said. Everything is worked together into a single, temporally seamless discourse. Thus if a unit of discourse draws upon ideas of authorities of the first half of the third century, such as Simeon b. Laqish and Yohanan, as well as those of figures of the second half of the fourth century, such as Yosé, Jonah, Huna, Zeira, and Yudan, while discourse will be continuous, discussion will always focus upon the logical point at hand.

III. Cogent Discourse and Well-Crafted Propositions

Now let us move on to evidence. We begin with a set of instances which illustrate the fundamental traits of discourse. What we see is that the discussion is coherent and harmonious, moving from beginning to what was, in fact, a predetermined end. The voice, "the Talmud Yerushalmi," speaks to us throughout, not the diverse voices of real people engaged in a concrete and therefore chaotic argument. As in Plato's dialogues, question and answer – the dialectical argument – constitute conventions through which logic is exposed and tested, not the reports of things people said spontaneously or even after the fact. The controlling voice is monotonous, lacking all points of differentiation of viewpoint, tone, mode of inquiry and thought. That is what I mean to illustrate here. To prove this same proposition incontrovertibly, I should have to cite a vast proportion of the Yerushalmi as a whole. A few instances must suffice. I refer to passages translated in my *Talmud of the Land of Israel. A Preliminary Translation and Explanation.*

In Y. Horayot 2:1, we have a sustained discussion on the exegetical foundations of a law of the Mishnah. The voice of the Talmud Yerushalmi is undifferentiated; the entire passage concentrates on the substance of matters. A single hand surely stands behind it all, for there is not a single seam or margin. So to give an account of the matter, we must speak in the name of "the Talmud Yerushalmi." That is, "the

Talmud Yerushalmi" wants to know the relationship of an anointed priest to a court, the reciprocal authority of autonomous institutions. Scripture has specified several autonomous persons and institutions or groups that atone with a bullock for erroneous actions committed inadvertently. So the Talmud Yerushalmi now raises the interesting question of the rule that applies when one of these autonomous bodies follows instructions given by another. The unit explores this question, first establishing that the anointed priest is equivalent to the community, just as Scripture states, and drawing the consequence of that fact. Then comes the important point that the anointed priest is autonomous of the community. He atones for what he does, but is not subject to atonement by, or in behalf of, others.

A.   [If] an anointed [high] priest made a decision for himself [in violation of any of the commandments of the Torah] doing so inadvertently, and carrying out [his decision] inadvertently,

B.   he brings a bullock [Lev. 4:3].

C.   [If] he [made an erroneous decision] inadvertently, and deliberately carried it out.

D.   deliberately [made an erroneous decision] and inadvertently carried it out,

E.   he is exempt.

F.   For [as to A-B] an [erroneous] decision of an anointed [high priest] for himself is tantamount to an [erroneous] decision of a court for the entire community.

I

A.   ["If any one sins unwittingly in any of the things which the Lord has commanded not to be done and does any one of them, if it is the anointed priest who sins, thus bringing guilt on the people, then let him offer for the sin which he has committed a young bull" (Lev. 4:23-30.] "Anyone...," "If it is the high priest...," – lo, [the Scripture would seem to imply that] the high priest is tantamount to an individual [and not, vs. M. Hor. 2:1F, to an embodiment of the community and thus not subject to a bullock-offering.]

B.   [In this case, Scripture's purpose is to say:] Just as an individual, if he ate [something prohibited] at the instruction of a court is exempt, so this one [subject to court authority], if he ate something at the instruction of the court, is exempt.

C.   Just as an individual, if he ate [something prohibited] without the instruction of a court is liable, so this one, if he ate something not at the instruction of a court, is liable.

D.   [To encounter that possible interpretation] Scripture states, "Thus bringing guilt on the people" [meaning] lo, [the high anointed priest's] guilt is tantamount to the guilt of the entire people [just as M. Hor. 2:1F states].

E.   Just as the people are not guilty unless they gave instruction [Lev. 4:13], so this one is not guilty unless he gave instruction.

F.   There is a Tannaitic tradition that interprets [the matter with reference to] the people [and] the court:

G.   Just as [if] the people gave instruction and other people did [what the people] said, [the people] are liable, so this one, [if] he gave [erroneous] instruction and others did [what he said], should be liable.

H.   [It is to counter that possible interpretation that] Scripture states, "[If it is the high priest] who sins," [meaning] for the sin that this one himself committed he brings [a bullock], but he does not have to bring a bullock on account of what other people do [inadvertently sinning because of his instruction].

I.   There is a Tannaitic tradition that interprets the [matter with reference to] the people [and] the community:

J.   Just as, in the case of the people, if others gave erroneous instruction and they [inadvertently] committed a sin, they are liable, so in the case of this one, [if] others gave erroneous instruction and he carried it out [and so sinned], he should be liable.

K.   [To counter that possible, wrong interpretation,] Scripture states, "[If it is the high priest] who sins," [meaning] for the sin that this one committed, he brings [a bullock], but he does not have to bring a bullock on account of what other people do [inadvertently sinning because of their instruction].

Y. San. 4:9: We find here a further instance in which the argument is so constructed as to speak to an issue, without regard to the source of sayings or the definition of the voices in conversation. A question is asked, then answered, because the rhetoric creates dialectic, movement from point to point. It is not because an individual speaks with, and interrogates, yet another party. The uniform voice of the Talmud Yerushalmi is before us, lacking all distinguishing traits, following a single, rather simple program of rhetorical conventions.

II

A.   And perhaps you might want to claim, "What business is it of ours to convict this man of a capital crime?"[M. San. 4:9].

B.   It is written, "And about sunset a cry went through the army" (1 Kings 22:36).

C.   What is this cry?

D.   Lo, it a song, as it is said, "When the wicked perish, there is a song" (Prov. 11:10).

E.   But, on the contrary, it also is said, "[That they should praise] as they went out before the army [and say, 'Give thanks unto the Lord, for his mercy endures for ever']" (2 Chr. 20:21).

F.   [Omitting the words, "for he is good,"] is to teach you that even the downfall of the wicked is no joy before the Omnipresent.

Y. Makkot 1:5: Here is yet another example in which a sustained conversation on a passage of Scripture, unfolding through questions and answers, conforms to a simple rhetorical program. The voice of the interlocutor is not differentiated from the source of the respondent, for the whole is a single discourse. Not a "real" conversation, but rather an effective presentation of a simple idea is at hand.

I

A.   [Scripture refers to the requirement of two or three witnesses to impose the death penalty, Deut. 17:6. Scripture further states, "Only on the evidence of two witnesses or of three witnesses shall a charge be sustained," (Deut. 19.15). The former deals with capital cases, the latter with property cases. Since both refer to two or three witnesses, the duplication is now explained:] Scripture is required to refer to property cases, and also to capital cases.

B.   For if it had referred to property cases and not to capital cases, I might have said, In the case of property cases, which are of lesser weight, three witnesses have the power to prove two to be perjurers, but two may not prove three to be perjurers.

C.   How do I know that that is so even of a hundred?

D.   Scripture states, "Witnesses."

E.   Now if reference had been made to capital cases, and not to property cases, I might have said, In capital cases, which are weightier, two witnesses have the power to prove that three are perjurers but three do not have the power to prove that two are perjurers.

F.   How do I know that that applies even to a hundred?

G.   Scripture says, "Witnesses." [It follows then the Scripture must refer to "two or three" in the context of each matter, since one could not have derived the one from the other.]

All of the units of discourse before us exhibit the same traits. In each instance we see that the conversation is artificial. What is portrayed is not real people but a kind of rhetoric. The presence of questions and answers is a literary convention, not a (pretended) transcription of a conversation. So we may well speak of "the Talmud Yerushalmi" and its voice: that is all we have. The absence of differentiation is not the sole striking trait. We observe, also, a well-planned and pointed program of inquiry, however brief, leading to a single purpose for each unit of discourse. While the various units in theme are completely unrelated to one another, in rhetoric and mode of analysis they are essentially uniform: simple questions, simple answers, uncomplex propositions, worked out through reference to authoritative sources of law, essentially an unfolding of information.

IV. Indifference to Chronology

Up to this point, we have seen only that the Talmud Yerushalmi takes on a persona, becomes a kind of voice. The voice is timeless. On the face of it, the units we have reviewed can have been made up at any time in the period in which the Talmud Yerushalmi was taking shape, from 200 to 400. The uniformity of style and cogency of mode of discourse can have served as powerful scholastic-literary conventions, established early, followed slavishly thereafter. The bulk of the units of discourse, however, are not anonymous. They constitute compilations of statements assigned to named authorities. These on the surface testify to specific periods in the two centuries at hand, since the authorities mentioned lived at specific times and places. If, now, we observe the same uniformity of tone and dialectic, we shall address a somewhat more refined problem.

This brings us to discourse involving named authorities. The important point in the examples that follow is that while named authorities and sayings assigned to them do occur, the dialectic of argument is conducted outside the contributions of the specified sages. Sages' statements serve the purposes of the anonymous voice, rather than defining and governing the flow of argument. So the anonymous voice, "the Talmud Yerushalmi," predominates even when individuals' sayings are utilized. Selecting and arranging whatever was in hand is the work of one hand, one voice.

Y. Abodah Zarah 1:5: What is interesting in this account of the language of the Mishnah is that the framer of the entire discussion takes over and uses what is attributed to Hiyya. The passage requires Hiyya's version of the Mishnah-rule. But Hiyya is not responsible for the formation of the passage. It is "the Talmud Yerushalmi" that speaks, drawing upon the information, including the name, of Hiyya. Only the secondary comment in the name of Bun bar Hiyya violates the monotone established by "the Talmud Yerushalmi." And at the end that same voice takes over and draws matters to their conclusion, a phenomenon we shall shortly see again. It is not uncommon for later fourth-century names to occur in such a setting.

I.   A   These are things [which it is] forbidden to sell to gentiles:
      B.   (1) fir cones, (2) white figs, (3) and their stalks, (4) frankincense, and (5) a white cock.

II.   A   We repeat in the Mishnah-pericope [the version]: A white cock.

B.   R. Hiyya repeated [for his version of] the Mishnah-pericope: "A cock of any sort."

C.   The present version of the Mishnah [specifying a white cock] requires also the version of R. Hiyya, and the version of R. Hiyya requires also the [present] version of the Mishnah.

D.   [Why both?] If we repeated [the present version of the Mishnah], and we did not repeat the version of R. Hiyya, we should have reached the conclusion that the sages state the rule only in regard to a white cock, but as to any sort of cock other than that, even if this was all by itself [M. A. Z. 1:5D], it is permitted. Thus there was need for the Mishnah-version of R. Hiyya.

E.   Now if one repeated the version of R. Hiyya, and we did not repeat the version before us in the Mishnah, we should have ruled that the rule applies only in the case of an unspecified cock [requested by the purchaser], but [if the purchaser requested] a white cock, then even if this was all by itself, it would be prohibited [to sell such a cock].

F.   Thus there was need for the Mishnah-version as it is repeated before us, and there also was need for the Mishnah-version as it is repeated by R. Hiyya.

G.   Said R. Bun bar Hiyya, "[In Hiyya's view, if a gentile said, 'Who has] a cock to sell?' one may sell him a white cock, [so Hiyya differs from, and does not merely complement, the version of the Mishnah-pericope]."

H.   [Now if the gentile should say, "Who has] a white cock to sell," we then rule that if the white cock is by itself, it is forbidden, but if it is part of a flock of cocks, it is permitted to sell it to him. [This clearly is the position of the Mishnah-pericope, so there is no dispute at all, merely complementary traditions, as argued at D-E.]

Y. Shebuot 3:7: Here is yet another instance, but a more complex and better articulated one, in which topically interesting sayings attributed to two principal authorities, Yohanan and Simeon b. Laqish, provide a pretext for a rather elaborate discussion. The discussion is conducted about what Yohanan and Simeon are supposed to have said. But the rhetoric is such that they are not presented as the active voices. Their views are described. But they, personally and individually, do not express views. Predictably, the language in no way differentiates between Yohanan's and Simeon b. Laqish's manner of speech. Only the substance of what is said tells us how and about what they differ. The reason is obvious. The focus of discourse is the principle at hand, the logic to be analyzed and fully spelled out. The uniform voice of "the Talmud Yerushalmi" speaks throughout.

I.   A   "I swear that I won't eat this loaf of bread," "I swear that I won't eat it," "I swear that I won't eat it" –

	B.	and he ate it –
	C.	he is liable on only one count.
	D.	This is a "rash oath" (Lev. 5:4).
	E.	On account of deliberately [taking a rash oath] one is liable to flogging, and on account of inadvertently [taking a rash oath] he is liable to an offering of variable value.
II.	A.	[If someone said], "I swear that I shall eat this loaf of bread today," and the day passed, but then he ate it –
	B.	R. Yohanan and R. Simeon b. Laqish – both of them say, "He is exempt [from flogging for deliberate failure]."
	C.	The reason for the position of one authority is not the same as the reason for the ruling of the other.
	D.	The reason for the ruling of R. Yohanan is on the grounds that the case is one in which there can be no appropriate warning [that what the man is about to do will violate the law, because the warning can come only too late, when the day has already passed].
	E.	The reason for the ruling, in R. Simeon b. Laqish's view, is that [by not eating] the man is thereby violating a negative rule which does not involve an actual, concrete deed.
	F.	What is the practical difference between the positions of the two authorities?
	G.	A case in which he burned the bread and threw it into the sea.
	H.	If you say that the reason is on the count that the man is not in a position to receive a warning, the man will be exempt [on the same grounds in the present case].
	I.	But if you say that the reason is that the matter involves a negative commandment in which there is no concrete deed, here we do have a concrete deed [namely, throwing the bread into the sea].

Y. Shebuot 3:9: Here we have a still more striking instance in which the entire focus of discourse is the logic. No rhetorical devices distinguish one party to the argument from the other one. The two speak in rigidly patterned language, so that what is assigned to the one always constitutes a mirror image of what is assigned to the other. That the whole, in fact, merely refers to positions taken by each is clear in the resort to third person and descriptive language, in place of the attributive, "said."

	A.	"I swear that I shall eat this loaf of bread," "I swear that I shall not eat it" – the first statement is a rash oath, and the second is a vain oath [M. Shebu. 3:9A-B].
	B.	How do they treat such a case [in which a man has taken these contradictory oaths, one of which he must violate]?
	C.	They instruct him to eat [the loaf].

D.   It is better to transgress a vain oath and not to transgress a rash oath.

E.   "I swear that I shall not eat this loaf of bread," "I swear that I shall eat it" – the first is rash oath, the second a vain oath.

F.   How do they treat such a case?

G.   They instruct him not to eat it.

H.   It is better to transgress a vain oath by itself, and not to transgress both a vain oath and a rash oath.

I.   "I swear that I shall eat this loaf of bread today," "I swear that I shall not eat it today," and he ate it –

J.   R. Yohanan said, "He has carried out the first oath and nullified the second."

K.   R. Simeon b. Laqish said, "He has nullified the first and not carried out the second."

L.   "I swear that I shall not eat this loaf of bread today," "I swear that I shall eat it today," and he ate it –

M.   R. Yohanan said, "He has nullified the first oath and carried out the second."

N.   R. Simeon b. Laqish said, "He has nullified the first oath and as to the second, they instruct him to carry it out with another loaf of bread."

O.   "I swear that I shall eat this loaf today," "I swear that I shall eat it today," and he ate it –

P.   R. Yohanan said, "He has carried out both oaths."

Q.   And R. Simeon b. Laqish said, "He has carried out the first, and as to the second, they instruct him to carry it out with another loaf of bread."

R.   "I swear that I shall not eat this loaf of bread," "I swear that I shall not eat it today," and he ate it –

S.   in the view of R. Yohanan, he is liable on only one count.

T.   In the view of R. Simeon b. Laqish, is he liable on two counts?

U.   [No.] Even R. Simeon b. Laqish will concede that he [has repeated himself] because he merely [wishes to] keep himself away from prohibited matters [and that is why he repeated the oath, but only one count is at hand].

Y. San. 5:2: The final example does utilize the attributive, with the implication that we have an effort to represent not merely the gist of an authority's opinion, but his exact words. Even if we assume that before us are *ipsissima verba* of Rab and Yohanan, however, we have still to concede the paramount role of "the Talmud Yerushalmi" in the formation and unpacking of the argument. For, as we notice, as soon as Rab and Yohanan have spoken, curiously mirroring one another's phrasing and wording, the monotonous voice takes over. At that point, the argument unfolds in a set of questions and answers, the standard dialectic thus predominating once again. The secondary expansion of the matter, beginning at O, then adduces a piece of evidence, followed by an anonymous discourse in which that evidence is absorbed into, and made to serve, the purposes of the analysis as a whole. Once more the fact that each item is balanced by the next is not the important point, though it is striking. What is important is that movement of the argument is defined by "the Talmud Yerushalmi," and not by the constituents of discourse given in the names of specific authorities. The mind and voice behind the whole are not Rab's and Yohanan's, or, so far as we can see, their immediate disciples'. The voice is "the Talmud's." "The Talmud Yerushalmi" does not tire, as its tertiary explication, testing the views of each and showing the full extent of the position taken by both principal parties, runs on and on. Only at the end, with Mana and Abin, fourth-century figures, do named authorities intervene in such a way as to break the uniform rhetorical pattern established by "the Talmud Yerushalmi."

A.   There we learned:

B.   He concerning whom two groups of witnesses gave testimony—

C.   these testify that he took a vow to be a Nazir for two spells,

D.   and those testify that he took a vow to be Nazir for five spells –

E.   The House of Shammai say, "The testimony is at variance, and no Naziriteship applies here at all."

F.   And the House of Hillel say, "In the sum of five are two spells, so let him serve out two spells of Naziriteship" [M. Naz. 3:7].

G.   Rab said, "As to a general number [the Houses] are in disagreement [that is, as to whether he has taken the Nazirite vow at all]. But as to a specific number, all parties agree that [the testimony is at variance]. [Following the versions of Y. Yeb. 15:5, Naz. 3:7: the sum of five includes two, as at M. 5:2F.]"

H.   R. Yohanan said, "As to spelling out the number of vows there is a difference of opinion, but as to a general number, all parties concur that [within the general principle of five spells of Naziriteship there are two upon which all parties concur]. [The testimony is at variance.]"

I.   What is meant by the "general number," and what is meant by "counting out the number of specific vows" [the man is supposed to have taken]? [Examples of each are as follows:]

J.   The general number – one party has said, "Two," and one party has said, "Five."

K.   Counting out the number of vows one by one is when one said "One, two," and the other said, "Three, four."

L.   Rab said, "If the essence of the testimony is contradicted, the testimony is not null."

M.   And R. Yohanan said, "If the essence of the testimony is contradicted, the testimony is null."

N.   All parties concede, however, [that] if testimony has been contradicted in its nonessentials, the testimony [of the first set of witnesses] is not nullified.

O.   The full extent of the position taken by R. Yohanan is seen in the following case:

P.   For Ba bar Hiyya in the name of R. Yohanan: "The assumption [that a loan has taken place is] confirmed [by testimony] that one has counted out [coins].

Q.   "If this witness says, 'From his pocket did he count out the money,' and that one says, 'From his pouch did he count out the money,'

R.   "we have a case in which a testimony is contradicted in its essentials [within the same pair of witnesses, who thus do not agree]. [This testimony is null.]"

S.   Here even Rab concedes that the testimony is null.

T.   Concerning what do they differ?

U.   Concerning a case in which there were two groups of witnesses.

V.   One states, "From the pocket did he count out the money," and the other says, "From the pouch did he count out the money."

W.   Here we have a case in which testimony is contradicted in its essentials. The effect of the testimony [in Yohanan's view] is null.

X.   But in the view of Rab, the effect of the testimony is not null.

Y.   If one witness says, "Into his vest did he count out the money," and the other says, "Into his wallet,"

Z.   in the opinion of all parties, the testimony is contradicted in its nonessentials and therefore the testimony is not nullified. [This testimony is not about the essence of the case.]

AA.   If one party says, "With a sword did he kill him," and the other party says, "With a staff did he kill him," we have a case in which testimony has been contradicted in its essentials [just as in a property case, so in a capital one].

BB.   Even Rab concedes that the effect of the entire testimony is null.

CC.   In what regard did they differ?

DD.   In a case in which there were two sets of two witnesses:

EE.   One group says, "With a sword...," and the other says, "With a staff..."

FF.   Here we have a case in which the testimony has been contradicted in its essentials, and the effect of the testimony is null.

GG.   But in the view of Rab, the effect of the testimony is not null.

HH.   One witness says, "[The murderer] turned toward the north [to flee]," and the other witness says, "He turned toward the south," in the opinion of all parties, the testimony [of one group] has been contradicted in its nonessentials, and the testimony has not been nullified.

II.   The full force of Rab's opinion is indicated in the following, which we have learned there:

JJ.   [If one woman says, "He died," and one says, "He was killed," R.
               Meir says, "Since they contradict one another in details of their
               testimony, lo, these women may not remarry."] R. Judah and R.
               Simeon say, "Since this one and that one are in agreement that he
               is not alive, they may remarry" [M. Yeb. 15:5B-D].

KK.   Now did he not hear that which R. Eleazar said, "R. Judah and R.
               Simeon concur in the matter of witnesses [that where they
               contradict one another in essentials, their testimony is null]?"

LL.   If so, what is the difference between such contradiction when it
               comes from witnesses and the same when it comes from co-
               wives?

MM.   They did not treat the statement of a co-wife concerning her
               fellow-wife as of any consequence whatsoever.

NN.   Said R. Yohanan, "If R. Eleazar made such a statement, he heard
               it from me and said it."

OO.   The Mishnah-pericope is at variance with the position of Rab. All
               the same are interrogation and examination in the following
               regard: When the witnesses contradict one another, their
               testimony is null [M. San. 5:2F]. [Rab does not deem it invariably
               null, as we have seen.]

PP.   Said R. Mana, "Rab interprets the Mishnah-rule to speak of a
               case in which one witness contradicts another [but not in which a
               set of witnesses contradicts another such set in some minor
               detail]."

QQ.   Said R. Abin, "Even if you interpret the passage to speak of
               contradictions between one set of witnesses and another, still Rab
               will be able to deal with the matter. For a capital case is subject to
               a different rule, since it is said, 'Justice, [and only] justice, will you
               pursue'" (Deut. 16:20).   [Thus capital trials are subject to a
               different set of rules of evidence from those applicable in
               property cases, of which Rab spoke above at L.]

Since this final example is somewhat protracted, we had best
review the point of citing it before we proceed. The issue of the
interpretation of the passage of the Mishnah, A-F, is phrased at G-H,
the conflict between Rab and Yohanan. We note that the former spent
most of his mature years in Babylonia, the latter, in the Land of Israel.
Accordingly, considerations of geographical or institutional
relationship play no role whatsoever. The language of the one is a
mirror image of what is given to the other.   Then the Talmud
Yerushalmi takes over, by providing an exegesis of the cited dispute, I-
K. This yields a secondary phrasing of the opinions of the two
authorities, L, M, with a conclusion at N. Then the position of Yohanan
is provided yet a further amplification, O-R. But what results, S, is a
revision of our view of Rab's opinion. Consequently, a further exegesis
of the dispute is supplied, T-U, spelled out at W-X, then with further

amplification still, now at Y-BB. Once more we attempt a further account of the fundamental point at issue between the two masters, CC-HH, and, in the model of the foregoing exercise with Yohanan, Rab's view is carried to its logical extreme, II-JJ. The final part of the passage, tacked on and essentially secondary, allows for some further discussion of Rab's view, with a late authority, Mana, and his contemporary, Abin, PP-QQ, writing a conclusion to the whole. Up to that point, it seems to me clear, what we have is a rather elegant, cogent, highly stylized mode of exposition through argument, with a single form of logic applied time and again.

When I claim that the Talmud's focus of interest is in the logical exposition of the law, here is a good instance of what I mean. The materials are organized so as to facilitate explanations of the law's inner structure and potentiality, not to present a mere repertoire of ideas and opinions of interest for their own sake. The upshot is a sustained argument, not an anthology of relevant sayings. But Halivni's theory requires the opposite, that is, an anthology of diverse materials, some changed, some not changed, from their "original" formulation. A null hypothesis offered by Halivni should turn up precisely the document as we now have it. A null hypothesis offered by me should turn up the opposite of what the Yerushalmi gives us.

V. The Unitary, Harmonious Voice of the Document Itself

Such a cogent and ongoing argument as we find characteristic of both Talmuds is more likely the work of a single mind than of a committee, let alone of writers who lived over a period of ten or fifteen decades. The role of individuals in the passages we have reviewed is unimportant. The paramount voice is that of "the Talmud Yerushalmi." The rhetoric of the Talmud Yerushalmi may be described very simply: a preference for questions and answers, a willingness, then, to test the answers and to expand through secondary and tertiary amplification, achieved through further questions and answers. The whole gives the appearance of the script for a conversation to be reconstructed, or an argument of logical possibilities to be reenacted, in one's own mind. In this setting we of course shall be struck by the uniformity of the rhetoric, even though we need not make much of the close patterning of language, e.g., Rab's and Yohanan's, where it occurs. The voice of "the Talmud Yerushalmi," moreover, authoritatively defines the mode of analysis. The inquiry is consistent and predictable; one argument differs from another not in supposition but only in detail. When individuals' positions occur, it is because what they have to say serves the purposes of "the Talmud Yerushalmi" and its uniform inquiry. The inquiry is into the logic and the rational potentialities of a passage. To these dimensions of thought, the details of place, time, and even of an individual's philosophy, are secondary. All details are turned toward a common core of discourse. This, I maintain, is possible only because the document as a whole takes shape in accord with an overriding program of inquiry and comes to expression in conformity with a single plan of rhetorical expression. To state the proposition simply: it did not just grow, but rather, someone made it up.

This view is reenforced by the innumerable instances of the predominance of logic over chronology. The talmudic argument is not indifferent to the chronology of authorities. But the sequence in which things may be supposed to have been said – an early third century figure's saying before a later fourth century figure's saying – in no way explains the construction of protracted dialectical arguments. The argument as a whole, its direction and purpose, always govern the selection, formation, and ordering of the parts of the argument and their relationships to one another. The dialectic is determinative. Chronology, if never violated, is always subordinated. Once that fact is clear, it will become further apparent that "arguments" – analytical units of discourse – took shape at the end, with the whole in mind, as part of a plan and a program. That is to say, the components of the argument, even when associated with the names of specific authorities who lived at different times, were not added piece by piece, in order of historical appearance. They were put together whole and complete, all at one time, when the dialectical discourse was made up. By examining a few units of discourse, we shall clearly see the unimportance of the sequence in which people lived, hence of the order in which sayings (presumably) became available.

The upshot is that chronological sequence, while not likely to be ignored, never determines the layout of a unit of discourse. We can never definitively settle the issue of whether a unit of discourse came into being through a long process of accumulation and agglutination, or was shaped at one point – then, at the end of the time in which named authorities flourished – with everything in hand and a particular purpose in mind. But the more likely of the two possibilities is clearly the latter. Let me first review a passage already set forth. It is at Y. San. 5:2. Here Rab and Yohanan both are assumed to have flourished in the middle of the third century. Placing their opinions in conflict does not violate chronology. There is a Mana who was a contemporary of Yohanan. The first Abin, a Babylonian, is supposed to have flourished about a half-century later. Perhaps Mana's saying at PP stood by itself for a while, and Abin's at QQ was added later on. But it is also possible that PP and QQ were shaped in response to one another – that is, at the same time, as yet another layer of argument. The flow of argument from Yohanan and Rab to Mana and Abin is smooth and uninterrupted. The addition at PP-QQ seems to me a colloquy to be read as a single statement. If that is the case, then the whole is a unity, formed no earlier than its final element. This seems confirmed by the fact that the set at PP-RR is made necessary by the question at OO, and that question is integral to the exposition of Rab's position in toto. Accordingly, it would appear that what we have in the names of the latest authorities is an integral part of the secondary expansion of the primary dispute. In that case, part of the plan of the whole, at the very outset, was the inclusion of these final sayings as elements of the amplification of the dispute. If so, the construction will have come into being as a whole not much earlier than the early or mid-fourth century. At the same time, we notice that the glosses of the positions of Rab and Yohanan do not reach us in the name of authorities who are assumed to have flourished prior to the times of the principal authorities. The main point must not be missed: the needs of the analysis of the positions of Rab and Yohanan, with attention, in particular, to the logic behind the view of each and the unfolding of the argument to expose that logic, explain the composition of the whole. So a clear conception of the direction and purpose of inquiry existed prior to the assembly of the parts and governed the layout of arguments and the dialectic of discourse. Let us now consider from the present perspective further instances in which the names of diverse authorities figure. What then dictates the composition of a passage? It is logic that forms the governing principle of construction, and that logic is prior to the construction and controls all components thereof.

I take as my example, among innumerable possibilities, Y. Baba Qamma 2:13. In this protracted discussion, we see how one authority cites another, earlier figure, with the result that the question of consistency of the view of the first authority comes under discussion. Simeon b. Laqish's interpretation of the Mishnah-passage is compared with a view of Hoshaiah, yet earlier by a generation and so cited by Simeon b. Laqish. A further discussion has Ami, slightly later than Simeon b. Laqish, interpret Simeon's view. Then an opinion of Hoshaiah – hence prior to both Ami and Simeon b. Laqish – comes under discussion. The reason is not that Hoshaiah is represented as conducting a face-to-face argument with Simeon or Ami. Hoshaiah's position is formulated quite separately from theirs. But it intersects in topic and logic. Therefore the framer of the whole found it quite natural to cite Hoshaiah's views. The context is the main thing. Ilfai-Hilfa was a contemporary of Yohanan. His position in the construction hardly has been dictated by that fact. Rather, what he has to say forms a final topic of discussion, in sequence after the view of Rab, who surely came earlier in the third century than Ilfai.

The main point bears repeating. We do not find that the chronology of authorities bears any important relationship to the arrangement of opinions. We also do not find violation of the order in which authorities flourished. The long argument has been laid out in accord with the principles of logical exposition at hand. For that purpose no attention needs to be paid to the sequence in which people may have expressed their views. But people of different centuries are not made to talk to one another.

	A.	"How is the tooth deemed an attested danger in regard to eating what is suitable for [eating]" [M. 1:4C]?
	B.	An ox is an attested danger to eat fruit and vegetables.
	C.	[If, however] it ate [a piece of] clothing or utensils, [the owner] pays half the value of the damage it has caused.
	D.	Under what circumstances?
	E.	[When this takes place] in the domain of the injured party.
	F.	But [if it takes place] in the public domain, he is exempt.
	G.	But if it [the ox] derived benefit [from damage done in public domain], the owner pays for the value of what [his ox] has enjoyed.
I.	A.	[To what does the statement, M. 2:3D-G, "Under what circumstances?" apply?] R. Simeon b. Laqish said, "It applies to the first clause. [If, in the public domain, a beast ate what it usually eats, the owner pays nothing. But if, even in the public domain, it ate clothing or utensils, the owner is liable because people commonly leave things in public domain, and the owner of the beast has the responsibility to watch out for such unusual events.]"
	B.	R. Yohanan said, "It applies to the entire pericope [including the consumption of unusual items, such as clothing or utensils]. [If someone left clothing or utensils in the public domain, the owner of the beast is exempt, because it is not common to leave such things in public domain.]"
	C.	The opinions imputed to R. Simeon b. Laqish are in conflict.
	D.	There R. Simeon b. Laqish has said in the name of R. Hoshaiah, "[If] an ox stood still and ate produce which was stacked in piles, [the owner] is liable." [Hence the owner of the beast is liable if the beast eats what it usually eats in the public domain. M. makes no distinction between the beast's doing so while walking along and while standing still.]
	E.	And here he has said that [the owner is exempt if the beast eats produce in the public domain, on the grounds that that is common.]

F.   They said, "There he spoke in the name of R. Hoshaiah while here he speaks in his own name."

II. A.   A statement which R. Simeon b. Laqish said: "[If there were two beasts in the public domain, one walking, one crouched and] the one which was walking along butted the one which was crouching, [the owner] is exempt [because the one which was crouching bore responsibility for changing the normal procedure, and it is not normal for a beast to crouch in public domain]."

B.   A statement which R. Yohanan said: "[If] the one which was walking along butted the one which was crouching, [the owner] is liable." [The owner of the crouching beast still may ask, "Who gave your beast the right to butt mine?"]

C.   [And, Yohanan further will maintain,] it is not the end of the matter that if the one which was walking along butts the one which was crouching, or the one which was crouching butts the one which was walking along, [the owner of the aggressor is liable].

D.   But even if the two of them were walking along, and one of those which was walking along butted the other which was walking along, [the owner] is liable [on the same grounds, namely, while both beasts had every right to be where they were, there is no right for one beast to butt the other].

E.   [Dealing with these same matters in behalf of Simeon b. Laqish,] R. Ami said, "R. Simeon b. Laqish's position applies only to a case in which a beast which was walking along butted a beast which was crouching, in which case [the owner] is exempt.

F.   "But if a beast which was crouching butted one which was walking along, or one which was walking along butted another which was walking along, [the owner in either case] will be liable."

G.   R. Hoshaiah taught, "In all cases, [the owner] is exempt."

H.   The basis for R. Hoshaiah's position is that liability for injury done by an ox's horn does not apply in public domain anyhow. [Pené Moshe prefers to read: "This is not a case of damages done by an ox's horn in the public domain."]

I.   Rab said, "If the beast stood still [in public domain] and ate up produce which was lying in piles –

J.   "now they have made a lenient rule in the case of tooth, in which case an ox walking along consumed produce lying in piles [and so] standing [still],

K.   "while they have made a more stringent rule in the case of damages done by the horn,

L.   "in which a beast which was walking along has butted a beast which was standing still. [That is, the beast which was walking along does not impose liability on its owner for produce eaten by the way. In this regard a more stringent rule applies to damages done by the beast's horn than those done by the beast's tooth, since if the beast walking along butted one lying down, the owner

> is liable, while, as we saw, in the case of tooth, the owner is exempt. If, to be sure, the beast had stood still and eaten produce, also in the case of damages done by tooth, the owner is liable.]"
>
> N.   Ilfai remarked, "If the beast had stood still and eaten the produce which was lying in piles, [the owner] would be liable.
>
> N.   "Now they have made a lenient rule in the case of tooth, in that if the beast which was walking along and ate produce which was lying around, the owner is exempt from paying damages.
>
> O.   "But a more stringent rule applies in the case of damages done by the horn when a beast which was walking along butted another beast which was walking along, [and the owner in this case would be liable to damages]."

The upshot is that we may speak about "the Talmud Yerushalmi," its voice, its purposes, its mode of constructing a view of the Israelite world. The reason is that, when we claim "the Talmud Yerushalmi" speaks, we replicate both the main lines of chronology and the literary character of the document. These point toward the formation of the bulk of materials – its units of discourse – in a process lasting (to take a guess) about half a century, prior to the ultimate arrangement of these units of discourse around passages of the Mishnah and the closure and redaction of the whole into the document we now know.

Now, admittedly, the arguments that constitute the exegetical and amplificatory work of the Talmud Yerushalmi often contain names of specific authorities. These figures are assumed to have lived not only at the end of the process of the formation of the document, but at the beginning and middle as well. If we could demonstrate that these authorities really said what was attributed to these authorities really was said by them, we should be able to compose a history of the exegetical process, not merely an account of its end product. And that is what Halivni claims in his *Sources and Traditions* to have accomplished. But as soon as we recognize the simple fact that attributions are just that – not facts but merely allegations as to facts – we realize the remarkably shallow foundations that underlie Halivni's towering construction.

VI. From Building Block to Document, or from Document to Building Block?

We have very good reason to suppose that the text as we have it speaks within the limited context of the period of the actual framing of the text's principal building blocks. As I have already pointed out, the evidence points to these traits of the writings:

(1) The building blocks – units of discourse – give evidence of having been put together in a moment of sustained deliberation, in

accordance with a plan of exposition, and in response to a finite problem of logical analysis.

(2) To state matters negatively, the units of discourse in no way appear to have taken shape slowly, over a long period of time, in a process governed by the order in which sayings were framed, now and here, then and there, later and anywhere else (so to speak). Before us is the result of considered redaction, not protracted accretion, mindful construction, not sedimentary accretion, such as Halivni's theory of matters requires.

As I said at the outset, the traits of the bulk of the Talmud Yerushalmi may be explained in one of only two ways. One way is this: the very heirs of the Mishnah, in the opening generation, ca. A.D. 200-225, agreed upon conventions not merely of speech and rhetorical formulation, but also of thought and modes of analysis. They further imposed these conventions on all subsequent generations, wherever they lived, whenever they did their work. Accordingly, at the outset the decision was made to do the work precisely in the way in which, two hundred years later, the work turns out to have been done. The alternative view is that, some time late in the formation of diverse materials in response to the Mishnah (and to various other considerations), some people got together and made a decision to rework whatever was in hand into a single, stunningly cogent document, the Talmud Yerushalmi as we know it in the bulk of its units of discourse. Whether this work took a day or a half-century, it was the work of sages who knew precisely what they wished to do and who did it over and over again. This second view is the one I take, and on the basis of it the remainder of this book unfolds. The consequence is that the Talmud Yerushalmi exhibits a viewpoint. It is portrayed in what I have called "the Talmud's one voice."

In claiming that we deal not only with uniform rhetoric, but with a single cogent viewpoint, we must take full account of the contrary claim of the Talmud's framers themselves. This claim they lay down through the constant citations of sayings in the names of specific authorities. It must follow that differentiation by chronology – the periods in which the several sages cited actually flourished – is possible. To be sure, the original purpose of citing named authorities was not to set forth chronological lines, but to establish the authority behind a given view of the law. But the history of viewpoints should be possible. As I argued earlier, it would be possible if we could show, on the basis of evidence external to the Talmud Yerushalmi itself, that the Talmud's own claim in attributing statements to specific people is subject to verification or falsification. But all that I can show is a general respect for chronology, not only authority, in the unfolding of discussion. That is, we are not likely to find in Talmud Yerushalmi that an authority of the early third century is made to comment on a statement in the name of a sage of the later fourth century.

But the organizing principle of discourse (even in anthologies) never derives from the order in which authorities lived. And that is the main point. The logical requirements of the analysis at hand determine the limits of applied and practical reason framed by the sustained discourses of which the Talmud Yerushalmi is composed. Now it may well be the case that sayings not reworked into the structure of a larger argument really do derive from the authority to whom they are ascribed. But if the discrete opinions at hand then do not provide us with a logical and analytical proposition, they also do not give us much else that is very interesting. They constitute isolated data, lacking all pattern, making no clear point. The fact that Rabbi X held opinion A, while Rabbi Y maintained position Q, is without sense, unless A and Q together say more than they tell us separately.

To conclude: in a given unit of discourse, the focus, the organizing principle, the generative interest – these are defined solely by the issue at hand. The argument moves from point to point, directed by the inner logic of argument itself. A single plane of discourse is established. All things are leveled out, so that the line of logic runs straight and true. Accordingly, a single conception of the framing and formation of the unit of discourse stands prior to the spelling out of issues. More fundamental still, what people in general wanted was not to create topical anthologies – to put together instances of what this one said about that issue – but to exhibit the logic of that issue, viewed under the aspect of eternity. Under sustained inquiry we always find a theoretical issue, freed of all temporal considerations and the contingencies of politics and circumstance.

VII. Halivni's Sources and Traditions and a Redefinition of "Sources" and "Traditions"

None of these traits exhibited by the literature Halivni purports to correct and explain favors Halivni's theory that the document took shape out of prior documents, some changed in the process of later (re)formulation and redaction, some not changed at all ("sources and traditions" once more), which the authorship preserved in such a way that we may identify them. Any claim, such as forms the basis for Halivni's massive exegetical exercise, that we deal with differentiable sources and traditions, contradicts the elementary facts of the Yerushalmi, and, obviously, the Bavli as well. What has gone wrong for Halivni is the simple fact that he never composed a null hypothesis and told us what sort of evidence would prove the proposition contrary to his own. Having failed to do that, he has built the entire edifice on nothing more than the presupposition that attributions of sayings to named authorities are – must be – valid. Without that premise, his whole hermeneutics proves hopeless because it contradicts the generative and indicative traits of the text he claims to expound. To dismiss the entire structure Halivni has erected as mere *pilpul* of the old yeshiva-type seems to me the only reasonable conclusion, and it is one that, after many years of careful study of his writings, I find myself constrained to adopt.

Let me close with my own view of how we should distinguish, in the Bavli, between sources and traditions, which forms the principal inquiry of Halivni's exegetical *ouevre*. The Talmud of Babylonia, or Bavli, draws upon prior materials. The document in no way was not made up out of whole cloth by its penultimate and ultimate authorship, the generations that drew the whole together and placed it into the form in which it has come down from the seventh century to the present day. The Bavli's authorship both received out of the past a corpus of *sources*, and also stood in a line of *traditions* of sayings and stories, that is, fixed wordings of thought the formulation and transmission of which took place not in completed documents but in ad hoc and brief sentences or little narratives. These materials, deriving from an indeterminate past through a now inaccessible process of literary history, constitute traditions in the sense defined in the preface: an incremental and linear process that step by step transmits out of the past an essential and unchanging fundament of truth and writing.

Traditions: some of these prior materials never reached redaction in a distinct document and come down as sherds and remnants within the Bavli itself. These are the ones that may be called traditions, in the sense of materials formulated and transmitted from one generation to the next, but not given a place in a document of their own.

Sources: others had themselves reached closure prior to the work on the Bavli and are readily identified as autonomous writings. Scripture, to take an obvious example, the Mishnah, tractate Abot (the Fathers), the Tosefta (so we commonly suppose), Sifra, Sifré to Numbers, Sifré to Deuteronomy, Genesis Rabbah, Leviticus Rabbah, the Fathers according to Rabbi Nathan, Pesiqta deRab Kahana, Pesiqta Rabbati, possibly Lamentations Rabbah, not to mention the Siddur and Mahzor (order of daily and holy day prayer, respectively), and various other writings had assuredly concluded their processes of formation before the Bavli's authorship accomplished their work. These we call *sources* – more or less completed writings. On that basis, what I believe to be a more critical, nuanced, and altogether productive exegetical task finds definition, one that Halivni may well wish to consider as well. The null hypothesis has called into question Halivni's fundamental premises, so the approach proposed here – working backward from the finished product, rather than forward from the smallest whole units of thought – will now have its hearing. The documentary approach advocated in this book now defines the future of inquiry.

3

When the Document Defines the Literary Protocol

I. When Redaction Governs Writing

Since I insist that a document may dictate the rhetorical and logical characteristics of its components, I have now to demonstrate what I mean. Can I show what kind of writing reflects the documentary program and plan of the ultimate redactors or authorship? The Mishnah provides the exemplary and strongest instance of a canonical writing, most (though not all) of which responds to a single redactional program, encompassing not merely how completed units of thought are joined into a cogent whole, but also how individual units of thought are themselves composed and crafted. When we see a sustained and detailed account of the role of the documentary program in the framing of the writing, we may discern cases in which the documentary plan plays no part in the composition of the units of which the document is composed.

II. Writing and Redaction in the Mishnah

One document alone in the entire canon of the Judaism of the Dual Torah as closed in late antiquity shows how the purposes of the framers dictate the literary traits of their writing. That is the Mishnah, which in the main, though not entirely, conforms to a literary protocol dictated only in the formation of the end product. While the Mishnah refers occasionally to, and often makes use of, conceptions formed prior to its closure in ca. A.D. 200, nonetheless its authorship imposes a single plan upon nearly the entire document. And that plan can have been effected only if it was imposed in the very writing, the act of composing, of the components of the document as a whole. The reason is that the Mishnah's literary protocol imposes mnemonic traits of pattern and form upon most of the components of the writing, and these traits are so pervasive, recur in such carefully enumerated patterns, that a sedimentary theory of the formation of the writing, with materials prepared first and only then inserted into the document that was in process of aggregation, cannot account for the facts in our hands. Only if the pattern was imposed systematically can we explain its pervasive presence. And that must mean that the process of redaction encompassed also the stage of composition of the writing; there is then no distinguishing between the framing of completed units of thought and the conglomeration of those units of thought into chapters and tractates and thence the Mishnah as a whole.[1]

III. The Topical Organization of the Document as a Whole

The Mishnah's tractates are readily distinguishable from one another since each treats a distinct topic.[2] So if Mishnah were to be copied out in a long scroll without the significance of lines of demarcation among the several tractates, the opening pericope of each tractate would leave no doubt that one topic had been completed and a new one undertaken. The same is so within the tractates ("chapters"). Intermediate divisions of these same principal divisions (we might call them chapters of parts of books) are to be discerned on the basis of internal evidence. That is accomplished through the confluence of theme or subject-matter and form or patterning of language. That is to say, a given intermediate division of a principal one (a chapter of a tractate) will be marked by a particular, recurrent, formal pattern in accord with which sentences are constructed, and also by a particular and distinct theme, to which these sentences are addressed. When a new theme commences, a fresh formal pattern will be used. Within the

---

[1]That is not the only possible explanation for the formal and redactional uniformity of the document. It is also possible that there was a very long history behind each individual unit, but that the framers of all units, during that long history, conformed to literary conventions that governed how they would express their ideas. But that theory does not account for the numerical patterns that govern, and these are independent of the sequences of the names to which materials are attributed, hence the (putative) stages or order in which a given set of sayings was put together. In my view, therefore, the only plausible explanation for the Mishnah's literary character is the one given here.

[2]We shall look in vain in the midrash compilations for topical unity of the sort that the Mishnah exhibits throughout. The counterpart, for some midrash compilations, is propositional cogency, but that is far from the same thing.

intermediate divisions, we are able to recognize the components, or smallest whole units of thought (hereinafter, cognitive units, defined at greater length presently), because there will be a recurrent pattern of sentence structure repeated time and again within the unit and a shifting at the commencement of the next theme. Each point at which the recurrent pattern commences marks the beginning of a new cognitive unit. In general, an intermediate division will contain a carefully enumerated sequence of exempla of cognitive units, in the established formal pattern, commonly in groups of three or five or multiples of three or five (pairs for the first division). A single rhetorical pattern will govern the whole set of topical instances of a logical proposition. When the logical-topical program changes, the rhetorical pattern will change too. None of these well-composed traits of order and form can have come about in a long-term process of agglutination; they are in my judgment conceivable only if the work of redaction was coexistensive with the work of formulation. That is to say, in the case of the Mishnah, the document defines the literary protocol. In the Mishnah, writing and redaction unite. Accordingly, the Mishnah's author imposes at the end the plan and program of the whole, and the work of writing is integral to the work of redaction and closure. The document presents its discourses as thematic expositions, with beginnings, middles, and endings, principles and secondary developments thereof. Throughout the Mishnah the preferred mode of layout is by themes, spelled out along the lines of the logic imbedded in those themes.

Seeing the writing as a whole – and here we cannot turn to an inductive examination of the evidence and the reader will have to trust me, or we shall have at this point to lay out the entire Mishnah, which, in my English translation, covers 1100 pages! – we observe that the Mishnah is divided up into six principal divisions, each expounding a single, immense topic. The tractates of each division furthermore take up subtopics of the principal theme. The chapters then unfold along the lines of the (to the framers) logic of the necessary dissection of the division. While that mode of organization may appear to be necessary or "self-evident" (it is how *we* should have written a law code, is it not?), we should notice that there are three other modes of organization found within the document. They show us what might have been done. Since these are not utilized extensively or systematically, however, they represent rejected options. One of the three alternative ways of putting things together is to collect diverse sayings around the name of a given authority. (The whole of tractate *Eduyyot* is organized in that way.) A second way is to express a given basic principle through diverse topics, e.g., a fundamental rule cutting across many areas of law, stated in one place through all of the diverse types of law through which the rule or principle may be expressed. A third way is to take a striking language pattern and collect sayings on diverse topics which conform to the given language pattern. But faced with these possible ways of organizing materials, the framers of the Mishnah chose to adhere to a highly disciplined thematic-logical principle of organization. So internal evidence suffices to tell us that we deal with a vast exposition on various themes, divided by major subjects and by still broader classifications of divisions.

This brings us to the formal cogency of the document, a cogency possible, in my view, only if redaction and writing form a union. The Mishnah's authorship constructs units of meaning, intermediate divisions composed of cognitive elements. The Mishnah's authorship conveys its message through uniform aesthetic expression: how things are said matters as much as what is said. The Mishnah's authorship took as its mode of expression not the statement of generalization, but the implicit communication of generalization only through grouped examples of a common rule, which rule would rarely be articulated. That is a subtle mode of discourse indeed, and, joined to the intent of memorization and transmission orally, represents an extraordinary compliment to the proposed audience of the document. The technology of mnemonics therefore forms the surface of a deep texture of thought about communication – but also, thought about thinking, that is, about conveying principles through details. What these fundamental traits tell us about our authorship is two important facts.

First, they proposed to make an autonomous, free-standing statement, which did not appeal to some other writing for order and proportion. Rather, they treated the topics of their choice within an autonomous logic dictated by the requirements of those topics. Specifically, they exhibit the sense that a given topic has its own inner tension and generates its own program of thought and exposition. Second, their free-standing statement was set forth in a highly systematic and rhetorically careful way. Since the exposition bore the burden of clarifying itself, unable to appeal to some other document for structure and cogency, the formulation of that exposition would have to exhibit those signals of sense, beginnings, middles, endings, that instructed the reader (or hearer) on how to follow the whole. These traits will strike us as consequential only when we take up other writings of the same set, in which discourse is not propositional, and in which the formalization of language is not critical to the exposition at all.

Let me summarize the criteria of formalization and organization of the Mishnah, criteria that apply throughout. The first of the two criteria derives from the nature of the principal divisions themselves:

theme. That is, it is, as I said at the outset, along thematic lines that the redactors organized vast corpora of materials into principal divisions, tractates. These fundamental themes themselves were subdivided into smaller conceptual units. The principal divisions treat their themes in units indicated by the sequential unfolding of their inner logical structure. Accordingly, one established criterion for the deliberation of an aggregate of materials from some other, fore or aft, will be a shift in the theme, or predominant and characteristic concern, of a sequence of materials. The second fundamental criterion is the literary character, the syntactical and grammatical pattern, which differentiates and characterizes a sequence of primitive (that is, undifferentiable, indivisible) units of thought. Normally, when the subject changes, the mode of expression, the formal or formulary character, the patterning of language, will change as well.

IV. Forms and the Formalization of Speech

From the basic traits of large-scale organization, which appeal to the characteristics of subject matter, we turn to the way in which sentences and paragraphs are put together. By a "paragraph" (which is a metaphor drawn from our own circumstance) I mean a completed exposition of thought, the setting forth of a proposition whole and complete, now without regard to the larger function, e.g., in a sustained discourse of argument or proposition, served by that thought. Two or more lapidary statements, e.g., allegations as to fact, will make up such a sustained cognitive unit. The cognitive units in the Mishnah in particular resort to a remarkably limited repertoire of formulary patterns, and the document as a whole exhibits remarkable formal uniformity.

For the authorship of the Mishnah manages to say whatever it wants in one of the following ways:

1.   the simple declarative sentence, in which the subject, verb, and predicate are syntactically tightly joined to one another, e.g., he who does so and so is such and such;

2.   the duplicated subject, in which the subject of the sentence is stated twice, e.g., He who does so and so, lo, he is such and such;

3.   mild apocopation, in which the subject of the sentence is cut off from the verb, which refers to its own subject, and not the one with which the sentence commences, e.g., He who does so and so..., it [the thing he has done] is such and such;

4.   extreme apocopation, in which a series of clauses is presented, none of them tightly joined to what precedes or follows, and all of them cut off from the predicate of the sentence, e.g., He who does so and so...,

it [the thing he has done] is such and such..., it is a matter of doubt whether...or whether...lo, it [referring to nothing in the antecedent, apocopated clauses of the subject of the sentence] is so and so.

5. In addition to these formulary patterns, in which the distinctive formulary traits are effected through variations in the relationship between the subject and the predicate of the sentence, or in which the subject itself is given a distinctive development, there is yet a fifth. In this last one we have a contrastive complex predicate, in which case we may have two sentences, independent of one another, yet clearly formulated so as to stand in acute balance with one another in the predicate, thus, *He who does...is unclean, and he who does not...is clean.*

It naturally will be objected, is it possible that "a simple declarative sentence" may be asked to serve as a formulary pattern, alongside the rather distinctive and unusual constructions which follow? True, by itself, a tightly constructed sentence consisting of subject, verb, and complement, in which the verb refers to the subject, and the complement to the verb, hardly exhibits traits of particular formal interest. Yet a sequence of such sentences, built along the same gross grammatical lines, may well exhibit a clear-cut and distinctive pattern. And here the mnemonics of the document enter into consideration. The Mishnah is not a generalizing document; it makes its points by repeating several cases that yield the same, ordinarily unarticulated, general principle. Accordingly, the Mishnah, as I said, utilizes sets of three or five repetitions of cases to make a single point. Now when we see that three or five "simple declarative sentences" take up one principle or problem, and then, when the principle or problem shifts, a quite distinctive formal pattern will be utilized, we realize that the "simple declarative sentence" has served the formulator of the unit of thought as aptly as did apocopation, a dispute, or another more obviously distinctive form or formal pattern. The contrastive predicate is one example; the Mishnah contains many more.

The important point of differentiation, particularly for the simple declarative sentence, therefore appears in the intermediate or the whole cognitive unit, thus in the interplay between theme and form. It is there that we see a single pattern recurring in a long sequence of sentences, e.g., *the X which has lost its Y is unclean because of its Z. The Z which has lost its Y is unclean because of its X.* Another example will be a long sequence of highly developed sentences, laden with relative clauses and other explanatory matter, in which a single syntactical pattern will govern the articulation of three or six or nine exempla. That sequence will be followed by one repeated terse sentence pattern, e.g., *X is so and so, Y is such and such, Z is thus and so.* The former group will treat one principle or theme, the latter some other. There can be no doubt, therefore, that the declarative sentence in recurrent patterns is, in its way, just as carefully formalized as a sequence of severely apocopated sentences or of contrastive predicates or duplicated subjects. None of the Mishnah's secondary and amplificatory companions, e.g., the Tosefta, the Talmud of the Land of Israel or Yerushalmi, the Talmud of Babylonia or Bavli, exhibits the same tight and rigidly adhered to rhetorical cogency. And none of the midrash compilations on which we concentrate in this book exhibit anything like the aesthetic cogency characteristic of the Mishnah. When, therefore, we want to see what a document written by its redactors looks like, in the rabbinic canon we can turn only to the Mishnah.[3]

V. The Mnemonic Plan of the Mishnah

The reason for the patterning of rhetoric becomes apparent when we appreciate the effect of doing so. It is vastly to facilitate memorizing the document. Exactly how does the formulation of the document facilitate remembering its exact words? The answer to that question derives from the smallest whole units of discourse, the cognitive units, defined as groups of sentences that make a point completely and entirely on their own, become intelligible on three bases: logical, topical, and rhetorical. What I now prove is simple: It is the confluence of logic, topic, and rhetoric that generates at the deepest structure of the Mishnah's language a set of mnemonic patterns. These mnemonics serve by definition to facilitate the easy memorization of the text of the Mishnah. First to define the matter: what marks the smallest whole unit of discourse – a handful of sentences – is that the several sentences of which it is composed are unintelligible or not wholly intelligible by themselves but are entirely intelligible when seen as a group. The smallest whole unit of discourse in the Mishnah *invariably* constitutes a syllogism, that is, a statement of a proposition, in which a condition or question, constituting a protasis, finds resolution in a rule or answer, the apodosis. "If such and such is the case, then so

---

[3]To revert to the concession made in the preface, that does seem to me to argue for that historical-ordinal sequence that I have posited, even though, admittedly, at one and the same moment a variety of types of writing can have gone on, some of them involving redactional planning in the writing of documents, others producing writing independent of the documents for which the writing was intended, and still others yielding writing that would stand without reference to later documentary inclusion.

and so is the rule" – that is the characteristic cognitive structure of the Mishnah's smallest whole unit of thought or discourse. Even if that statement were made up of two or three or even five declarative sentences, it is only when the proposition is fully exposed, both protasis and apodosis, that the declarative sentences reach the level of full and complete expression, that is, sense and intelligibility.[4]

For the purpose of making this point about recurrent patterns clear, let me take up a brief example, drawn from Mishnah-tractate Sanhedrin Chapter Two paragraph two, hence M. San. 2:2:

[1]	A.	*A high priest judges, and [others] judge him;*
[2]	B.	*gives testimony, and [others] give testimony about him;*
[3]	C.	*performs the rite of removing the shoe [Deut. 25:7-9], and [others] perform the rite of removing the shoe with his wife.*
[4]	D.	*[Others] enter levirate marriage with his wife, but he does not enter into levirate marriage,*
	E.	because he is prohibited to marry a widow.

Thus far we have simple declarative sentences, subject, verb. Now the syntax shifts to conditional sentences or other qualified statements.

	F.	[If] he suffers a death [in his family], he does not follow the bier.
	G.	"But when [the bearers of the bier] are not visible, he is visible; when they are visible, he is not.
	H.	"And he goes with them to the city gate," the words of R. Meir.
	I.	R. Judah says, "He never leaves the sanctuary,
	J.	"since it says, *'Nor shall he go out of the sanctuary'* (Lev. 21:12)."
	K.	And when he gives comfort to others
	L.	the accepted practice is for all the people to pass one after another, and the appointed [prefect of the priests] stands between him and the people.
	M.	And when he receives consolation from others,
	N.	all the people say to him, "Let us be your atonement."
	O.	And he says to them, "May you be blessed by Heaven."
	P.	And when they provide him with the funeral meal,
	Q.	all the people sit on the ground, while he sits on a stool.

M. Sanhedrin 2:1

I have emphasized the simple declarative sentence, because of the match to follow. But we shall see other correspondences, e.g., the *and when...* type.

---

[4]And it goes without saying, if the presence of these traits indicates an intent on mnemonic composition, the absence should suggest the contrary: no reliance upon mnemonics, hence no interest in memorization. That calls into question the insistence of Halivni, discussed in the conclusion, that individual sayings (lemmas) circulated in memory out of all relationship to documentary locus.

[1] A.   *The king does not judge, and [others] do not judge him;*

[2] B.   *does not give testimony, and [others] do not give testimony about him;*

[3] C.   *does not perform the rite of removing the shoe, and others do not perform the rite of removing the shoe with his wife;*

[4] D.   *does not enter into levirate marriage, nor [do his brothers] enter levirate marriage with his wife.*

E.   R. Judah says, "If he wanted to perform the rite of removing the shoe or to enter into levirate marriage, his memory is a blessing."

F.   They said to him, "They pay no attention to him [if he expressed the wish to do so]."

G.   [Others] do not marry his widow.

H.   R. Judah says, "A king may marry the widow of a king.

I.   "For so we find in the case of David, that he married the widow of Saul,

J.   "For it is said, 'And I gave you your master's house and your master's wives into your embrace' (2 Sam. 12:8)."

M. Sanhedrin 2:2

Now if we wish to ask what point emerges in the carefully crafted details before us, we do not have far to go to find the answer. It is that the high priest and the king form a single genus, but two distinct species, and the variations between the species form a single set of taxonomic indicators. The one is like the other in these ways, unlike the other in those ways. Does that information yield a proposition? Without doubt. Does the proposition generate further propositions, so that it constitutes a syllogism? Without doubt. How so? The remainder of the passage shows us the secondary amplification and discussion of the implication of the established principle, and that principle proves generative of further syllogisms, proposed and debated in the secondary details of the passage. We now have a clear picture of the unit of discourse and its rhetorical components as well as its syllogistic character.

VI. Syntax and Syllogism

The patterns of language, e.g., syntactic structures, of the apodosis and protasis of the Mishnah's smallest whole units of discourse are framed in formal, mnemonic patterns. They follow a few simple rules. These rules, once known, apply nearly everywhere and form stunning evidence for the document's cogency. They permit anyone to reconstruct, out of a few key phrases, an entire cognitive unit, and even complete intermediate units of discourse. Working downward from the surface, therefore, anyone can penetrate into the deeper layers of meaning of the Mishnah. Then and at the same time, while discovering the principle behind the cases, one can easily memorize the whole by mastering the recurrent rhetorical pattern dictating the expression of the cogent set of cases.   For it is easy to note the shift from one rhetorical pattern to another and to follow the repeated cases, articulated in the new pattern downward to its logical substrate.   So syllogistic propositions, in the Mishnah's authors' hands, come to full expression not only in *what* people wish to state but also in *how* they choose to say it.   The limits of rhetoric define the arena of topical articulation.   Once we ask what three or five joined topical propositions have in common, we state the logic and can therefore propose the syllogism that is shared among them all.

The analysis of the Mishnah's linguistic formalization requires brief attention to the forms not only of cognitive units ("paragraphs") but also of sentences ("smallest whole units of thought").   The smallest whole unit of discourse is made up of fixed, recurrent formulas, clichés, patterns, or little phrases, out of which whole pericopes, or large elements in pericopes, e.g. complete sayings, are constructed.   Small units of tradition, while constitutive of pericopes, do not generate new sayings or legal problems, as do apophthegmatic formulae.   An example of part of a pericope (smallest whole unit of thought) composed primarily of recurrent formulas is as follows:

> *A basket of fruit intended for the Sabbath*
> House of Shammai declare exempt
> *And* the House of Hillel declare liable.

The italicized words are not fixed formulas.   *And* is redactional; the formulation of the statement of the problem does not follow a pattern. The Houses-sentences, by contrast, are formed of fixed, recurrent phrases, which occur in numerous pericopes.   Similarly:

> *House of Shammai say ... House of Hillel say ...*

are fixed small units, whether or not the predicate matches; when it balances, we have a larger unit of tradition composed of two small units.   By definition these small formulas cannot be random, or they would not constitute formulas.   Such small units are whole words, not syntactical or grammatical particles.   They also are not mere redactional devices used to join together discrete pericopes in the later processes of collection and organization, such as connecting words, editorial conventions, formulaic introductions to Scriptures, and other redactional clichés.

Some of the patterning or formalization of language serves in the expression of the proposition at hand.   The pattern, then, is internal to the idea which is expressed and which predominates in the formulation of that idea, its linguistic formalization. If this pattern recurs for two or more cognitive units, then we have a formulary trait internal to the pattern of language of each element in a subdivision. Each and every cognitive unit within said subdivision will express its particular concept or thought in conformity with this common pattern, which therefore is to be designated as internal to the whole. The recurrent pattern of syntax or language is both tradental and redactional, in that what is to be expressed is the work of those responsible for both the formulary and formalized character and the cognitive substance of the subdivision in all of its parts and as a whole. In the sample passage given earlier, the following illustrates the formulary pattern just now described:

8:1

B. The House of Shammai *say, "One blesses over the* [1] day, *and afterward one blesses over the* [2] wine."

C. And the House of Hillel *say, "One blesses over the* [2] wine, *and afterward one blesses over the* [1] day."

8:2

A. The House of Shammai say, "They wash [1] the hands and afterward mix [2] the cup."

B. And the House of Hillel say, "They mix [2] the cup and afterward wash [1] the hands."

8:4

A. The House of Shammai say, "They clean [1] the house, and afterward they wash [2] the hands."

B. And the House of Hillel say, "They wash [2] the hands, and afterward they clean [1] the house."

M. Berakhot 8:1-4

Here we have a highly coherent theme ("concerning the meal") and a rigidly adhered to formulary pattern, 1, 2 vs. 2, 1.

The formal pattern may also stand external to the idea which is expressed and superficial, and which occurs chiefly at the outset of a cognitive unit. The arrangement of words of said unit will ignore this external formulary trait. What is to be said can be, and is, stated without regard to the superficial trait shared among several cognitive units. Indeed, we may readily discern that the formulary trait of a series of cognitive units is external to the formulation of all of them, simply because each cognitive unit goes its own way, stating its ideas in its own form or formulary pattern, without any regard whatsoever for the formal traits of other units to which it is joined. The joining – the shared language or formulary or formal pattern – is therefore external to the several units. An example of a unit presenting a coherent theme but lacking a coherent formulary pattern derives from the passage of tractate Sanhedrin cited above.

VII. Rhetoric and Redaction

Now to state my main point in heavy emphasis:

The Mishnah's formal traits of rhetoric indicate that the document has been formulated all at once, and not in an incremental, linear process extending into a remote (mythic) past, (e.g., to Sinai).

These traits, common to a series of distinct cognitive units, are redactional, because they are imposed at that point at which someone intended to join together discrete (finished) units on a given theme. The varieties of traits particular to the discrete units and the diversity of authorities cited therein, including masters of two or three or even four strata from the turn of the first century to the end of the second, make it highly improbable that the several units were formulated in a common pattern and then preserved, until, later on, still further units, on the same theme and in the same pattern, were worked out and added. The entire indifference, moreover, to historical order of authorities and concentration on the logical unfolding of a given theme or problem without reference to the sequence of authorities, confirm the supposition that the work of formulation and that of redaction go forward together. The principal framework of formulation and formalization in the Mishnah is the intermediate division rather than the cognitive unit. The least-formalized formulary pattern, the simple declarative sentence, turns out to yield many examples of acute formalization, in which a single distinctive pattern is imposed upon two or more (very commonly, groups of three or groups of five) cognitive units. While an intermediate division of a tractate may be composed of several such conglomerates of cognitive units, it is rare indeed for cognitive units formally to stand wholly by themselves. Normally, cognitive units share formal or formulary traits with others to which they are juxtaposed and the theme of which they share.

It follows that the principal unit of formulary formalization is the intermediate division and not the cognitive unit. And what that means for our inquiry, is simple: we can tell when it is that the ultimate or penultimate redactors of a document do the writing. Now let us see that vast collection of writings that exhibit precisely the opposite trait: a literature in which, while doing some writing of their own, the redactors collected and arranged available materials. In the comparison of writing governed by redactional considerations and writing indifferent to redactional considerations we see the emergence of the indicative criteria on the basis of which the experiments of Part Two depend.

4

When the Document Does Not Define the Literary Protocol: Stories Told But Not Compiled

A Reprise of the Argument of
Why No Gospels in Talmudic Judaism?

I. The Three Types of Received Compositions,
the Dual Structure of their Ultimate Redaction

In *Why No Gospels?* I performed an experiment similar to that worked out in these pages. That is, I assembled materials that (as in Chapter Six) can have yielded a compilation unlike any now in our hands, but (as in Chapter Seven) did not do so. So when, later on, I claim to identify kinds of writing – complete and well-exposed essays – that were not framed into cogent documents, readers will know precisely that to which I refer. Then the very notion that a kind of writing was going on in response to the requirements of compiling documents, which we can differentiate by appeal to objective traits from a kind of writing that was produced not in relationship to the task of redaction, will prove less strange. In order to make sense of the whole, let us first of all take our sighting on the basic redactional repertoire of the canon of the Judaism of the Dual Torah. Precisely what kinds of compilations do we have, and how were these formed into documents? We begin with the final document, the Bavli, ca. A.D. 600, and ask about what the compilers of that document had in hand and how they chose to organize their materials. From there we work our way backward to other documents.

The final organizers of the Bavli, the Talmud of Babylonia had in hand a tripartite corpus of inherited materials awaiting composition into a final, closed document. The first type of material, in various states and stages of completion, addressed the Mishnah or took up the principles of laws that the Mishnah had originally brought to articulation. These the framers of the Bavli organized in accord with the order of those Mishnah-tractates that they selected for sustained attention.

Second, they had in hand received materials, again in various conditions, pertinent to Scripture, both as Scripture related to the Mishnah and also as Scripture laid forth its own narratives. These they set forth as Scripture commentary. In this way, the penultimate and ultimate redactors of the Bavli laid out a systematic presentation of the two Torahs, the oral, represented by the Mishnah, and the written, represented by Scripture.

And, third, the framers of the Bavli also had in hand materials focused on sages. These in the received form, attested in the Bavli's pages, were framed around twin biographical principles, either as strings of stories about great sages of the past or as collections of sayings and comments drawn together solely because the same name stands behind all the collected sayings. These can easily have been composed into biographies. In the context of Christianity and of Judaism, it is appropriate to call the biography of a holy man or woman, meant to convey the divine message, a gospel.[1] Hence the question raised here: why no gospels in Judaism? The question is an appropriate one, because, as I shall show, there could have been. The final step – assembling available stories into a coherent narrative, with a beginning, middle, and end, for example – was not taken.

The Bavli as a whole lays itself out as a commentary to the Mishnah. So the framers wished us to think that whatever they wanted to tell us would take the form of Mishnah commentary. But a second glance indicates that the Bavli is made up of enormous composites, themselves closed prior to inclusion in the Bavli. Some of

---

[1] I use the word "gospel" with a small G as equivalent to "didactic life of a holy man, portraying the faith." Obviously, the Christian usage, with a capital G, must maintain that there can be a Gospel only about Jesus Christ. Claims of uniqueness are, of course, not subject to public discourse. In the present context, I could as well have referred to lives of saints, since Judaism of the Dual Torah produced neither a gospel about a central figure nor lives of saints. Given the centrality of Moses "our rabbi," for example, we should have anticipated a "Gospel of Moses" parallel to the Gospels of Jesus Christ, and, lacking that, at least a "life of Aqiba," scholar, saint, martyr, parallel to the lives of various saints. We also have no autobiographies of any kind, beyond some "I"-stories, which themselves seem to me uncommon.

these composites – around 35 percent to 40 percent of Bavli's, if my sample is indicative[2] – were selected and arranged along lines dictated by a logic other than that deriving from the requirements of Mishnah commentary. The components of the canon of the Judaism of the Dual Torah prior to the Bavli had encompassed amplifications of the Mishnah, in the Tosefta and in the Yerushalmi, as well as the same for Scripture, in such documents as Sifra to Leviticus, Sifré to Numbers, another Sifré, to Deuteronomy, Genesis Rabbah, Leviticus Rabbah, and the like. But there was no entire document, now extant, organized around the life and teachings of a particular sage. Even The Fathers According to Rabbi Nathan, which contains a good sample of stories about sages, is not so organized as to yield a life of a sage, or even a systematic biography of any kind. Where events in the lives of sages do occur, they are thematic and not biographical in organization, e.g., stories about the origins, as to Torah study, of diverse sages; death scenes of various sages. The sage as such, whether Aqiba or Yohanan ben Zakkai or Eliezer b. Hyrcanus, never in that document defines the appropriate organizing principle for sequences of stories or sayings. And there is no other in which the sage forms an organizing category for any material purpose.[3]

Accordingly, the decision that the framers of the Bavli reached was to adopt the two redactional principles inherited from the antecedent century or so and to reject the one already rejected by their predecessors, even while honoring it. [1] They organized the Bavli around the Mishnah. But [2] they adapted and included vast tracts of antecedent materials organized as scriptural commentary. These they inserted whole and complete, not at all in response to the Mishnah's

---

[2]I compared Bavli and Yerushalmi tractates Sukkah, Sanhedrin, and Sotah, showing the proportion of what I call Scripture-units of thought to Mishnah-units of thought. See my *Judaism. The Classic Statement. The Evidence of the Bavli* (Chicago, 1986: University of Chicago Press).

[3]The occasion, in the history of Judaism, at which biography defines a generative category of literature, therefore also of thought, will therefore prove noteworthy. The model of biography surely existed from the formation of the Pentateuch, with its lines of structure, from Exodus through Deuteronomy, set forth around the biography of Moses, birth, call, career, death. And other biographies did flourish prior to the Judaism of the Dual Torah. Not only so, but the wall of the Dura synagogue highlights not the holy people so much as saints, such as Aaron and Moses. Accordingly, we must regard as noteworthy and requiring explanation the omission of biography from the literary genres of the canon of the Judaism of the Dual Torah. One obvious shift is marked by Hasidism, with its special interest in stories about saints and in compiling those stories.

program. But, finally, [3] while making provision for small-scale compositions built upon biographical principles, preserving both strings of sayings from a given master (and often a given tradent of a given master) as well as tales about authorities of the preceding half millennium, they *never* created redactional compositions, of a sizable order, that focused upon given authorities. But sufficient materials certainly lay at hand to allow doing so.

In the three decisions, two of what to do and one of what not to do, the final compositors of the Bavli indicated what they proposed to accomplish: to give final form and fixed expression, through their categories of the organization of all knowledge, to the Torah as it had been known, sifted, searched, approved, and handed down, even from the remote past to their own day. So in our literary categories the compositors of the Bavli were encyclopaedists. Their creation turned out to be the encyclopaedia of Judaism, its *summa*, its point of final reference, its court of last appeal, its definition, it conclusion, its closure – so they thought, and so said those that followed, to this very day.

Shall we then draw so grand a conclusion from so modest a fact as how people sorted out available redactional categories? Indeed so, if we realize that the modes by which thinkers organize knowledge leads us deep into the theses by which useful knowledge rises to the surface while what is irrelevant or unimportant or trivial sinks to the bottom. If we want to know what people thought and how they thought it, we can do worse than begin by asking about how they organized what they knew, on the one side, and about the choices they made in laying out the main lines of the structure of knowledge, on the other.

II. The Compositions No One Made: Collections of Wise Sayings and Biographies

The Yerushalmi and the collections of scriptural exegeses comprise compositions made up of already worked out units of discourse focused upon the Mishnah and Scripture, respectively. Other completed units of thought, such as we might call paragraphs or even short chapters, deal with individual sages. Midrash compilations and Mishnah commentaries, both the Yerushalmi and the Bavli, contain a sizable quantity of sage units of discourse. These can surely have coalesced in yet a third type of book. Specifically, sayings and stories about sages could have been organized into collections of wise sayings attributed to various authorities (like Avot), on the one side, or sequences of tales, e.g., brief snippets of biographies or lives of the saints, on the other. Let me spell out what we do find, which will underline the noteworthy character of the fact at hand: materials not used for their obvious purpose, in the way in which materials of a parallel character were used for their purpose.

Let me define more fully the character of the discourse that focuses upon the sage. In this type of composition, e.g., a paragraph of thought, a story, things that a given authority said are strung together or tales about a given authority are told at some length. Whoever composed and preserved units of discourse on the Mishnah and on Scripture ultimately preserved in the two Talmuds did the same for the sage. What that fact means is simple. In the circles responsible for making up and writing down completed units of discourse, three distinct categories of interest defined the task: (1) exegesis of the Mishnah, (2) exegesis of Scripture, and (3) preservation and exegesis, in exactly the same reverential spirit, of the words and deeds of sages. Not only so, but the kind of analysis to which Mishnah- and Scripture-exegesis were subjected also applied to the exegesis of sage stories.

That fact may be shown in three ways. First, just as Scripture supplied prooftexts, so deeds or statements of sages provided prooftexts. Second, just as a verse of Scripture or an explicit statement of the Mishnah resolved a disputed point, so what a sage said or did might be introduced into discourse as ample proof for settling a dispute. And third, it follows that just as Scripture or the Mishnah laid down Torah, so what a sage did or said laid down Torah. In the dimensions of the applied and practical reason by which the law unfolded, the sage found a comfortable place in precisely the taxonomic categories defined, to begin with, by both the Mishnah and Scripture. Let us examine a few substantial examples of the sorts of sustained discourse in biographical materials turned out by circles of sages. What we shall see is an important fact. Just as these circles composed units of discourse about the meaning of a Mishnah passage, a larger theoretical problem of law, the sense of scriptural verse, and the sayings and doings of scriptural heroes seen as sages, so they did the same for living sages themselves.

In the simplest example we see that two discrete sayings of a sage are joined together. The principle of conglomeration, therefore, is solely the name of the sage at hand. One saying has to do with overcoming the impulse to do evil, and the other has to do with the classifications of sages' program of learning. What the two subjects have in common is slight. But to the framer of the passage, that fact meant nothing. For he thought that compositions joined by the same tradent and authority – Levi and Simeon – should be made up.

B. Berakhot 4B

XXIII

A.   Said R. Levi bar Hama said R. Simeon b. Laqish, "A person should always provoke his impulse to do good against his impulse to do evil,

B.   "as it is said, 'Provoke and do not sin' (Ps. 4:5).

C.   "If [the good impulse] wins, well and good. If not, let him take up Torah study,

D.   "as it is said, 'Commune with your own heart' (Ps. 4:5).

E.   "If [the good impulse] wins, well and good. If not, let him recite the Shema,

F.   "as it is said, 'upon your bed' (Ps. 4:5).

G.   "If [the good impulse] wins, well and good. If not, let him remember the day of death,

H.   "as it is said, 'And keep silent. Sela' (Ps. 4:5)."

I.   And R. Levi bar Hama said R. Simeon b. Laqish said, "What is the meaning of the verse of Scripture, 'And I will give you the tables of stone, the law and the commandment, which I have written, that you may teach them' (Ex. 24:12).

J.   "'The tables' [here] refers to the Ten Commandments.

K.   "'Torah' refers to Scripture.

L.   "'Commandment' refers to Mishnah.

M.   "'Which I have written' refers to the Prophets and the Writings.

N.   "'That you may teach them' refers to the Gemara.

O.   "This teaches that all of them were given to Moses from Sinai."

The frame of the story at hand links A-H and I-O in a way unfamiliar to those accustomed to the principles of conglomeration in legal and biblical-exegetical compositions. In the former, a given problem or principle of law will tell us why one item is joined to some other. In the latter, a single verse of Scripture will account for the joining of two or more otherwise discrete units of thought. Here one passage, A-H, takes up Ps. 4:5; the other, I-O, Ex. 24:12. The point of the one statement hardly goes over the ground of the other. So the *sole* principle by which one item has joined the other is biographical: a record of what a sage said about topics that are, at best, contiguous, if related at all.

A second way of stringing together materials illustrative of the lives and teachings of sages is to join incidents involving a given authority or (as in the following case) two authorities believed to have stood in close relationship with one another, disciple and master, for instance. Often these stories go over the same ground in the same way. In the following, the two farewell stories make essentially the same point but in quite different language. What joins the stories is not only the shared theme but the fact that Eliezer is supposed to have studied with Yohanan b. Zakkai.

B. Sanhedrin 68A

II

A.   Our rabbis have taught on Tannaite authority:

B.   When R. Eliezer fell ill, his disciples came in to pay a call on him. They said to him, "Our master, teach us the ways of life, so that through them we may merit the world to come."

C.   He said to them, "Be attentive to the honor owing to your fellows, keep your children from excessive reflection, and set them among the knees of disciples of sages, and when you pray, know before whom you stand, and on that account you will merit the life of the world to come."

D.   And when R. Yohanan b. Zakkai fell ill, his disciples came in to pay a call on him. When he saw them, he began to cry. His disciples said to him, "Light of Israel! Pillar at the right hand! Mighty hammer! On what account are you crying?"

E.   He said to them, "If I were going to be brought before a mortal king, who is here today and tomorrow gone to the grave, who, should he be angry with me, will not be angry forever, and, if he should imprison me, will not imprison me forever, and if he should put me to death, whose sentence of death is not for eternity, and whom I can appease with the right words or bribe with money, even so, I should weep.

F.   "But now that I am being brought before the King of kings of kings, the Holy One, blessed be he, who endures forever and ever, who, should he be angry with me, will be angry forever, and if he should imprison me, will imprison me forever, and if he should put me to death, whose sentence of death is for eternity, and whom I cannot appease with the right words or bribe with money,

G.   "and not only so, but before me are two paths, one to the Garden of Eden and the other to Gehenna, and I do not know by which path I shall be brought,

H.   "and should I not weep?"

I.   They said to him, "Our master, bless us."

J.   He said to them, "May it be God's will that the fear of Heaven be upon you as much as the fear of mortal man."

K.   His disciples said, "Just so much?"

L.   He said to them, "Would that it were that much. You should know that, when a person commits a transgression, he says, 'I hope no man sees me.'"

M.   When he was dying, he said to them, "Clear out utensils from the house, because of the uncleanness [of the corpse, which I am about to impart when I die], and prepare a throne for Hezekiah king of Judah, who is coming."

The links between B-C and D-M are clear. First, we have stories about sages' farewells. Second, people took for granted, because of the lists of

M. Abot 2:2ff., that Eliezer was disciple of Yohanan b. Zakkai. Otherwise, it is difficult to explain the joining of the stories, since they scarcely make the same point, go over the same matters, or even share a common literary or rhetorical form or preference. But a framer of a composition of lives of saints, who is writing a tractate on how saints die, will have found this passage a powerful one indeed.

Yet another approach to the utilization of tales about sages was to join together stories on a given theme but told about different sages. A tractate or a chapter of a tractate on a given theme, for example, suffering and its reward, can have emerged from the sort of collection that follows. The importance of the next item is that the same kinds of stories about different sages are strung together to make a single point.

B. Berakhot 5B
XXXI

A.   R. Hiyya bar Abba got sick. R. Yohanan came to him. He said to him, "Are these sufferings precious to you?"

B.   He said to him, "I don't want them, I don't want their reward."

C.   He said to him, "Give me your hand."

D.   He gave him his hand, and [Yohanan] raised him up [out of his sickness].

E.   R. Yohanan got sick. R. Hanina came to him. He said to him, "Are these sufferings precious to you?"

F.   He said to him, "I don't want them. I don't want their reward."

G.   He said to him, "Give me your hand."

H.   He gave him his hand and [Hanina] raised him up [out of his sickness].

I.   Why so? R. Yohanan should have raised himself up?

J.   They say, "A prisoner cannot get himself out of jail."

B. Berakhot 5B
XXXII

A.   R. Eliezer got sick. R. Yohanan came to see him and found him lying in a dark room. [The dying man] uncovered his arm, and light fell [through the room]. [Yohanan] saw that R. Eliezer was weeping. He said to him, "Why are you crying? Is it because of the Torah that you did not learn sufficiently? We have learned: 'All the same are the ones who do much and do little, so long as each person will do it for the sake of heaven.'

B.   "Is it because of insufficient income? Not everyone has the merit of seeing two tables [Torah and riches, as you have. You have been a master of Torah and also have enjoyed wealth].

C.   "Is it because of children? Here is the bone of my tenth son [whom I buried, so it was no great loss not to have children, since you might have had to bury them]."

D.   He said to him, "I am crying because of this beauty of mine which will be rotting in the ground."

E.   He said to him, "For that it certainly is worth crying," and the two of them wept together.

F.   He said to him, "Are these sufferings precious to you?"

G.   He said to him, "I don't want them, I don't want their reward."

H.   He said to him, "Give me your hand."

I.   He gave him his hand, and [Yohanan] raised him up [out of his sickness].

B. Berakhot 5B
XXXIII

A.   Four hundred barrels of wine turned sour on R. Huna. R. Judah, brother of R. Sala the Pious, and rabbis came to see him (and some say it was R. Ada bar Ahba and rabbis). They said to him, "The master should take a good look at his deeds."

B.   He said to them, "And am I suspect in your eyes?"

C.   They said to him, "And is the Holy One, blessed be he, suspect of inflicting a penalty without justice?"

D.   He said to them, "Has anybody heard anything bad about me? Let him say it."

E.   They said to him, "This is what we have heard: the master does not give to his hired hand [the latter's share of] vine twigs [which are his right]."

F.   He said to them, "Does he leave me any! He steals all of them to begin with."

G.   They said to him, "This is in line with what people say: 'Go steal from a thief but taste theft too!' [Simon: If you steal from a thief, you also have a taste of it.]"

H.   He said to them, "I pledge that I'll give them to him."

I.   Some say that the vinegar turned back into wine, and some say that the price of vinegar went up so he sold it off at the price of wine.

The foregoing composite makes the same point several times: "Not them, not their reward." Sufferings are precious, but sages are prepared to forego the benefits. The formally climactic entry at XXXIII makes the point that, if bad things happen, the victim has deserved punishment. In joining these several stories about sages – two involving Yohanan, the third entirely separate – the compositor of the passage made his point by juxtaposing two like biographical snippets to a distinct one. Collections of stories about saints can have served quite naturally when formed into tractates on pious virtues, expressing these virtues through strong and pictorial language such as is before us.

The foregoing sources have shown two important facts. First, a principle of composition in the sages' circles was derived from interest in the teachings associated with a given sage, as well as in tales and stories told about a sage or groups of sages. The first of the passages shows us the simplest composition of sayings, the latter, an equivalent conglomeration of related stories. Up to this point, therefore, the reader will readily concede that biographical materials on sages, as much as Mishnah exegesis and Scripture exegesis, came forth out of circles of sages. But I have yet to show that such materials attained sufficient volume and cogency from large-scale compilations – conglomerates so substantial as to sustain entire books.

III. Chapters and Tractates on Lives of Sages: What Might Have Been

At the risk of taxing the reader's patience, I shall now demonstrate that, had the framers of large-scale rabbinic compositions wished, they could readily have made up tractates devoted to diverse sayings of a given authority (or, tradent and authority). What follows to demonstrate the possibility are two enormous compositions, which together can have made up as much as half of a Talmud chapter in volume. If anyone had wanted to compose a chapter around rabbinical authorities' names, he is thus shown to have had the opportunity.

The first shows us a string of sayings not only in a single set of names but also on discrete subjects. We also see how such a string of sayings could form the focus of exactly the kind of critical analysis and secondary amplification to which any other talmudic passage would be subjected. So there can have been not only a Talmud based on the Mishnah and a midrash composition based on the Scripture but also a life of a saint (a gospel?) based on a set of rabbis' sayings. Here is the Talmud that can have served a collection of sayings of Yohanan-in-the-name-of-Simeon b. Yohai.

B. Berakhot 7B-8A

LIX

A.   [7B] Said R. Yohanan in the name of R. Simeon b. Yohai, "From the day on which the Holy One, blessed be he, created the world, there was no man who called the Holy One, blessed be he, 'Lord,' until Abraham came along and called him Lord.

B.   "For it is said, 'And he said, O Lord, God, whereby shall I know that I shall inherit it' (Gen. 15:8)."

C.   Said Rab, "Daniel too was answered only on account of Abraham.

D.   "For it is said, 'Now therefore, O our God, hearken to the prayer of your servant and to his supplications and cause your face to shine upon your sanctuary that is desolate, for the Lord's sake' (Dan. 9:17).

E.   "'For your sake' is what he should have said, but the sense is, 'For the sake of Abraham, who called you Lord.'"

B. Berakhot 7B-8A
LX

A   And R. Yohanan said in the name of R. Simeon b. Yohai, "How do we know that people should not seek to appease someone when he is mad?

B.   "As it is said, 'My face will go and then I will give you rest' (Ex. 33:14)."

B. Berakhot 7B-8A
LXI

A   And R. Yohanan said in the name of R. Simeon b. Yohai, "From the day on which the Holy One, blessed be he, created his world, there was no one who praised the Holy One, blessed be he, until Leah came along and praised him.

B.   "For it is said, 'This time I will praise the Lord' (Gen. 29:35)."

C.   As to Reuben, said R. Eleazar, "Leah said, 'See what is the difference [the name of Reuben yielding reu (see) and ben (between)] between my son and the son of my father-in-law.

D.   "The son of my father-in-law, even knowingly, sold off his birthright, for it is written, 'And he sold his birthright to Jacob' (Gen. 25:33).

E.   "See what is written concerning him: 'And Esau hated Jacob' (Gen. 27:41), and it is written, 'And he said, is he not rightly named Jacob? for he has supplanted me these two times' (Gen. 27:36).

F.   "My son, by contrast, even though Joseph forcibly took away his birthright, as it is written, 'But for as much as he defiled his father's couch, his birthright was given to the sons of Joseph' (1 Chron. 5:1), did not become jealous of him, for it is written, 'And Reuben heard it and delivered him out of their hand' (Gen. 37:21)."

G.   As to the meaning of the name of Ruth, said R. Yohanan, "It was because she had the merit that David would come forth from her, who saturated (RWH) the Holy One, blessed be he, with songs and praises."

H.   How do we know that a person's name affects [his life]?

I.   Said R. Eleazar, "It is in line with the verse of Scripture: 'Come, behold the works of the Lord, who has made desolations in the earth' (Ps. 46:9).

J.   "Do not read 'desolations' but 'names' [which the same root yields]."

B. Berakhot 7B-8A

LXII

A.   And R. Yohanan said in the name of R. Simeon b. Yohai, "Bringing a child up badly is worse in a person's house than the war of Gog and Magog.

B.   "For it is said, 'A Psalm of David, when he fled from Absalom, his son' (Ps. 3:1), after which it is written, 'Lord how many are my adversaries become, many are they that rise up against me' (Ps. 3:2).

C.   "By contrast, in regard to the war of Gog and Magog it is written, 'Why are the nations in an uproar? And why do the peoples mutter in vain?' (Ps. 2:1).

D.   "But it is not written in that connection, 'How many are my adversaries become.'"

E.   "A Psalm of David, when he fled from Absalom, his son (Ps. 3:1):

F.   "'A Psalm of David'? It should be, 'A lamentation of David'!

G.   Said R. Simeon b. Abishalom, "The matter may be compared to the case of a man against whom an outstanding bond was issued. Before he had paid it, he was sad. After he had paid it, he was glad.

H.   "So too with David, when he the Holy One had said to him, 'Behold, I will raise up evil against you out of your own house,' (2 Sam. 2:11), he was sad.

I.   "He thought to himself, 'Perhaps it will be a slave or a bastard child, who will not have pity on me.'

J.   "When he saw that it was Absalom, he was happy. On that account, he said a psalm."

B. Berakhot 7B-8A

LXIII

A.   And R. Yohanan said in the name of R. Simeon b. Yohai, "It is permitted to contend with the wicked in this world,

B.   "for it is said, 'Those who forsake the Torah praise the wicked, but those who keep the Torah contend with them' (Prov. 28:4)."

C.   It has been taught on Tannaite authority along these same lines:

D.   R. Dosetai bar Matun says, "It is permitted to contend with the wicked in this world, for it is said, 'Those who forsake the Torah praise the wicked, but those who keep the Torah contend with them' (Prov. 28:4)."

E.   And if someone should whisper to you, "But is it not written, 'Do not contend with evildoers, nor be envious against those who work unrighteousness' (Ps. 37:1)," say to him, "Someone whose conscience bothers him thinks so.

F.   "In fact, 'Do not contend with evildoers' means, do not be like them, 'nor be envious against those who work unrighteousness,' means, do not be like them.

G.   "And so it is said, 'Let your heart not envy sinners, but fear the Lord all day' (Prov. 23:17)."

H.   Is this the case? And lo, R. Isaac has said, "If you see a wicked person for whom the hour seems to shine, do not contend with him, for it is said, 'His ways prosper at all times' (Ps. 10:5).

I.   "Not only so, but he wins in court, as it is said, 'Your judgments are far above, out of his sight' (Ps. 10:5).

J.   "Not only so, but he overcomes his enemies, for it is said, 'As for all his enemies, he farts at them' (Ps. 10:5)."

K.   There is no contradiction. The one [Isaac] addresses one's own private matters [in which case one should not contend with the wicked], but the other speaks of matters having to do with Heaven [in which case one should contend with them].

L.   And if you wish, I shall propose that both parties speak of matters having to do with Heaven. There is, nonetheless, no contradiction. The one [Isaac] speaks of a wicked person on whom the hour shines, the other of a wicked person on whom the hour does not shine.

M.   And if you wish, I shall propose that both parties speak of a wicked person on whom the hour shines, and there still is no contradiction.

N.   The one [Yohanan, who says the righteous may contend with the wicked] speaks of a completely righteous person, the other [Isaac] speaks of someone who is not completely righteous.

O.   For R. Huna said, "What is the meaning of this verse of Scripture: 'Why do you look, when they deal treacherously, and hold your peace, when the wicked swallows up the man that is more righteous than he' (Hab. 1:13)?

P.   "Now can a wicked person swallow up a righteous one?

Q.   "And lo, it is written, 'The Lord will not leave him in his hand' (Ps. 37:33). And it is further written, 'No mischief shall befall the righteous' (Prov. 12:21).

R.   "The fact therefore is that he may swallow up someone who is more righteous than he, but he cannot swallow up a completely righteous man."

S.   And if you wish, I shall propose that, when the hour shines for him, the situation is different.

B. Berakhot 7B-8A

LXIV

A.   And R. Yohanan said in the name of R. Simeon b. Yohai, "Beneath anyone who establishes a regular place for praying do that person's enemies fall.

B.   "For it is said, 'And I will appoint a place for my people Israel, and I will plant them, that they may dwell in their own place and be disquieted no more, neither shall the children of wickedness afflict them any more as at the first' (2 Sam. 7:10)."

C.   R. Huna pointed to a contradiction between two verses of
         Scripture: "It is written, 'To afflict them,' and elsewhere, 'To
         exterminate them' (1 Chron. 17:9).

D.   "To begin with, merely to afflict them, but, at the end, to
         exterminate them."

B. Berakhot 7B-8A
LXV

A.   And R. Yohanan said in the name of R. Simeon b. Yohai, "Greater
         is personal service to Torah than learning in Torah [so doing
         favors for a sage is of greater value than studying with him].

B.   "For it is said, 'Here is Elisha, the son of Shaphat, who poured
         water on the hands of Elijah' (2 Kings 3:11).

C.   "It is not said, 'who learned' but 'who poured water.'

D.   "This teaches that greater is service to Torah than learning in
         Torah."

It is not difficult to pick up the main beams of the foregoing
construction, since they are signified by Yohanan-Simeon sayings,
LIX.A, LX.A, LXI.A, LXII.A, LXIII.A, LXIV.A, LXV.A – seven entries in
line. The common theme is not prayer; no other topic is treated in a
cogent way either. The sort of inner coherence to which any student of
the Bavli is accustomed does not pass before us. Rather we have a
collection of wise thoughts on diverse topics, more in the manner of
Proverbs than in the style of the great intellects behind the sustained
reasoning in passages of the Bavli and much of the Yerushalmi as well.
What is interesting is that, at a later stage, other pertinent materials
have been inserted, for example, Rab's at LIX.C-E, and so on down.
There is no reason to imagine that these sayings were made up in
response to Yohanan-Simeon's statement. Quite to the contrary, framed
in their own terms, the sayings were presumably tacked on at a point at
which the large-scale construction of Yohanan-Simeon was worked
over for a purpose beyond the one intended by the original compositor.
For what he wanted to do he did, which is, compose a collection of
Yohanan-Simeon sayings. If he hoped that his original collection
would form part of a larger composition on Yohanan, he surely was
disappointed. But even if he imagined that he would make up
material for compositions of lives and sayings of saints, he cannot have
expected his little collection to end up where and how it did, as part of
a quite different corpus of writing from one in which a given authority
had his say or in which stories were told in some sort of sensible
sequence about a particular sage. The type of large-scale composition,
for which our imagined compositor did his work, in the end never came
into being in the rabbinic canon.

In the following, still longer example I begin with the passage to which the entire composition, organized in the name of a tradent and a sage, is attached. At B. Berakhot 6B/1:1 XLI, we have a statement that a synagogue should have a regular quorum. Then the next passage, 1:1 XLII, makes the secondary point that a person should pray in a regular place – a reasonable amplification of the foregoing. That is, just as there should be a quorum routinely organized in a given location, so should an individual routinely attach himself to a given quorum. This statement is given by Helbo in Huna's name. What follows is a sizable set of sayings by Helbo in Huna's name, all of them on the general theme of prayer but none of them on the specific point at hand. Still more interesting, just as in the foregoing, the passage as a whole was composed so that the Helbo-Huna materials themselves are expanded and enriched with secondary accretions. For instance, at XLIII the base materials are given glosses of a variety of types. All in all, we see what we may call a little tractate in the making. But, as we shall hardly have to repeat, no one in the end created a genre of rabbinic literature to accommodate the vast collections of available compositions on sages' sayings and doings.

B. Berakhot 6B
XLI
A.   Said R. Yohanan, "When the Holy One, blessed be he, comes to a synagogue and does not find ten present, he forthwith becomes angry.

B.   "For it is said, 'Why when I came was there no one there? When I called, there was no answer' (Isa. 50:2)."

B. Berakhot 6B
XLII
A.   Said R. Helbo said R. Huna, "For whoever arranges a regular place for praying, the God of Abraham is a help, and when he dies, they say for him, 'Woe for the humble man, woe for the pious man, one of the disciples of Abraham, our father.'

B.   "And how do we know in the case of Abraham, our father, that he arranged a regular place for praying?

C.   "For it is written, 'And Abraham got up early in the morning on the place where he had stood' (Gen. 19:27).

D.   "'Standing' refers only to praying, for it is said, 'Then Phinehas stood up and prayed' (Ps. 106:30)."

E.   Said R. Helbo to R. Huna, "He who leaves the synagogue should not take large steps."

F.   Said Abayye, "That statement applies only when one leaves, but when he enters, it is a religious duty to run [to the synagogue].

G.   "For it is said, 'Let us run to know the Lord' (Hos. 6:3)."

H.   Said R. Zira, "When in the beginning I saw rabbis running to the lesson on the Sabbath, I thought that the rabbis were profaning the Sabbath. But now that I have heard what R. Tanhum said R. Joshua b. Levi said,

I.   "namely, 'A person should always run to take up a matter of law, and even on the Sabbath, as it is said, "They shall walk after the Lord who shall roar like a lion [for he shall roar, and the children shall come hurrying]" (Hos. 11:10),'

J.   "I too run."

B. Berakhot 6B
XLIII

A.   Said R. Zira, "The reward for attending the lesson is on account of running [to hear the lesson, not necessarily on account of what one has learned.]"

B.   Said Abayye, "The reward for attending the periodic public assembly [of rabbis] is on account of the crowding together."

C.   Said Raba [to the contrary], "The reward for repeating what one has heard is in reasoning about it."

D.   Said R. Papa, "The reward for attending a house of mourning is on account of one's preserving silence there."

E.   Said Mar Zutra, "The reward for observing a fast day lies in the acts of charity one performs on that day."

F.   Said R. Sheshet, "The reward for delivering a eulogy lies in raising the voice."

G.   Said R. Ashi, "The reward for attending a wedding lies in the words [of compliment paid to the bride and groom]."

B. Berakhot 6B
XLIV

A.   Said R. Huna, "Whoever prays behind the synagogue is called wicked,

B.   "as it is said, 'The wicked walk round about' (Ps. 12:9)."

C.   Said Abayye, "That statement applies only in the case of one who does not turn his face toward the synagogue, but if he turns his face toward the synagogue, we have no objection."

D.   There was a certain man who would say his prayers behind the synagogue and did not turn his face toward the synagogue. Elijah came by and saw him. He appeared to him in the guise of a Tai Arab.

E.   He said to him, "Are you now standing with your back toward your master?" He drew his sword and killed him.

F.   One of the rabbis asked R. Bibi bar Abayye, and some say, R. Bibi asked R. Nahman bar Isaac, "What is the meaning of the verse, 'When vileness is exalted among the sons of men' (Ps. 12:9)?"

G.   He said to him, "This refers to matters that are exalted, which people treat with contempt."

H.   R. Yohanan and R. Eleazar both say, "When a person falls into need of the help of other people, his face changes color like the kerum, for it is said, 'As the kerum is to be reviled among the sons of men' (Ps. 12:9)."

I.   What is the meaning of kerum?

J.   When R. Dimi came, he said, "There is a certain bird among the coast towns, called the kerum. When the sun shines, it turns many colors."

K.   R. Ammi and R. Assi both say, "[When a person turns to others for support], it is as if he is judged to suffer the penalties of both fire and water.

L.   "For it is said, 'When you caused men to ride over our heads, we went through fire and through water' (Ps. 66:12)."

B. Berakhot 6B
XLV

A.   And R. Helbo said R. Huna said, "A person should always be attentive at the afternoon prayer.

B.   "For lo, Elijah was answered only at the afternoon prayer.

C.   "For it is said, 'And it came to pass at the time of the offering of the late afternoon offering, that Elijah the prophet came near and said, "Hear me, O Lord, hear me"' (1 Kings 18:36-37)."

D.   "Hear me" so fire will come down from heaven.

E.   "Hear me" that people not say it is merely witchcraft.

F.   R. Yohanan said, "[A person should also be attentive about] the evening prayer.

G.   "For it is said, 'Let my prayer be set forth as incense before you, the lifting up of my hands as the evening sacrifice' (Ps. 141:2)."

H.   R. Nahman bar Isaac said, "[A person should also be attentive about] the morning prayer.

I.   "For it is said, 'O Lord, in the morning you shall hear my voice, in the morning I shall order my prayer to you, and will look forward' (Ps. 5:4)."

B. Berakhot 6B
XLVI

A.   And R. Helbo said R. Huna said, "Whoever enjoys a marriage banquet and does not felicitate the bridal couple violates five 'voices.'

B.   "For it is said, 'The voice of joy and the voice of gladness, the voice of the bridegroom and the voice of the bride, the voice of those who say, "Give thanks to the Lord of hosts"' (Jer. 33:11)."

C.   And if he does felicitate the couple, what reward does he get?

D.   Said R. Joshua b. Levi, "He acquires the merit of the Torah, which was handed down with five voices.

E.   "For it is said, 'And it came to pass on the third day, when it was morning, that there were voices [thus two], and lightnings, and a thick cloud upon the mount, and the voice of a horn, and when the voice of the horn waxed louder, 'Moses spoke and God answered him by a voice.' (Ex. 19:16, 19) [thus five voices in all]."

F. Is it so [that there were only five voices]?

G. And lo, it is written, "And all the people saw the voices" (Ex. 20:15). [So this would make seven voices.]

H. These voices came before the giving of the Torah [and do not count].

I. R. Abbahu said, "It is as if the one [who felicitated the bridal couple] offered a thanksgiving offering.

J. "For it is said, 'Even of them that bring thanksgiving offerings into the house of the Lord' (Jer. 33:11)."

K. R. Nahman bar Isaac said, "It is as if he rebuilt one of the ruins of Jerusalem.

L. "For it is said, 'For I will cause the captivity of the land to return as at the first, says the Lord' (Jer. 33:11)."

B. Berakhot 6B
XLVII

A. And R. Helbo said R. Huna said, "The words of any person in whom is fear of Heaven are heard.

B. "For it is said, 'The end of the matter, all having been heard: fear God and keep his commandments, for this is the whole man' (Qoh. 12:13)."

C. What is the meaning of the phrase, "For this is the whole man" (Qoh. 12:13)?

D. Said R. Eleazar, "Said the Holy One, blessed be he, 'The entire world has been created only on account of this one.'"

E. R. Abba bar Kahana said, "This one is worth the whole world."

F. Simeon b. Zoma says, "The entire world was created only to accompany this one."

B. Berakhot 6B
XLVIII

A. And R. Helbo said R. Huna said, "Whoever knows that his fellow regularly greets him should greet the other first.

B. "For it is said, 'Seek peace and pursue it' (Ps. 34:15).

C. "If he greeted him and the other did not reply, the latter is called a thief.

D. "For it is said, 'It is you who have eaten up the vineyard, the spoil of the poor is in your houses' (Isa. 3:14)."

What we noted in connection with the Yohanan-Simeon collection needs no restatement here. The scope and dimensions of the passage prove impressive. Again we must wonder for what sort of composition the framer of the Helbo-Huna collection planned his writing. Whatever it was, it hardly fit the ultimate destination of his work.

IV. The Standing and Authority of the Sage

One reason for not forming gospels can have been that the sage did not stand at the level of the Torah, while the Mishnah and Scripture constituted the Torah. Hence forming documents around the lives of the sage, as much as around the amplification of Scripture and the Mishnah, can have made no sense. But the opposite is the fact. The sage stood at that same level of authority as did the Torah, on the one side, and the Mishnah, on the other. Therefore the failure to compose gospels alongside midrash compilations and Mishnah-exegesis is not to be explained away as a by-product of the conception of revelation through words but not through persons that is imputed to the Judaism of the Dual Torah. Quite to the contrary, God reveals the Torah not only through words handed down from Sinai in the form of the Torah, written and oral, but also through the lives and deeds of saints, that is, sages. Reference to the discussion of Torah in Chapter Two will suffice to make the simple point that the same modes of exegetical inquiry pertaining to the Mishnah and Scripture apply without variation to statements made by rabbis of the contemporary period themselves.

We turn to the way in which the rabbis of the Yerushalmi proposed to resolve differences of opinion. Precisely in the same way in which talmudic rabbis settled disputes in the Mishnah and so attained a consensus about the law of the Mishnah, they handled disputes among themselves. The importance of that fact for our argument again is simple. The rabbis, represented in the Yerushalmi, treated their own contemporaries exactly as they treated the then-ancient authorities of the Mishnah. In their minds the status accorded to the Mishnah, as a derivative of the Torah, applied equally to sages' teachings. In the following instance we see how the same discourse attached to (1) a Mishnah rule is assigned as well to one in (2) the Tosefta and, at the end, to differences among (3) the Yerushalmi's authorities.

Yerushalmi Ketubot 5:1

VI

A. R. Jacob bar Aha, R. Alexa in the name of Hezekiah: "The law accords with the view of R. Eleazar b. Azariah, who stated, If she was widowed or divorced at the stage of betrothal, the virgin collects only two hundred zuz and the widow, a maneh. If she was widowed or divorced at the stage of a consummated marriage, she collects the full amount [M. Ket. 5:1E,D]."

B. R. Hananiah said, "The law accords with the view of R. Eleazar b. Azariah."

C. Said Abayye, "They said to R. Hananiah, 'Go and shout [outside whatever opinion you like.' But] R. Jonah, R. Zeira in the name of R. Jonathan said, 'The law accords with the view of R. Eleazar b.

Azariah.' [Yet] R. Yosé bar Zeira in the name of R. Jonathan said, 'The law does not accord with the view of R. Eleazar b. Azariah.' [So we do not in fact know the decision.]"

D.   Said R. Yosé, "We had a mnemonic: Hezekiah and R. Jonathan both say one thing."

E.   For it has been taught:

F.   He whose son went abroad, and whom they told, "Your son has died,"

G.   and who went and wrote over all his property to someone else as a gift,

H.   and whom they afterward informed that his son was yet alive –

I.   his deed of gift remains valid.

J.   R. Simeon b. Menassia says, "His deed of gift is not valid, for if he had known that his son was alive, he would never have made such a gift" [T. Ket. 4:14E-H].

K.   Now R. Jacob bar Aha [=A] said, "The law is in accord with the view of R. Eleazar b. Azariah, and the opinion of R. Eleazar b. Azariah is the same in essence as that of R. Simeon b. Menassia."

L.   Now R. Yannai said to R. Hananiah, "Go and shout [outside whatever you want].

M.   "But, said R. Yosé bar Zeira in the name of R. Jonathan, 'The law is not in accord with R. Eleazar b. Azariah.'"

N.   But in fact the case was to be decided in accord with the view of R. Eleazar b. Azariah.

What is important here is that the Talmud makes no distinction whatever when deciding the law of disputes (1) in the Mishnah, (2) in the Tosefta, and (3) among talmudic rabbis. The same already formed colloquy applied at the outset to the Mishnah's dispute is then held equally applicable to the Tosefta's. The process of thought is the main thing, without regard to the document to which the process applies. Scripture, the Mishnah, the sage – the three spoke with equal authority. True, one had to come into alignment with the other, the Mishnah with Scripture, the sage with the Mishnah. But it was not the case that one component of the Torah, of God's word to Israel, stood within the sacred circle, another beyond. Interpretation and what was interpreted, exegesis and text, belonged together. The sage, or rabbi, constitutes the third component in a tripartite canon of the Torah, because, while Scripture and the Mishnah govern what the sage knows, in the Yerushalmi as in the Bavli it is the sage who authoritatively speaks about them. What sages were willing to do to the Mishnah in the Yerushalmi and Bavli is precisely what they were prepared to do to Scripture – impose upon it their own judgment of its meaning.

V. The Sage and the Torah

The sage speaks with authority about the Mishnah and the Scripture. As much as they, he therefore has authority deriving from revelation. He himself may participate in the process of revelation. There is no material difference. Since that is so, the sage's book, whether the Yerushalmi or the Bavli to the Mishnah or midrash to Scripture, is Torah, that is, revealed by God. It also forms part of the Torah, a fully canonical document. The reason, then, is that the sage is like Moses, "our rabbi," who received torah and wrote the Torah. So while the canon was in three parts – Scripture, Mishnah, sage – the sage, in saying what the other parts meant and in embodying that meaning in his life and thought, took primacy of place. If no document organized itself around sayings and stories of sages, it was because that was superfluous. Why so? Because all documents, equally, whether Scripture, whether Mishnah, whether Yerushalmi, gave full and complete expression of deeds and deliberations of sages, beginning, after all, with Moses, our rabbi.

VI. The Topical Repertoire of Sage-Stories in The Fathers According to Rabbi Nathan: The Insufficiency of Sage-Stories for Forming Gospels

The sage-stories in The Fathers According to Rabbi Nathan do not cover a broad variety of topics but attend only to a few selected subjects. Only certain aspects of the lives and doings of sages demanded attention, and then for highly particular purposes. That fact again has important bearing upon our problem. What it tells us is that while the raw-materials for gospels – miracle-stories, biographical materials – do present themselves, sage-stories in point of fact cannot in the end coalesce into gospels. They serve a different purpose than biography, and biography in the end does not define the classification for these stories. I shall show that fact in some detail, because it carries us a considerable distance toward our goal.

To demonstrate that fact, I classify the stories in The Fathers According to Rabbi Nathan by topics because the most superficial trait is subject-matter. The sage-stories in this document[4] attend to only four topics: the sage's beginning in Torah-study, his character and his deeds

---

[4]We could, of course, collect among diverse canonical writings of the formative period stories on all the subjects not treated in a coherent setting in the document under study. That underlines two points critical to my argument. First, the materials for gospels were at hand. Second, where sage-stories formed the definitive component of a document, it was not so as to produce anything like gospels.

in relationship to the Torah, the role of the sage in important historical events, and at the end, the death of sages. Out of such a repertoire, a gospel is not possible. In point of fact, the sole theme characteristic of sage-stories in The Fathers According to Rabbi Nathan is the theme of the Torah, study of the Torah and the power gained by study of the Torah. Let me state with emphasis the main point at hand:

Sage-stories turn out not to tell about sages at all; they are stories about the Torah personified.

Sage-stories cannot yield a gospel because they are not about sages anyhow. They are about the Torah. Gospels by contrast tell the life of a human being, whom the narrator represents as holy and capable of miracles. The sage-stories do not differentiate one sage from another and do not underline traits of individuality. Quite to the contrary, the sage is represented always as exemplary, rarely as individual and distinct from other sages except by the standard of the Torah: more or less Torah, not difference between one sage's Torah and another sage's Torah. The sage-story, dealing with the individual, homogenizes sage with sage. The gospel does just the opposite, with its focus on the uniqueness of the hero.[5]

A list of the topics of sage-stories in The Fathers According to Rabbi Nathan that in fact are neglected, for example, the sage's childhood and wonderful precocity in Torah-study, the sage's supernatural deeds, the sage's everyday administration of the community's affairs, the sage's life with other sages and with disciples – such a list could be extended over many pages. But it suffices to notice that our document has chosen a highly restricted list of topics, but then differentiated, within these topics, by telling quite diverse stories about different sages as to their origins, deaths, and the like. The upshot is that when the authorship of The Fathers According to Rabbi Nathan resorted to narrative in general and storytelling in particular, with special attention to sage-stories, those compositors had in mind a very particular purpose and message indeed. There was nothing random or episodic in their choices of topics, and the medium of storytelling served the message conveyed by the story set forth in our composition.

---

[5]The fact that hagiography tends toward a certain homogeneity is not pertinent here. A study of hagiographical literature will yield differentiation between one saint and another, so that while all saints in common exhibit certain virtues, nonetheless, each saint bears traits of his or her own, which make the stories individual, even though of a common type.

VII. The Birth of Jesus Christ in Matthew's Gospel and the Origins of Aqiba and Eliezer

The contrast between sage-story and Gospel-story is readily drawn when we compare Matthew's story of the birth of Jesus Christ with the stories about the origins of Aqiba and Eliezer in The Fathers According to Rabbi Nathan. The interest of the former is well known. "Now the birth of Jesus Christ took place in this way" (Mt. 2:18): the birth of the child was announced to the virgin mother, Mary. Herod was told that the king of the Jews has been born. The Magi worshipped the infant. Herod killed the newborn babes; Joseph and Mary fled to Egypt. When Herod died, Joseph and Mary returned. And so on. The well-known story covers a variety of details. Not a single detail concerning the annunciation of the birth, the conditions of the birth, or the immediate events that succeeded the birth, of a sage, exists in the entire rabbinic canon of late antiquity. But the specific contrast I wish to draw concerns not what people do not say, but the things they choose to emphasize. We have in our document no birth-stories at all, but we do have "origins-in-Torah" stories, to which we turn.

The Fathers According to Rabbi Nathan contains stories of not the birth but "the origins" as masters of the Torah of two sages, Aqiba and Eliezer. By "origins," the storytellers mean the beginnings of the Torah-study of a famed authority. Life begins at birth, but when we wish to tell sage-stories, beginnings are measured differently. The sage begins life when he begins Torah-study. And the sages whose origins are found noteworthy both began in mature years, not in childhood (despite the repeated emphasis of The Fathers upon the unique value of beginning Torah-study in childhood). The proposition implicit in origins-stories then is that any male may start his Torah-study at any point in life and hope for true distinction in the Torah-community. But that does not account for the germ of the story, the critical tension that creates an event worthy of narrative, that poses a question demanding an answer, a problem requiring a solution through a tale with a beginning, middle, and end.

As everyone knows, Matthew tells the origins of a supernatural person, a unique individual. The critical tension of "origins" derives from the formation of supernatural, in contrast to natural, *relationships.* Life begins in the womb. But Torah-life does not begin in the natural birth, treated as supernatural in one case only, but begins at a supernatural birth of an already existing natural man, and, within that logic, there must be a tension between the natural beginning and the supernatural one. It is expressed through contrasting natural ties and relationships, to father and mother and brothers and sisters, or to one's wife, and supernatural ties to Torah-study. When a man undertakes to study the Torah, in the stories before us he abandons his natural relationships to his family, in the one case to his wife, in the other to his father. The point of origination of the sage marks the beginning of the wedding of the sage to the Torah, with the concomitant diminution of his relationship to his wife, who may be abandoned and indeed required to support the nascent sage's children as well as herself. The nascent sage furthermore gains a new father, the master or sage, and cuts his ties to the natural father, with the consequence that he loses his share in the estate to be provided by the father. These tensions generate the stories before us.

While told each in its own terms and subject to differentiation from the other, the stories make essentially the same point, which is that one can begin Torah-study in mature years and progress to the top, when one does so, one also goes from poverty to wealth through public recognition of one's mastery of the Torah, and a range of parallel propositions along the same lines. The supernatural relationship, which has superceded the natural ones to wife and father, generates glory and honor, riches and fame, for the sage, and, through reflection, for the natural family as well. That is the point of the stories of the origins of sages, which take up what is clearly a pressing question and answer it in a powerful way. (I give in boldface type citations of language in The Fathers.)

The Fathers According to Rabbi Nathan
VI:IV
1.   A.   Another comment on the statement, **And wallow in the dust of their feet:**
     B.   This refers to R. Eliezer.
     C.   **...and drink in their words with gusto:**
     D.   This refers to R. Aqiba.

This pericope serves as a prologue to the vast stories to follow, first on Aqiba, then on Eliezer.

VI:V
1.   A.   How did R. Aqiba begin [his Torah-study]?
     B.   They say: He was forty years old and had never repeated a tradition. One time he was standing at the mouth of a well. He thought to himself, "Who carved out this stone?"
     C.   They told him, "It is the water that is perpetually falling on it every day."
     D.   They said to him, "Aqiba, do you not read Scripture? *The water wears away stones* (Job. 4:19)?"

E.   On the spot R. Aqiba constructed in his own regard an argument *a fortiori*: now if something soft can [Goldin:] wear down something hard, words of Torah, which are as hard as iron, how much the more so should wear down my heart, which is made of flesh and blood."

F.   On the spot he repented [and undertook] to study the Torah.

G.   He and his son went into study session before a children's teacher, saying to him, "My lord, teach me Torah."

H.   R. Aqiba took hold of one end of the tablet, and his son took hold of the other end. The teacher wrote out for him *Alef Bet* and he learned it, *Alef Tav* and he learned it, *the Torah of the Priests* [the books of Leviticus and Numbers] and he learned it. He went on learning until he had learned the entire Torah.

I.   He went and entered study-sessions before R. Eliezer and before R. Joshua. He said to them, "My lords, open up for me the reasoning of the Mishnah."

J.   When they had stated one passage of law, he went and sat by himself and said, "Why is this *alef* written? why is this *bet* written? Why is this statement made?" He went and asked them and, in point of fact, [Goldin:] reduced them to silence.

Clearly, our opening component in the *magnalia Aqibae* is a narrative. The tone and program establish the mood of narrative: he was...he had...he did.... But how shall we classify the narrative, and by what criteria? One important criterion is whether the narrative describes a situation or tells about something that happened, with a beginning, middle, and end. The one is at rest, the other in movement. These constitute questions with objective answers. Do we have a tableau or a story, or, for that matter, a parable, or any of those other types of narratives we have already classified? By the simple criterion that a story has a beginning, middle, end, which dictate points of narrative tension, and a clearly delineated program of action, we have a story. The components do more than merely set up pieces in a static tableau. They flow from one to the next and yield movement – hence narrative action.

What about the Scripture-story? The blatant differences require slight amplification. We note that verses of Scripture scarcely intervene, and there is no focus on the exegesis of a verse of Scripture. At D, Aqiba and his interlocutors do not interpret the verse but simply draw upon its statement of fact. A sage-story, as I said, following the pattern determined by Aristotle has a beginning, middle, and end: movement from tension to resolution. In the present story there is a beginning: he had not studied; a middle, he went and studied; and an end, following Goldin's persuasive rendering, "he reduced them to silence." True, the action takes place mainly in what Aqiba thought rather than in what he did. But in the nature of things, the action of going to study the Torah forms the one genuinely dramatic deed that is possible with the present subject-matter. The beginning then works its way out at B-F. The middle is at G-H: Aqiba was so humble as to study with his own son. Then at I-J we have a climax and conclusion: Aqiba proved so profound in his question asking that he reduced the great authorities to silence. That conclusion hardly flows from A-H, but it is absolutely necessary to make the entire sequence into a cogent story. Otherwise we have merely bits and pieces of an uncompleted narrative.

Let us proceed to what follows in the context of the telling of the story of Aqiba's origins. Here we shall see most strikingly how, given the opportunity for a sustained narrative of the life of a man, the framers of The Fathers According to Rabbi Nathan do not exploit the occasion. Rather than dealing with other tales about the man, they focus upon the theme which he has served to realize in his own life, Torah-study.

VI:V

2.   A   R. Simeon b. Eleazar says, "I shall make a parable for you. To what is the matter comparable? To a stonecutter who was cutting stone in a quarry. One time he took his chisel and went and sat down on the mountain and started to chip away little sherds from it. People came by and said to him, 'What are you doing?'

     B.   "He said to them, 'Lo, I am going to uproot the mountain and move it into the Jordan River."

     C.   "They said to him, 'You will never be able to uproot the entire mountain.'

     D.   "He continued chipping away at the mountain until he came to a huge boulder. He quarried underneath it and unearthed it and uprooted it and tossed it into the Jordan.'

     E.   "He said to the boulder, 'This is not your place, but that is your place.'

     F.   "Likewise this is what R. Aqiba did to R. Eliezer and to R. Joshua."

The parable without F simply says that with patience one may move mountains. The parable by itself – not applied – amplifies or at least continues VI:V.1.E, the power of words of Torah to wear down the hard heart of a human being. But the parable proves particular to the preceding story, since the add-on, E, F, applies the parable to VI:V.1.J, the humiliation of Joshua and Eliezer. We may wonder whether, without the announcement at A that we have a parable, the parabolic character of the tale would have impressed us. The answer is that the general traits of a parable – an anonymous illustration in concrete and everyday terms of an abstract proposition – do occur in A-D, at which point the par worked out its proposition: "he continued chipping away...." Even E, without F, can remain within the limits of the announced proposition of the parable, that is, the power of patience and persistence. So only F is jarring. It clearly serves the redactor's purpose. It does not transform the parable into a story (!), since it does not impose upon the prior narrative that particularity and concrete one-time-ness that form the indicative traits of the story alone. In all, we may dismiss from the evidence of the story the present complement to the foregoing.

VI:V
3. A.   Said R. Tarfon to him, "Aqiba, in your regard Scripture says, *He stops up streams so that they do not trickle, and what is hidden he brings into the light* (Job 28:11).
    B.   "Things that are kept as mysteries from ordinary people has R. Aqiba brought to light."

"He said to him" does not make a story, and what is said does not bear the marks of a story, whole or in part.

VI:V
4. A.   Every day he would bring a bundle of twigs [Goldin: straw], half of which he would sell in exchange for food, and half of which he would use for a garment.
    B.   His neighbors said to him, "Aqiba, you are killing us with the smoke. Sell them to us, buy oil with the money, and by the light of a lamp do your studying."
    C.   He said to them, "I fill many needs with that bundle, first, I repeat traditions [by the light of the fire I kindle with] them, second, I warm myself with them, third, I sleep on them."

VI:V
5. A.   In time to come R. Aqiba is going to impose guilt [for failing to study] on the poor [who use their poverty as an excuse not to study].
    B.   For if they say to them, "Why did you not study the Torah," and they reply, "Because we were poor," they will say to them, "But was not R. Aqiba poorer and more poverty-stricken?"
    C.   If they say, "Because of our children [whom we had to work to support]," they will say to them, "Did not R. Aqiba have sons and daughters?"
    D.   So they will say to them, "Because Rachel, his wife, had the merit [of making it possible for him to study, and we have no equivalent helpmates; our wives do not have equivalent merit at their disposal]."

It is hard to classify VI:V.4 as other than a narrative setting for a conversation. But the conversation makes no point by itself. In fact the whole forms a prologue to VI:V.5, which does make a powerful point.

VI:V

6.   A.   It was at the age of forty that he went to study the Torah. Thirteen years later he taught the Torah in public.

   B.   They say that he did not leave this world before there were silver and golden tables in his possession,

   C.   and before he went up onto his bed on golden ladders.

   D.   His wife went about in golden sandals and wore a golden tiara of the silhouette of the city [Jerusalem].

   E.   His disciples said to him, "My lord, you have shamed us by what you have done for her [since we cannot do the same for our wives]."

   F.   He said to them, "She bore a great deal of pain on my account for [the study of] the Torah."

This item completes the foregoing, the narrative of how Rachel's devotion to Aqiba's study of the Torah produced a rich reward. The "they said to him...he said to him..."-sequences do not comprise a story or even establish much of a narrative framework. The upshot is that for Aqiba we have a sequence of narratives but only one story, that at the beginning. The composite does not hang together very well, but it does make a few important points.

This brings us to the story of the origins, in the Torah, of Eliezer. Let us turn directly to the account:

VI:VI

1.   A.   How did R. Eliezer ben Hyrcanus begin [his Torah-study]?

   B.   He had reached the age of twenty-two years and had not yet studied the Torah. One time he said, "I shall go and study the Torah before Rabban Yohanan ben Zakkai."

   C.   His father Hyrcanus said to him, "You are not going to taste a bit of food until you have ploughed the entire furrow."

   D.   He got up in the morning and ploughed the entire furrow.

   E.   They say that that day was Friday. He went and took a meal with his father-in-law.

   F.   And some say that he tasted nothing from the sixth hour on Friday until the sixth hour on Sunday.

The narrative is rather strange, since none of the actions is given a motivation. That immediately evident difference between Eliezer's and Aqiba's story will later on prove still more striking than it does now. But it suffices to note the points in which the two stories diverge in narrative technique. While in the case of Aqiba, we know why the great master originally determined to study the Torah, in the instance of Eliezer we do not. All we know is that at the mature age of twenty-two, he determined to study in the session of Yohanan ben Zakkai. My judgment is that the storyteller has in mind the task of explaining Eliezer's origins as Yohanan's disciple, not working out the inner motivation of the disciple. That accounts, also, for the random details, none of which fits together with the next. I see only a sequence of unintegrated details: he was twenty-two and decided to study the Torah. His father said, "Do not eat until you plough the furrow." He ploughed the furrow. Then he went and ate with his father-in-law. Some say he did not eat until Sunday. These details, scarcely connected, produce no effect either of narrative or of a propositional character.

VI:VI

2.   A   On the way he saw a rock. He picked it up and took it and put it into his mouth.

    B.   And some say that what he picked up was cattle dung.

    C.   He went and spent the night at his hostel.

Even if we read VI:VI.2 as part of VI:VI.1, all we have is more unintegrated details. Nothing in VI:VI.1-2 points to a cogent narrative, let alone a story. All we have are odd bits of information about what someone "said." The whole conglomerate does serve, however, to set the stage for VI:VI.3. The details necessary to understand what is coming have now made their appearance, and the climax is before us: he went and studied, and, because he had not eaten, produced bad breath. Yohanan recognized the bad breath and said, "Just as you suffered, so you will enjoy a reward."

VI:VI

3.   A   He went and entered study-session before Rabban Yohanan ben Zakkai in Jerusalem.

    B.   Since a bad odor came out of his mouth, Rabban Yohanan ben Zakkai said to him, "Eliezer my son, have you taken a meal today?"

    C.   He shut up.

    D.   He asked him again, and he shut up again.

    E.   He sent word and inquired at his hostel, and asked, "Has Eliezer eaten anything with you?"

    F.   They sent word to him, "We thought that he might be eating with my lord."

    G.   He said, "For my part, I thought that he might be eating with you. Between me and you, we should have lost R. Eliezer in the middle."

H.   He said to him, "Just as the odor of your mouth has gone forth, so will a good name in the Torah go forth for you."

VI:VI

4.   A.   Hyrcanus, his father, heard that he was studying the Torah with Rabban Yohanan ben Zakkai. He decided, "I shall go and impose on Eliezer my son a vow not to derive benefit from my property."

B.   They say that that day Rabban Yohanan ben Zakkai was in session and expounding [the Torah] in Jerusalem, and all the great men of Israel were in session before him. He heard that he was coming. He set up guards, saying to them, "If he comes to take a seat, do not let him."

C.   He came to take a seat and they did not let him.

D.   He kept stepping over people and moving forward until he came to Ben Sisit Hakkesset and Naqdimon b. Gurion and Ben Kalba Sabua. He sat among them, trembling.

E.   They say, On that day Rabban Yohanan ben Zakkai looked at R. Eliezer, indicating to him, "Cite an appropriate passage and give an exposition."

F.   He said to him, "I cannot cite an appropriate passage."

G.   He urged him, and the other disciples urged him.

H.   He went and cited an opening passage and expounded matters the like of which no ear had ever heard.

I.   And at every word that he said, Rabban Yohanan ben Zakkai arose and kissed him on his head and said, "My lord, Eliezer, my lord, you have taught us truth."

J.   As the time came to break up, Hyrcanus his father stood up and said, "My lords, I came here only to impose a vow on my son, Eliezer, not to derive benefit from my possession. Now all of my possessions are given over to Eliezer my son, and all my other sons are disinherited and will have no share in them."

We have a beginning: Hyrcanus plans to go and place Eliezer under a vow of ostracism. That not only begins the story, but it also creates an enormous tension. A dramatic setting is set up: do not let the father sit down at the back, so that the father will sit among the greatest men of Jerusalem (B-D). Yohanan then calls upon Eliezer to speak, and, after appropriate urging, he does. The tension is resolved at the climax, which also is the conclusion. I cannot think of a more perfect story, since every detail contributes to the whole, and the storyteller's intent – to underline the reward coming to the disciple, even though his family originally opposes his joining the sage – is fully realized. We note, therefore, that the conglomerate of narratives involving both Aqiba and Eliezer in fact rest in each case on a single story, and that story forms the redactional focus, permitting the aggregation of further materials, not all of them of a finished character, and some of them not stories at all.

Let us now stand back and review the whole composite involving both Aqiba and Eliezer, which, in the aggregate, makes the point that one can start Torah-study in mature years. VI:IV.1 serves only as a preface to the autonomous materials collected on the theme of how two famous masters began their studies late in life, having had no prior education. Both figures, moreover, started off poor but got rich when they became famous. These are Eliezer and Aqiba. There is no clear connection between the materials and the original saying. Perhaps the reference to wallowing in the dust of their feet in connection with Eliezer is meant to link up to the detail that he put a piece of dirt or cow dung in his mouth, but that seems to me farfetched. We refer first to Eliezer, then to Aqiba, but tell the stories in reverse order.

The diverse stories on Aqiba are hardly harmonious, since one set knows nothing of his wife, while the other introduces her as the main figure. The first set, No. 2ff., emphasizes how slow and steady wins the race. The lesson is that if one persists, one may ultimately best one's masters. No. 3 goes over the same matter, now with a parable to make the point that if one persists, he can uproot mountains. This seems to me appropriately joined to the foregoing, with the notion that Joshua and Eliezer are the mountains, as is made explicit. Tarfon then goes over the same matter in yet another way, No. 4. No. 5 then goes over the theme of studying in poverty. No. 5 seems to me a rather pointless story, but it leads to No. 6, which presents its own message explicitly. I treat No. 6 as distinct from No. 5 because it introduces the distinct theme of Aqiba's wife, and that has nothing to do with studying in poverty, but rather, the wife's toleration of the husband's long absences. No. 7 then carries forward the second theme of the foregoing, Aqiba's wealth later on and how he lavished it on Rachel. I find puzzling the failure of the storyteller to take an interest in the source of Aqiba's great wealth. The sequence on Eliezer goes over a recurrent theme, but is as incoherent as the foregoing. No. 1 presents a number of problems of continuity, since 1.1-D are simply gibberish, there being no clear relationship between C and B. How E-F fit in I cannot say. One may make a good case for treating VI:VI.1 and VI:VI.2 as continuous. But because of the detail of 9.A, on the way he saw a rock, it seems to me that we are on good ground in treating the latter as a fragment of yet another story, rather than as a bridge. VI:VI.3 is on its own coherent and complete, a cogent and readily comprehended statement on its own. VI:VI.4 also works well, beginning to end. The details given in D then account for the appendix which follows, VI:VII-X.

VIII. The Passion of Jesus Christ in Mark's Gospel and the Story of How the Sage Dies

Mark 14-16 tell the story of the passion, death, and resurrection of Jesus Christ. The story emphasizes the supernatural prescience of the hero, his preparation for the last supper, betrayal, sacramental deeds, distress at the prospect of suffering and death but acceptance of the father's will, trial, suffering, crucifixion, and resurrection. The narrative is not only rich, but it is full of action; the message is carried by both what is said and what is done. The range of themes and messages is remarkably broad, and, while the force of the narrative holds the whole, beginning to end, the variety of scenes and stages in the narrative yields a rich and diverse tale. It is not a tableau but a vivid sequence of events heavy with meaning. When we contrast the story of the passion of Jesus Christ as Mark (and the other evangelists) portray it with the story of the death scenes of great sages, the representation of the Judaic saints presents a sharp contrast. If I may point to the single difference between the passion of Christ and the death of Rabbi Aqiba or Rabbi Eliezer, it is that the former is represented as an event, the latter is represented as routine and ordinary. The death of the sage serves as an occasion once again to demonstrate the serenity that study of the Torah brings to the sage: there is nothing to fear, no occasion for distress, no reason for anguish. Let us turn forthwith to the representation of sages' deaths. Here again we shall grasp why no gospels could emerge: there is nothing exceptional, nothing, really, to tell, because nothing remarkable happens, though a critical truth is once again realized. And that accounts, also, for the medium of the story, which is wholly worked out in dialogue. Where nothing happens, dialogue bears the burden of the tale.

Two moments in the life of the sage formed the center of interest: origins, meaning, beginnings as a Torah-disciple, and death. The death stories are told under the aspect of the Torah and serve to show the supernatural power of the Torah to transform even the moment of death into an occasion of Torah-learning. The two points, start and finish, served to define and delineate the middle. How a sage coped with the death of a loved one had to draw into alignment with how a sage studied the Torah; the Torah obviously provided the model of the correct confrontation. How a sage died – the death scene, with its quiet lessons – likewise presented a model for others. The encounter with death took narrative shape in the account of how the sage accepted comfort:

The Fathers According to Rabbi Nathan
XIV:IV

1. A   When the son of Rabban Yohanan ben Zakkai died, his disciples came in to bring him comfort.

    B.   R. Eliezer came in and took a seat before him and said to him, "My lord, with your permission, may I say something before you."

    C.   He said to him, "Speak."

    D.   He said to him, "The first Man had a son who died, and he accepted comfort in his regard. And how do we know that he accepted comfort in his regard?

    E.   "As it is said, *And Adam knew his wife again* (Gen. 4:25). You, too, be comforted."

    F.   Said he to him, "Is it not enough for me that I am distressed on my own account, that you should mention to me the distress of the first Man?"

    G.   R. Joshua came in and said to him, "My lord, with your permission, may I say something before you."

    H.   He said to him, "Speak."

    I.   He said to him, "Job had sons and daughters who died, and he accepted comfort in their regard. And how do we know that he accepted comfort in their regard?

    J.   "As it is said, *The Lord gave and the Lord has taken away, blessed be the name of the Lord* (Job 1:21). You too, be comforted."

    K.   Said he to him, "Is it not enough for me that I am distressed on my own account, that you should mention to me the distress of Job?"

    L.   R. Yosé came in and took a seat before him and said to him, "My lord, with your permission, may I say something before you."

    M.   He said to him, "Speak."

    N.   He said to him, "Aaron had two grown-up sons who died on the same day, and he accepted comfort in their regard.

    O.   "For it is said, *And Aaron held his peace* (Lev. 10:3). and silence means only comfort. You too, be comforted."

    P   Said he to him, "Is it not enough for me that I am distressed on my own account, that you should mention to me the distress of Aaron?"

    Q.   R. Simeon came in and said to him, "My lord, with your permission, may I say something before you."

    R.   He said to him, "Speak."

    S.   He said to him, "King David had a son who died, and he accepted comfort in his regard. You too, be comforted. And how do we know that he accepted comfort in his regard?

    T.   "As it is said, *And David comforted Bath Sheba his wife and went in unto her and lay with her and she bore a son and called his name Solomon* (2 Sam. 12:24). You too, be comforted."

U.   Said he to him, "Is it not enough for me that I am distressed on
        my own account, that you should mention to me the distress of
        King David?"

V.   R. Eleazar b. Arakh came in. When he saw him, he said to his
        servant, "Take my clothes and follow me to the bathhouse [so that
        I can prepare to accept consolation], for he is a great man and I
        shall not be able to resist his arguments."

W.   He came in and took a seat before him and said to him, "I shall
        draw a parable for you. To what may the matter be compared?
        To the case of a man with whom the king entrusted a treasure.
        Every day he would weep and cry saying, 'Woe is me, when shall I
        get complete and final relief from this treasure that has been
        entrusted to me.'

X.   "You too, my lord, had a son, he recited from the Torah, Prophets
        and Writings, Mishnah, laws, lore, and has departed from this
        world without sin. You have reason, therefore, to accept
        consolation for yourself that you have returned your treasure,
        entrusted to you, whole and complete."

Y.   He said to him, "R. Eleazar b. Arakh, my son, you have given
        comfort to me in the right way in which people console one
        another."

The structure of the story, focused on the superiority of Eleazar b.
Arakh (counterpart to the constructions in The Fathers 2:2ff. built along
the same lines), should not obscure its larger sense. The first four
disciples, Eliezer, Joshua, Yosé, and Simeon, all invoke biblical models.
Scripture is insufficient. Eleazar then presents an argument resting on
the Oral Torah: the son had studied the Torah, inclusive of the
Mishnah, laws and lore. He departed from this world without sin, so
"you have returned the treasure entrusted to you." The Written Torah
presents a mere set of examples. The Oral Torah, by contrast, provides
not only the model but also the measure and the meaning. The sequence
of names, to which our attention is first attracted, allows the message
to be stated with great force, and the climactic statement underlines
the power of the Oral Torah to define the appropriate response to the
death of the child. The polemic is clear, and, we find, consistent with
that of Hillel.

    We come now to the stories about the death of a sage, with special
reference to Yohanan ben Zakkai and his disciple, Eliezer, the only two
death scenes (other than those of martyrs, below) presented in The
Fathers According to Rabbi Nathan. Both death scenes respond to lists
of omens pertinent to one's condition at death. In the first, Yohanan's,
there is no correspondence at all, since Yohanan is not represented as
dying with a serene mind:

XXV:I

1. A.   Ben Azzai says, "Whoever has a serene mind on account of his learning has a good omen for himself, and who does not have a serene mind on account of his learning has a bad omen for himself.

B.   "Whoever has a serene mind on account of his impulse, has a good omen for himself, but [Goldin:] if his mind is distressed because of his impulse, it is a bad sign for him.

C.   "For him with whom the sages are satisfied at the hour of death it is a good sign, and for him with whom sages are not satisfied at the hour of death it is a bad sign.

D.   "For whoever has his face turned upward [at death] it is a good sign, and for whoever has his face turned toward the bed it is a bad sign.

E.   "If one is looking at people, it is a good sign, at the wall, a bad sign.

F.   "If one's face is glistening, it is a good sign, glowering, a bad one."

XXV:II

1. A.   At the time that Rabban Yohanan ben Zakkai was departing from this life, he raised up his voice and wept. His disciples said to him, "Lord, tall pillar, eternal light, mighty hammer, why are you weeping?"

B.   He said to them, "Now am I going to appear before a mortal king, who, should he be angry with me, is angry only in this world, and if he should imprison me, imposes imprisonment only in this world, and if he should put me to death, imposes death only in this world, and not only so, but whom I can appease with words and bribe with money?

C.   "Lo, I am going to appear before the King of kings of kings, the Holy One, blessed be he, who, should he be angry with me, is angry both in this world and in the world to come, whom I cannot appease with words or bribe with me.

D.   "And furthermore, before me are two paths, one to the Garden of Eden, the other to Gehenna, and I do not know on which road, whether I shall be drawn down to Gehenna or whether I shall be brought into the Garden of Eden."

E.   And in this regard it is said, *Before him shall be sentenced all those who go down to the dust, even he who cannot keep his soul alive* (Ps. 22:30).

XXV:II

2. A.   In regard to Moses Scripture says, *And I will take away my hand and you shall see my back, but my face shall not be seen* (Ex. 33:23).

B.   And further, *And he spread it before me and it was written on its face and on its back* (Ezek. 2:10).

C.   *Its face* refers to this world, *its back*, to the world to come.

    D.   Another interpretation: *its face* refers to the distress of the righteous in this world and the prosperity of the wicked in this world, *its back*, to the reward given to the righteous in the world to come, and the punishment inflicted on the wicked in Gehenna.

XXV:II
3. A.   *And there was written therein lamentations and jubilant sound and woe* (Ezek. 2:10):

    B.   *Lamentations* refers to the penalty inflicted on the wicked in this world, as it is said, *This is the lamentation with which they shall lament, the daughters of the nations shall lament with it* (Ezek. 32:16).

    C.   *...and jubilant sound and woe* refers to the reward of the righteous in the world to come, as it is said, *With an instrument of ten strings and with the psaltery, with a jubilant sound on the harp* (Ps. 92:4).

    D.   *...and woe*: refers to the punishment that is coming to the wicked in the world to come, as it is said, *Calamity shall come upon calamity, and rumor upon rumor* (Ezek. 7:26).

XXV:II
4. A.   [Yohanan ben Zakkai] would say, "Clear the house on account of uncleanness and prepare a throne for King Hezekiah of Judah."

The narrative of XXV:II.1 hardly qualifies as a story, since we have little more than a tableau: the setting of the stage, the giving of a speech. Yohanan is dying and "he said to him...he said to him...." The message is very powerful. Yohanan reminds the disciples that the judgment at hand is inexorable and incorruptible, and he does not know the way in which he will now go. The colloquy hardly qualifies as a story, and, when we come to Eliezer's, we see the possibilities for action as a vehicle for the unfolding of the narrative, characterization as a mode of making its point(s), and sustained sequences of exchange – whether word or deed – as the deep structure of the story. The essentially stationary character of the present death scene is shown at XXV:II.2-3, which form little more than exegeses of Scripture. At XV:II.4, then, we have a further "would say" for Yohanan. These snippets scarcely qualify as a story by any definition.

XXV:III
1. A.   [Ben Azzai] would say, "If one dies in a serene mind, it is a good omen from him, in derangement, it is a bad omen.

    B.   "...while speaking, it is a good omen, in silence, a bad omen.

    C.   "...in repeating words of the Torah, it is a good omen for him, in the midst of discussing business, it is a bad omen.

    D.   "...while doing a religious duty, it is a good omen, while involved with a trivial matter, it is a bad omen.

E.   "...while happy, it is a good omen, while sad, a bad omen.
F.   "...while laughing, a good omen, while weeping, a bad omen.
G.   "...on the eve of the Sabbath, a good omen, at the end of the Sabbath, a bad omen.
H.   "...on the eve of the Day of Atonement a bad omen, at the end of the Day of Atonement a good omen.

After the sizable interruption illustrating the first unit of the sayings, we revert to the completion of Ben Azzai's statement on this theme. A mark of the end of a systematic list is the change in the established pattern, as at H.

XXV:IV

1.   A.   When R. Eliezer was dying – they say it was the eve of the Sabbath [toward dusk] – R. Aqiba and his colleagues came in to see him, and he was dozing in the room, sitting back [Goldin:] on a canopied couch. They took seats in the waiting room. Hyrcanus his son came in to remove his phylacteries [which are worn on week days but not on the Sabbath, about to begin]. But he did not let him do so, and he was weeping.

     B.   Hyrcanus went out and said to the sages, "My lords, it appears to me that my father is deranged."

     C.   [Eliezer] said to him, "My son, I am not the one who is deranged, but you are the one who is deranged. For you have neglected to light the lamp for the Sabbath, on which account you may become liable to death penalty inflicted by heaven, but busied yourself with the matter of the phylacteries, on account of which liability is incurred, at worst, merely on the matter of violating the rules of Sabbath rest."

     D.   Since sages saw that he was in full command of his faculties, they came in and took up seats before him, but at a distance of four cubits [as was required, because Eliezer was in a state of ostracism on account of his rejection of the decision of the majority in a disputed case]. [Bringing up the case subject to dispute, so to determine whether he had finally acceded to the decision of the majority,] they said to him, "My lord, as to a round cushion, a ball, [a shoe when placed on] a shoemaker's last, an amulet, and phylacteries that have been torn, what is the law as to their being susceptible to uncleanness? [Are they regarded as completed and useful objects, therefore susceptible, or as useless or incomplete and therefore not susceptible?]"

     E.   [Maintaining his earlier position,] he said to them, "They remain susceptible to uncleanness, and should they become unclean, immerse them as is [without undoing them, e.g., exposing their contents to the water], and take great pains in these matters, for these represent important laws that were stated to Moses at Sinai."

F.   They persisted in addressing to him questions concerning matters of insusceptibility and susceptibility to uncleanness as well as concerning immersion pools, saying to him, "My lord, what is the rule on this matter?"

G.   He would say to them, "Clean."

H.   And so he went, giving the answer of susceptible to uncleanness to an object that could become unclean, and insusceptible to one that could not become unclean."

I.   After a while R. Eliezer said to sages, "I am amazed at the disciples of the generation, perhaps they may be liable to the death penalty at the hand of Heaven."

J.   They said to him, "My lord, on what account?"

K.   He said to them, "Because you never came and performed the work of apprenticeship to me."

L.   Then he said to Aqiba b. Joseph, "Aqiba, on what account did you not come before me and serve as apprentice to me?"

M.   He said to him, "My lord, I had no time."

N.   He said to him, "I shall be surprised for you if you die a natural death."

O.   And some say, He said nothing to him, but when R. Eliezer spoke as he did to his disciples, forthwith [Aqiba's] [Goldin:] heart melted within him.

P.   Said to him R. Aqiba, "My lord, how will I die?"

Q.   He said to him, "Aqiba, yours will be the worst."

XXV:IV

2   A.   R. Aqiba entered and took a seat before him and said to him, "My lord, now repeat traditions for me."

B.   He opened a subject and repeated for him three hundred rules concerning the bright spot [to which Lev. 13:1ff. refers in connection with the skin ailment translated as leprosy].

C.   Then R. Eliezer raised his two arms and folded them on his breast and said, "Woe is me for these two arms, which are like two scrolls of Torahs, which now are departing from the world.

D.   "For were all the oceans ink, all the reeds quills, all men scribes, they could not write down what I have learned in Scripture and repeated in Mishnah-traditions, and derived as lessons from my apprenticeship to sages in the session.

E.   "Yet I have taken away from my masters only as much as does a person who dips his finger into the ocean, and I have taken away for my disciples only so much as a paintbrush takes from a paint tube.

F.   "And furthermore, I can repeat three hundred laws on the rule: *You shall not permit a sorceress to live.*"

G.   Some say, "Three thousand."

XXV:IV

3. A. "But no one ever asked me anything about it, except for Aqiba b. Joseph.

   B. "For one time he said to me, 'My lord, teach me how people plant cucumbers and how they pull them up.'

   C. "I said something and the entire field was filled with cucumbers.

   D. "He said to me, 'My lord, you have taught me how they are planted. Teach me how they are pulled up.'

   E. "I said something, and all of the cucumbers assembled in a single place."

XXV:IV

4. A. Said R. Eleazar b. Azariah to him, "My lord, as to a shoe that is on the shoemaker's list, what is the law? [Is it susceptible to uncleanness, as a useful object, or insusceptible, since it is not fully manufactured and so finished as a useful object?]"

   B. He said to him, "It is insusceptible to uncleanness."

   C. And so he continued giving answers to questions, ruling of an object susceptible to uncleanness that it is susceptible, and of one insusceptible to uncleanness that it is permanently clean, until his soul went forth as he said the word, "Clean."

   D. Then R. Eleazar b. Azariah tore his clothes and wept, going forth and announcing to sages, "My lords, come and see R. Eliezer, for he is not in a state of purity as to the world to come, since his soul went forth with the word pure on his lips."

XXV:IV

5. A. After the Sabbath R. Aqiba came and found [Eliezer's corpse being conveyed for burial] on the road from Caesarea to Lud. Then he tore his clothes and ripped his hair, and his blood flowed, and he fell to the earth, crying out and weeping, saying, "Woe is me for you, my Lord, woe is me, my master, for you have left the entire generation orphaned."

   B. At the row of mourners he commenced [the lament,] saying, "*My father, my father, chariot of Israel and its horsemen!* I have coins but no expert money changer to sort them out."

The snippets of death scenes of Eliezer are sewn together, but the distinct components are fairly easy to recognize, through the repetitions, on the one side, and the shifts in setting and premise as to the location of authorities, on the other. But the flow is smooth, beginning to end, a credit to the compiler. The detail of No. 1 becomes a main point later on, that is, the ruling on objects Eliezer had held subject to uncleanness, sages taking the opposite view. No. 1 moves along to the complaint of Eliezer that the disciples had kept their distance from him. No. 2 picks up at this point, but by introducing Aqiba, suggests that the tale is distinct from the foregoing, which already has him on the scene. The same happens later with Eleazar b. Azariah's paragraph. No. 3 then goes back over the matter of No. 2 – the distance of the disciples – and goes over its own point. No. 4 does not appear to know anything about much that has gone before, as I said, and No. 5 is independent as well, since up to now we have had Aqiba at the death scene, while here Aqiba finds out about the death only after the Sabbath and in a different set.

The story serves as a good illustration for three of the positive omens Ben Azzai has listed, while speaking, while repeating words of the Torah, and on the eve of the Sabbath. But he clearly is not represented as happy or cheerful or laughing, so, in the aggregate, I think that an illustration of the omens of Ben Azzai formed a negligible consideration in the mind of the storytellers. The center of interest of the story is Eliezer's complaint against the disciples, who did not study Torah through service to him. The interplay of Eliezer and Aqiba then forms the centerpiece, with Nos. 1, 2, 3, and 5 placing Aqiba at the heart of matters; Eleazar b. Azariah dominates in No. 4. The materials form a nuanced and powerful story on their own. Each detail points toward the next, each sequence of action, the one to follow. The master, very much an individual and not a type, leaves a legacy of reproach, a distinctive and particular message. We have slight experience in dealing with sages as distinctive individuals, since stories over all represent them as either symbols on their own – e.g., the sage as against the emperor – or as models of virtues for the many to emulate, e.g., Hillel's patience, Yohanan b. Zakkai's resort to the Torah to cope with the destruction of the Temple.

Since the Passion narratives deal with a martyrdom, our comparison of the Gospel of Jesus Christ with the Torah of our sages of blessed memory requires attention to a story of the same kind. Here is how a sage's narrative is represented, once more, as an exercise in Torah-study:

XXXVIII:V

1. A   **A sword comes into the world because of the delaying of justice and perversion of justice, and because of those who teach the Torah not in accord with the law.**

XXXVIII:V

2. A   When they seized Rabban Simeon b. Gamaliel and R. Ishmael on the count of death, Rabban Simeon b. Gamaliel was in session and was perplexed, saying, "Woe is us! For we are put to death like those who profane the Sabbath and worship idols and practice fornication and kill."

B. Said to him R. Ishmael b. Elisha, "Would it please you if I said something before you?"

C. He said to him, "Go ahead."

D. He said to him, "Is it possible that when you were sitting at a banquet, poor folk came and stood at your door, and you did not let them come in and eat?"

E. He said to him, "By heaven [may I be cursed] if I ever did such a thing! Rather, I set up guards at the gate. When poor folk came along, they would bring them in to me and eat and drink with me and say a blessing for the sake of Heaven."

F. He said to him, "Is it possible that when you were in session and expounding [the Torah] on the Temple mount and the vast populations of Israelites were in session before you, you took pride in yourself?"

G. He said to him, "Ishmael my brother, one has to be ready to accept his failing. [That is why I am being put to death, the pride that I felt on such an occasion.]"

H. They went on appealing to the executioner for grace. This one [Ishmael] said to him, "I am a priest, son of a high priest, kill me first, so that I do not have to witness the death of my companion."

I. And the other [Simeon] said, "I am the patriarch, son of the patriarch, kill me first, so that I do not have to witness the death of my companion."

J. He said to him, "Cast lots." They cast lots, and the lot fell on Rabban Simeon b. Gamaliel.

K. The executioner took the sword and cut off his head.

L. R. Ishmael b. Elisha took it and held it in his breast and wept and cried out: "Oh holy mouth, oh faithful mouth, oh mouth that brought forth beautiful gems, precious stones and pearls! Who has laid you in the dust, who has filled your mouth with dirt and dust.

M. "Concerning you Scripture says, *Awake, O sword, against my shepherd and against the man who is near to me* (Zech. 13:7)."

N. He had not finished speaking before the executioner took the sword and cut off his head.

O. Concerning them Scripture says, *My wrath shall wax hot, and I will kill you with the sword, and your wives shall be widows, and your children fatherless* (Ex. 22:23).

The story establishes the tension at the outset: why do we die as do sinners? This question is resolved in the colloquy at C-H, at which act I concludes. The second act has the sages appeal to the executioner to spare the one the sight of the martyrdom of the other, I-L. The third and final component has Ishmael's lament: the mouth that taught the Torah will be avenged. The sage who dies in peace addresses his lessons to the Torah-community: the decline of the great tradition because of the failure of the sages and their disciples. The sage who dies as a martyr teaches a lesson of hope to Israel at large: God will ultimately exact justice of those who sin by persecuting Israel, just as God exacts strict justice even for the peccadillo of pride. The death scenes yield a variety of lessons, since they present nuanced, and not merely conventional, portraits, with a measure of action and not merely set-piece speeches. If I had to single out the main point sages wished through the topic at hand to underline, it is God's perfect justice.

IX. Individuality and Consensus: From Gospels and Named Authors to Mishnah- or Scripture-Commentaries (Talmuds, Midrash Compilations) and Authorships

Instead of authors the canonical writings of the Dual Torah come from what I call authorships. Let me explain what I mean by an authorship. All classics of the Judaism of the Dual Torah exhibit one definitive characteristic. It is that none is signed by a named author or is so labeled (except in a few instances long after the fact) as to represent the opinion of a lone individual. In their intrinsic traits of discourse all speak out of the single, undifferentiated voice of Sinai, and each makes a statement of the Torah of Sinai and within that Torah. That anonymity, indicative for theological reasons, comes to expression in the highly formalized rhetoric of the canonical writings, which denies the possibility of the individuation not only of the writings themselves, but also of the sayings attributed to authorities in those writings.[6] Why the sedulous anonymity of the writings of the canon of the Judaism of the Dual Torah?

Books such as the Mishnah, Sifré to Deuteronomy, Genesis Rabbah, or the Bavli, that after formulation were accepted as part of the canon of Judaism, that is, of "the one whole Torah of Moses our rabbi revealed by God at Sinai," do not contain answers to questions of definition that commonly receive answers within the pages of a given book. Such authors as (the school of) Matthew or Luke, Josephus, even the writers of Ezra-Nehemiah, will have found such a policy surprising. And while Socrates did not write, Plato and Aristotle did – and they signed their own names (or did the equivalent in context). In antiquity books or other important writings, e.g., letters and treatises, ordinarily, though not always, bore the name of the author or at least an attribution, e.g.,

---

[6]That is not to claim that no traits of individual speech are preserved in any canonical document. That is self-evidently false in specific instances. It is only to claim that, in general, authorships have their authorities speak in pretty much the same syntactic and grammatical patterns, with very slight provision for stylistic individuation.

Aristotle's or Paul's name, or the attribution to Enoch or Baruch or Luke. For no document in the canon of Judaism produced in late antiquity, by contrast, is there a named author internal to the document. No document in that canon contains within itself a statement of a clear-cut date of composition, a defined place or circumstance in which a book is written, a sustained and ongoing argument to which we readily gain access, or any of the other usual indicators by which we define the authorship, therefore the context and the circumstance, of a book.

Let me now give my simple reason for the phenomenon of the anonymous authorship, presenting the consensus of sages rather than the individual opinion of a single writer.[7] The purpose of the sages who in the aggregate created the canonical writings of the Judaism of the Dual Torah is served by not specifying differentiating traits such as time, place, and identity of the author or the authorship. The canon – "the one whole Torah of Moses, our rabbi" – presents single books as undifferentiated episodes in a timeless, ahistorical setting: Torah revealed to Moses by God at Mount Sinai, but written down long afterward.

Our rapid comparison of the Gospels of Jesus Christ and the Torah of our sages of blessed memory yields a simple point of difference. Individual authors, Matthew, Mark, Luke, John, tell the story of the unique individual. A consensus of an entire community reaches its full human realization in the sage, and the writing down of that consensus will not permit individual traits of rhetoric to differentiate writer from writer or writing from writing. The individual obliterates the marks of individuality in serving the holy people by writing a work that will become part of the Torah, and stories about individuals will serve, in that context, only so far as they exemplify and realize traits characteristic of all Torah-sages. That is why, in my view, Christianity produced Gospels about a unique individual, and lives of saints later on, and that also explains why the Gospels have named authors. It also accounts for why the Judaism of the Dual Torah, while valuing exemplary stories about sages, did not make provision for the counterpart, about Aqiba, of Mishnah- (and therefore also Yerushalmi- or Bavli-) tractates, or, about Eliezer, of midrash compilations either.

---

[7]And, the reader should remember, where an individual opinion is given, the reason is that that opinion is thereby marked as not normative and not to be followed. The individual is named so that the opinion may be signified as not that of the consensus. Gaining a hearing for one's ideas requires in both rhetoric and larger presentation conformity to the norms of the community and the representation of private opinion as public and anonymous.

This brings us back to our starting point: materials written without regard to the requirements of compiling a complete document, as distinct from materials written in response to the program of a documentary compilation. While, as I have shown, the raw materials in hand, inclusive of stories about wonder-working by sages and also stories about incidents in the lives of sages, can have generated gospels or lives of saints, no one compiled the stories into biographies. It was a literary category that was excluded by the fundamental and indicative traits of the system as a whole. To state the result simply: Christianity was Christianity because of the Gospels, and Judaism was Judaism because of the Torah: different people, talking about different things, to different people. And that, by the way, also is why Talmudic Judaism had no gospels. It had what it wanted, which was, and is, the Torah of Moses, our rabbi, revealed by God at Sinai. The upshot is simple. Whatever materials lay at hand, the makers of the classics of Judaism produced compilations – completed documents – of one kind, rather than of some other, because of well-considered theological convictions that came to expression, also, in aesthetic and literary choices.

The upshot for the experiment of Part Two is simple. We have now seen that some writings carry out a redactional purpose. The Mishnah was our prime example. Some writings ignore all redactional considerations we can identify. The stories about sages in the Fathers According to Rabbi Nathan has shown us kinds of writing that are wholly out of phase with the program of the document that collects and compiles them. We may therefore turn to midrash compilations and find the traits of writing that clearly are imposed by the requirements of compilation. These will then characterize one sort of composition in such compilations. In Chapter Five we have a sizable sample, drawn from the ten midrash compilations that reached closure in late antiquity. We further identify writings that clearly respond to a redactional program, but not the program of any compilation we now have in hand. There is little speculation about the identification of such writings. They will conform to the redactional patterns we discern in the known compilations, but presuppose a collection other than one now known to us. These are in Chapter Six. Finally, as in the materials we have reviewed in this chapter, we turn to pieces of writing that respond to no redactional program known to us or susceptible to invention in accord with the principles of defining compilations known to us. In Chapter Seven in the context of a rich repertoire of examples, I explain why, within the modes of thought of the canonical writings before us, we cannot imagine compilations to encompass other kinds of writing, besides stories about sages, that we find in abundance in the ten midrash compilations subject to this probe.

Part Two
THE DOCUMENTARY CLASSIFICATION OF WRITING: THE THREE STAGES OF LITERARY FORMATION

5

Pericopes Framed for the Purposes
of the Particular Document
in Which They Occur

I. Prologue. Definition

Let us now review the definitions given in Chapter One. The remainder of this chapter then sets forth examples of this kind of writing in the classics of Judaism in the first and second classifications; there is no need to distinguish writings of these two types, since, by definition, both kinds of writings fall into the same stratum, the one defined by the composition of writings by the penultimate and ultimate redactors of documents we now have.

[1] Some writings clearly serve the redactional program of the framers of the document in which those writings occur.

[2] Some writings serve not the redactional program of the document in which they occur, but some other document, now in our hands.

The first of those four kinds of completed units of thought (pericopes) as matter of hypothesis fall into the final stage of literary formation. That is to say, at the stage at which an authorship has reached the conclusion that it wishes to compile a document of a given character, that authorship will have made up pieces of writing that serve the purposes of the document it wishes to compile. The second through fourth kinds of completed units of thought come earlier than this writing in the process of the formation of the classics of Judaism represented by the compilation in which this writing now finds its place.

My analytical taxonomy of the writings now collected in various midrash compilations point to not only three stages in the formation of the classics of Judaism. It also suggests that writing went on outside of the framework of the editing of documents, and also within the limits of the formation and framing of documents. Writing of the former kind then constituted a kind of literary work to which redactional planning proved irrelevant. But the second and the third kinds of writing respond to redactional considerations. So in the end we shall wish to distinguish between writing intended for the making of books – compositions of the first three kinds listed just now – and writing not in response to the requirements of the making of compilations.

The distinctions upon which these analytical taxonomies rest are objective and no way subjective since they depend upon the fixed and factual relationship between a piece of writing and a larger redactional context.

[1] We know the requirements of redactors of the several documents of the rabbinic canon – I have already shown what they are in the case of a large variety of documents. When, therefore, we judge a piece of writing to serve the program of the document in which that writing occurs, it is not because of a personal impulse or a private and incommunicable insight, but because the traits of that writing self-evidently respond to the documentary program of the book in which the writing is located.

[2] When, further, we conclude that a piece of writing belongs in some other document than the one in which it is found, that too forms a factual judgment.

II. Mekhilta

Mekhilta Beshallah Chapter Six
XXIV: I

4.	A.	"on dry ground, the waters being a wall to them:"
	B.	He made the water into a kind of wall at their right and at their left.
5.	A.	"on their right hand and on their left:"
	B.	this refers to prayer.
6.	A.	Another interpretation of the phrase, "on their right hand and on their left:"
	B.	"On their right hand" refers to the amulet on the doorpost [at the right].
	C.	"and on their left" refers to the phylacteries that are put on the left hand.
8.	A.	Another interpretation of the clause, "And in the morning watch:"
	B.	this was at the dawn's early light.

9. A.   "in the pillar of fire and of cloud looked down upon the host of the Egyptians:"

    B.   For the pillar of cloud went down and made [the ground] like mud, and the pillar of fire heated it up,

    C.   and the hooves of the horses were dislocated [Lauterbach:] the node above and its socket below coming apart,

    D.   as it is said, "Then did the horses' hooves stamp by reason of the prancing, the prancings of their mighty ones" (Judges 5:22).

10. A.   "and discomfited the host of the Egyptians:"

    B.   He disorganized them and confused them.

    C.   He took away their signals, and they did not know what they were doing.

11. A.   Another interpretation of the verse, "and discomfited the host of the Egyptians:"

    B.   "discomfit" means through pestilence: "And shall discomfit them with great discomfiture until they be destroyed" (Dt. 7:23).

12. A.   "clogging their chariot wheels:"

    B.   R. Judah says, "On account of the fire from above, the wheels down below burned up.

    C.   "But the yokes and chariots ran onward despite the [drivers],

    D.   "for [the chariots with their yokes] were encrusted with silver and gold utensils, precious stones and pearls, so that the Israelis would take them as spoil."

13. A.   R. Nehemiah says, "On account of the rumblings from above the pins of the wheels down below flew off: 'The voice of your thunder was upon the wheel, the lightnings lighted up the world' (Ps. 77:19).

    B.   "But the yokes and chariots ran onward despite the [animals].

    C.   "Earlier, the mules had pulled the chariots; now the chariots pulled the mules."

14. A.   "so that they drove heavily:"

    B.   R. Judah says, "With the measure with which they meted out was their measure meted.

    C.   "They had said, 'Let the work be laid on heavily' (Ex. 5:9).

    D.   "So you paid them back with that same measure: 'so that they drove heavily.'"

15. A.   "and the Egyptians said, 'Let us flee from before Israel; [for the Lord fights for them against the Egyptians']:"

    B.   The evil and foolish among them were saying, "Are we going to flee before these miserable and rootless people?"

    C.   The smart ones among them said, "Let us flee from before Israel, for the Lord fights for them against the Egyptians."

    D.   They said, "The one who did wonders for them in Egypt is the one who is doing wonders for them at the sea."

16. A.   R. Yosé says, "How do we know that by the same plagues that those who were at the sea were smitten those in Egypt were smitten, and these saw those?

B.   "It is in that connection that it is said, 'and the Egyptians said, "Let
          us flee from before Israel; for the Lord fights for them against the
          Egyptians."'

C.   "And not against the Egyptians alone, but against all those who
          trouble the Israelites in all generations: 'And he smote his
          adversaries backward, he made them a perpetual reproach' (Ps.
          78:66); 'Even my adversaries and my foes stumbled and fell' (Ps.
          27:2); 'I would soon subdue their enemies' (Ps. 81:15); 'That I will
          break Assyria in my land' (Is. 14:25); 'The envy also of Ephraim
          shall depart, and those who harass Judah shall be cut off' (Is.
          11:13).

D.   "And that rule runs through all generations: 'This is the counsel
          that is advised for all the earth' (Is. 14:26).

E.   "On what account? 'For the Lord of hosts has advised, and who
          will nullify it' (Is. 14:27).

F.   "So you learn that it was not against the Egyptians alone, but
          against all those who trouble the Israelites in all generations.

G.   "Therefore it is said, 'for the Lord fights for them against the
          Egyptians."'

While the subterranean proposition that the redemption at the sea
prefigures the redemption at the end of time figures, that is not an
articulated motif in the whole. These materials have been compiled
for the purposes of a phrase-by-phrase amplification of the cited
verses of Exodus. They adhere closely to the necessary form, which is
citation then amplification, and they are formulated in such a way as
to serve only a commentary. Here therefore are writings that have
been framed in such a way as to serve the purposes of the redactors. The
authorship that compiled the document need not have made up the
individual entries; but the entries, whether made up all in one
afternoon or over the course of a hundred years, all are aimed at
adhering to a single uniform literary protocol.

III. Sifra

To show that the framers of a document may impose their program
on virtually every aspect of the writing that they include in their
document, I turn not to a narrowly exegetical passage, in which one
word after another is expounded, but rather I point to a monumental
intellectual program, worked out in vast detail, in which the exegesis
of a document takes second place to the formation and representation of
large-scale and general propositions, expressed in the main (though not
entirely) through the exegesis of the document. For that purpose I give
the first two *parashiyyot* of Sifra. Here we see with great clarity how
a program of general analysis is joined with the form of exegesis of a

single verse. The paramount program is that of the compilers of the document as a whole, we see time and again, and we cannot claim that before us is writing aimed at some document other than an exegesis of the book of Leviticus. That is more or less beside the point. What we have is a cogent piece of writing, important in relationship to the book of Leviticus and framed in order to re-present the book of Leviticus. The writing is not (merely) exegetical – it is propositional in a profound sense – but the propositions find their particular exemplification in response to the stimuli supplied by the book of Leviticus. Giving this sample here shows some of the subtlety of the distinctions between the items classified here and those classified in the next part of this book.

Parashat Vayyiqra Dibura Denedabah Parashah One
I:I
1.   A   "The Lord called [to Moses] and spoke [to him from the tent of meeting, saying, 'Speak to the Israelite people and say to them']" (Lev. 1:1):
     B.   He gave priority to the calling over the speaking.
     C.   That is in line with the usage of Scripture.
     D.   Here there is an act of speaking, and in connection with the encounter at the bush [Ex. 3:4: "God called to him out of the bush, 'Moses, Moses'"], there is an act of speaking.
     E.   Just as in the latter occasion, the act of calling is given priority over the act of speaking [even though the actual word, "speaking" does not occur, it is implicit in the framing of the verse], so here, with respect to the act of speaking, the the act of calling is given priority over the act of speaking.
2.   A   No [you cannot generalize on the basis of that case,] for if you invoke the case of the act of speaking at the bush, which is the first in the sequence of acts of speech [on which account, there had to be a call prior to entry into discourse],
     B.   will you say the same of the act of speech in the tent of meeting, which assuredly is not the first in a sequence of acts of speech [so there was no need for a preliminary entry into discourse through a call]?
     C.   The act of speech at Mount Sinai [Ex. 19:3] will prove to the contrary, for it is assuredly not the first in a sequence of acts of speech, yet, in that case, there was an act of calling prior to the act of speech.
3.   A   No, [the exception proves nothing,] for if you invoke in evidence the act of speech at Mount Sinai, which pertained to all the Israelites, will you represent it as parallel to the act of speech in the tent of meeting, which is not pertinent to all Israel?
     B.   Lo, you may sort matters out by appeal to comparison and contrast, specifically:

C.   The act of speech at the bush, which is the first of the acts of speech, is not of the same classification as the act of speech at Sinai, which is not the first act of speech.

D.   And the act of speech at Sinai, which is addressed to all Israel, is not in the same classification as the act of speech at the bush, which is not addressed to all Israel.

4. A   What they have in common, however, is that both of them are acts of speech, deriving from the mouth of the Holy One, addressed to Moses, in which case, the act of calling comes prior to the act of speech,

B.   so that, by way of generalization, we may maintain that every act of speech which comes from the mouth of the Holy One to Moses will be preceded by an act of calling.

5. A   Now if what the several occasions have in common is that all involve an act of speech, accompanied by fire, from the mouth of the Holy One, addressed to Moses, so that the act of calling was given priority over the act of speaking, then in every case in which there is an act of speech, involving fire, from the mouth of the Holy One, addressed to Moses, should involve an act of calling prior to the act of speech.

B.   But then an exception is presented by the act of speech at the tent of meeting, in which there was no fire.

C.   [That is why it was necessary for Scripture on this occasion to state explicitly,] "The Lord called [to Moses and spoke to him from the tent of meeting, saying, 'Speak to the Israelite people and say to them']" (Lev. 1:1).

D.   That explicit statement shows that, on the occasion at hand, priority was given to the act of calling over the act of speaking.

I:II

1. A   ["The Lord called to Moses and spoke to him from the tent of meeting, saying, 'Speak to the Israelite people and say to them'" (Lev. 1:1)]: Might one suppose that the act of calling applied only to this act of speaking alone?

B.   And how on the basis of Scripture do we know that on the occasion of all acts of speaking that are mentioned in the Torah, [there was a prior act of calling]?

C.   Scripture specifies, "from the tent of meeting,"

D.   which bears the sense that on every occasion on which it was an act of speaking from the tent of meeting, there was an act of calling prior to the act of speaking.

2. A   Might one suppose that there was an act of calling only prior to the acts of speech alone?

B.   How on the basis of Scripture do I know that the same practice accompanied acts of saying and also acts of commanding?

C. Said R. Simeon, "Scripture says not only, '...spoke,...,' but '...and he spoke,' [with the inclusion of the *and*] meant to encompass also acts of telling and also acts of commanding."

The exercise of generalization addresses the character of God's meeting with Moses. The point of special interest is the comparison of the meeting at the bush and the meeting at the tent of meeting. And at stake is asking whether all acts of God's calling and talking with, or speaking to, the prophet are the same, or whether some of these acts are of a different classification from others. In point of fact, we are able to come to a generalization, worked out at I:I.5.A. And that permits us to explain why there is a different usage at Lev. 1:1 from what characterizes parallel cases. I:II.1-2 proceeds to generalize from the case at hand to other usages entirely, a very satisfying conclusion to the whole. I separate I:II from I:I because had I:I ended at 5, it could have stood complete and on its own, and therefore I see I:II as a brief appendix.

I.III

1. A. Might one maintain that is also the case for free-standing statements [which do not commence with a reference either to speaking or to saying, as at Lev. 1:10, which opens, simply, "If his offering..."]?

   B. Scripture says, "...spoke...," meaning that on an occasion of an act of speech there was also an act of calling, but there was no act of calling prior to the setting forth of a free-standing statement.

2. A. What purpose was there in setting forth free-standing statements [such as those that commence without reference to speaking or saying]?

   B. It was so as to give Moses a pause to collect his thoughts between the statement of one passage and the next, between the presentation of one topic and the next.

3. A. And lo, that yields an argument *a fortiori*:

   B. If one who was listening to words from the mouth of the Holy One, and who was speaking by the inspiration of the Holy Spirit, nonetheless had to pause to collect his thoughts between one passage and the next, between one topic and the next,

   C. all the more so an ordinary person in discourse with other common folk [must speak with all due deliberation].

We proceed to a quite separate matter, at No. 1, asking about passages that do not begin with "and he called, and he spoke," of which the writing before us contains a great many. The fact that there are such is worked out at No. 1, and these are explained at No. 2. No. 3 then provides a rule applicable to ordinary folk.

I:IV

1. A. How on the basis of Scripture do we know that every act of speech involved the call to Moses, Moses [two times]?

   B. Scripture says, "God called to him out of the bush, 'Moses, Moses'" (Ex. 3:4).

   C. Now when Scripture says, "And he said," it teaches that every act of calling involved the call to Moses, Moses [two times].

2. A. And how on the basis of Scripture do we know, furthermore, that at each act of calling, he responded, "Here I am"?

   B. Scripture says, "God called to him out of the bush, 'Moses, Moses,' and he said, 'Here I am'" (Ex. 3:4).

   C. Now when Scripture says, "And he said," it teaches that in response to each act of calling, he said, "Here I am."

3. A. "Moses, Moses" ((Ex. 3:4), "Abraham, Abraham" (Gen. 22:11), "Jacob, Jacob" (Gen. 46:2), Samuel, Samuel" (1 Sam. 3:10).

   B. This language expresses affection and also means to move to prompt response.

4. A. Another interpretation of "Moses, Moses:"

   B. This was the very same Moses both before he had been spoken with [by God] and also afterward.

The final unit completes the work of generalization which began with the opening passage. The point throughout is that there are acts of calling and speech, and a general rule pertains to them all. No. 3 and No. 4 conclude with a observations outside of the besought generalization. The first of the two interprets the repetition of a name, the second, a conclusion particular to Moses personally. These seem to me tacked on.

Parashat Vayyiqra Dibura Denedabah Pereq Two

II:I

1. A. "[The Lord called to Moses and spoke] to him [from the tent of meeting, saying, 'Speak to the Israelite people and say to them']" (Lev. 1:1):

   B. [The explicit reference to] "to him [Moses]" serves to exclude Aaron.

2. A. Said R. Judah b. Betera, "There are thirteen passages in the Torah which were addressed to both Moses and Aaron, and, as a counterpart, thirteen passages were stated with an exclusion [parallel to this one,] so informing you that these passages were stated not to Aaron but only to Moses, who was then to inform Aaron."

3. A. And these are they: "When Moses came to the tent of meeting to speak with him, he heard the voice speaking to him, and it said to him" (Num. 7:9).

   B. "And I shall meet you and I shall speak to you" (Ex. 25:22).

C.   "Where I shall meet (Ex. 30:6), "with you to speak to you" (Ex. 29:42).

D.   "On the day on which the Lord commanded him" (Lev. 7:38).

E.   "Whom he will command" (Ex. 34:34).

F.   "...all that I shall command you for the Israelites" (Ex. 25:22).

G.   "And it happened on the day on which the Lord spoke to Moses in the land of Egypt" (Ex. 6:28).

H.   "And these are the generations of Aaron and Moses on the day on which the Lord spoke with Moses at Mount Sinai" (Num. 3:1).

I.   "The Lord called to Moses and spoke to him from the tent of meeting, saying, 'Speak to the Israelite people and say to them'" (Lev. 1:1).

4.   A   R. Yosé the Galilean says, "In three passages in the entire Torah it is so stated, specifically, in the land of Israel, at Mount Sinai, and in the tent of meeting.

B.   "What is stated with reference to the land of Egypt? 'It happened on the day on which the Lord spoke to Moses in the land of Egypt' (Ex. 6:28), thus excluding Aaron from the acts of speech that took place in the land of Egypt.

C.   "At Mount Sinai, what is stated? 'These are the generations of Aaron and Moses on the day on which the Lord spoke with Moses at Mount Sinai' (Num. 3:1), thus excluding Aaron from the acts of speech that took place at Mount Sinai.

D.   "At the tent of meeting, what does Scripture then say? 'The Lord called to Moses and spoke to him from the tent of meeting, saying, "Speak to the Israelite people and say to them"'" (Lev. 1:1), thus excluding Aaron from the acts of speech that took place at the tent of meeting."

5.   A   R. Eleazar says, "Lo, Scripture says, 'And I shall meet there with the Israelites and I shall be sanctified in my glory' (Ex. 29:43).

B.   "'I am destined to meet with them and to be sanctified through them.

C.   "'When will that come about?   On the eighth day of the consecration of the tent of meeting,' for it is said, 'And the entire people saw and cried out and fell on their faces' (Lev. 9:24).

D.   "Or perhaps the sense of the passage is only to assign to them status as having been part of the meeting for the acts of speech [for when the fire came down from heaven, the people saw it, but they did not hear what the Lord said to Moses. Hence the purpose of the passage may be to indicate that they did in fact take part in the meeting.]

E.   "Scripture says, 'I shall meet you' (Ex. 25:22), that is to say, you in particular will be an actual meeting, but all the Israelites other than yourself will have no place in the actual meeting."

6.   A   But while, on that basis, I might exclude the Israelites in general, who in any event were not worthy of going up on the mountain,

perhaps I should not exclude the elders, who were indeed worthy of going up on the mountain?

B.   And along these same lines, perhaps I might exclude the elders, who in no passage appear to have participated in the dialogue between Moses [and the Lord], but I should not exclude the sons of Aaron, who did participate in the dialogue with Moses [and the Lord] [at Ex. 29:42, Num. 17:19].

C.   And perhaps I might indeed exclude the sons of Aaron, who did not actually participate in the dialogue with Moses, but I should not exclude Aaron himself, who indeed did participate in the dialogue with Moses.

D.   That is why Scripture makes the matter explicit, when it says, "And I shall meet with you" (Ex. 30:6), meaning, with you in particular I shall hold a meeting, but there will be no meeting with any of the rest of them.

7. A   Now perhaps I might exclude them from the meeting, but I should not exclude them from the acts of speech [which they can have heard from a distance]?

B.   Scripture says, "I shall speak with you" (Ex. 25:22).

C.   Perhaps I should exclude the Israelites, but not the elders, the elders, but not the sons of Aaron, the sons of Aaron, but not Aaron himself?

D.   Scripture says, "To speak with you" (Ex. 30:6).

E.   With you will be the act of speech, and the act of speech will not be with any of the others.

8. A   Might one say that while they may not hear the actual speech [understanding what is said in detail], they should hear the voice [of God]?

B.   Scripture says, "...the voice [talking with] him" (Num. 7:89).

C.   Then perhaps while I shall exclude the Israelites, I should not exclude the elders, the elders, but not the sons of Aaron, the sons of Aaron, but not Aaron himself?

D.   Scripture says, "...the voice [talking with] him" (Num. 7:89).

9. A   Perhaps I should exclude all of them, except for the ministering angels,

B.   for Moses himself cannot enter into their territory until he is called.

C.   Scripture says, "...the voice...to him...the voice...to him," bearing the sense that Moses could heard the voice of God, and none of these could hear the voice of God.

The entire passage forms a single sustained discourse, aiming at making the simple point that Moses was distinguished from all others, ordinary folk, elders, the priests, Aaron himself, and even, at the climax, the ministering angels. This theme is introduced in two distinct ways, first, at 1-2+3, then through the remainder. No. 4 carries forward the basic point of 1-2. No. 5 plays with the same theme but moves in its own direction. Then No. 6-9 restates the whole in its powerful and compelling way, again and again, appealing to the proof-texts in fact set forth at No. 3. So while we can identify as individual pieces Nos. 1-2 with its valuable appendix at No. 3, then Nos. 4, 5, and Nos. 6-9 as a single unit, the authorship behind the whole has done more than tack together some discrete items that say the same things. The editorial work has given to these items a flow and an urgency that standing by themselves (e.g., Nos. 4, 5) they lack. The hand of the authorship here is very heavy indeed.

II:II

1.   A.   "[The Lord called to Moses and spoke to him] from the tent of meeting, [saying, 'Speak to the Israelite people and say to them']" (Lev. 1:1):

    B.   [The stress on Moses's receiving the message] indicates that the voice came to an end [at the bound of the tent of meeting] and did not resonate outside of the tent. [Only Moses heard it.]

    C.   Might one suppose that this was because it was a subdued voice?

    D.   Scripture says, "And he heard the voice" (Num. 7:89).

    E.   For Scripture refers to "the voice" to indicate that it is only that voice to which Scripture makes explicit reference.

    F.   And what indeed is that voice to which Scripture makes explicit reference?

    G.   It is the one to which the following verses of Scripture refer:

    H.   "The voice of the Lord is power, the voice of the Lord is majesty; the voice of the Lord breaks cedars; the Lord shatters the cedars of Lebanon. [He makes Lebanon skip like a calf, Sirion like a young wild ox.] The voice of the Lord kindles flames of fire; the voice of the Lord convulses the wilderness; the Lord convulses the wilderness of Kadesh; the voice of the Lord causes hinds to calve and strips forests bare" (Ps. 29:4-7).

    I.   If that is the case, why does it say, "from the tent of meeting"?

    J.   [The stress on Moses's receiving the message] indicates that the voice came to an end [at the bound of the tent of meeting] and did not resonate outside of the tent. [Only Moses heard it.]

2.   A.   Along these same lines: "The sound of the cherubs' wings could be heard as far as the outer court, like the voice of God Almighty when he speaks" (Ez. 10:5):

    B.   Might one suppose that this was because it was a subdued voice?

    C.   Scripture says, "...like the voice of God Almighty when he speaks at Sinai."

    D.   If so, why is it said, "...as far as the outer court"?

    E.   Once the sound got to the outer court, it no longer resonated.

1.I-J is simply tacked on to revert to the opening; there is no sense to "if that is the case...." No. 2 goes over the same proposition, that the sound of God's voice could be kept within the bounds of the holy space. But the pair is inserted here because it underlines the thesis of the passage as a whole, that is, the unique standing of Moses.

II:III

1.   A.   "[The Lord called to Moses and spoke to him] from the tent of meeting, [saying, 'Speak to the Israelite people and say to them']" (Lev. 1:1):

       B.   "Might one suppose that it could be heard throughout the entire house?

       C.   "Scripture says, '[When Moses went into the tent of meeting to speak with him, he would hear the voice addressing him] from above the cover [that was on the top of the ark of the pact between the two cherubim, thus he spoke to him]' (Num. 7:89).

       D.   "If Scripture says, 'From above the cover,' might one suppose that it was from the entire expanse of the cover?

       E.   "Scripture says, '...between the two cherubim,'" the words of R. Aqiba.

       F.   Said Simeon b. Azzai, "I take up a position not in contention with the view of my lord, but only so as to amplify his opinion.

       G.   "Concerning the glory of God it is written, 'Do I not fill heaven and earth' (Jer. 23:24).

       H.   "Now see the extent to which affection is shown to Israel, for lo, it made this divine glory, which is so vast, as if it were straitened so as to appear to be talking from on top of the cover, between the two cherubs."

2.   A.   R. Dosa says, "Lo, Scripture says, 'For a person will not see me and live' (Ex. 33:20).

       B.   "In mortals' life, they may not see it, but they do see it at the moment of their death.

       C.   "And so it is said, 'All those in full vigor shall eat and prostrate themselves; all those at death's door, whose spirits flag, shall bend the knee before him' (Ps. 22:30 [JPS, verbatim])."

3.   A.   R. Aqiba says, "Lo, Scripture says, 'For a person will not see me and live' (Ex. 33:20).

       B.   "Even the holy chayyoth that carry the seat of glory cannot see the divine glory."

       C.   Said Simeon b. Azzai, "I take up a position not in contention with the view of my lord, but only so as to amplify his opinion.

       D.   "'For a person will not see me and live' (Ex. 33:20).

       E.   "Even ministering angels, who live forever, cannot see the glory of God."

This is somewhat misleading, since No. 1 seems to move in its own direction, namely, to identify the particular spot at which the Lord spoke. The message then seems to concern that passage, with pertinent comments to it. But the punchline at No. 3 is that Moses could see what even ministering angels cannot see, and that is consonant with the theme and proposition of the entire chapter as a whole.

II:IV

1. A. "[The Lord called to Moses and spoke to him from the tent of meeting,] saying, ['Speak to the Israelite people and say to them']" (Lev. 1:1):

   B. [The sense of "saying" is this:] "Go and state to them a persuasive message, namely,

   C. "'It is upon your account that I am spoken with.'"

   D. For so we find that for the entire thirty-eight years that the Israelites were as though they were under a ban, [the Lord] would not speak with Moses.

   E. That is in line with this verse of Scripture: "When all the warriors among the people had died off, the Lord spoke to me, saying" (Dt. 2:16).

2. A. Another matter concerning "saying:"

   B. "Go and say to them and bring me a reply."

   C. How on the basis of Scripture do we know that Moses would go out and speak with them?

   D. As it is said, "Whenever Moses went in before the Lord to speak with him, he would leave the veil off until he came out; and when he came out and told the Israelites what he had been commanded..." (Ex. 34:34).

   E. How on the basis of Scripture do we know that Moses would bring before the Omnipresent a reply [from the people] to the matters [under discussion]?

   F. As it is said, "And Moses brought back the people's words to the Lord" (Ex. 19:8).

3. A. Eleazar b. Ahbai says, "Might one suppose that he would not speak with him solely on his own account?

   B. "Scripture says, '...saying,'

   C. "'saying,' 'saying to Israel,' merely for the sake of Israel alone, he would not have spoken with him. He spoke with him only on his own account."

The amplification of the next clause in the base verse, "saying," brings a new proposition, which is that the entire purpose of God's encounter with Moses, already represented as unique among prophets, is for the sake of Israel. This is then the climax of the exposition of the verse: Moses is unique, and his unique encounter with God is because of Israel's unique relationship with God. That point is made in the very specific setting of II:IV.1 C. Nos. 2, 3 are merely tacked on as amplifications of the same usage, "saying," but I see no basis in the fundamental message for including these points as well. The net effect of No. 3 is to contradict No. 1.

IV. Sifré to Numbers

Sifré to Numbers

I:VII

1. A. "[The Lord said to Moses, 'Command the people of Israel that they put out of the camp every leper and everyone having a discharge, and everyone that is unclean through contact with the dead.] You shall put out both male and female, putting them outside the camp, that they may not defile their camp, in the midst of which I dwell'" (Gen. 5:1-4)

   B. I know, on the basis of the stated verse, that the law applies only to male and female [persons who are suffering from the specified forms of cultic uncleanness]. How do I know that the law pertains also to one lacking clearly defined sexual traits or to one possessed of the sexual traits of both genders?

   C. Scripture states, "...putting *them* outside the camp." [This is taken to constitute an encompassing formulation, extending beyond the male and female of the prior clause.]

   D. I know, on the basis of the stated verse, that the law applies only to those who can be sent forth. How do I know that the law pertains also to those who cannot be sent forth?

   E. Scripture states, "...putting them outside the camp." [This is taken to constitute an encompassing formulation, as before.]

   F. I know on the basis of the stated verse that the law applies only to persons. How do I know that the law pertains also to utensils?

   G. Scripture states, "...putting *them* outside the camp." [This is taken to constitute an encompassing formulation.]

I:VII

2. A. [Dealing with the same question as at 1.F,] R. Aqiba says, "'You shall put out both male and female, putting them outside the camp.' Both persons and utensils are implied."

   B. R. Ishmael says, "You may construct a logical argument, as follows:

   C. "Since man is subject to uncleanness on account of *negaim* ["plagues"], and clothing [thus: utensils] are subject to uncleanness on the same count, just as man is subject to being sent forth [ostracism], likewise utensils are subject to being sent forth."

   D. No, such an argument is not valid [and hence exegesis of the actual language of Scripture, as at A, is the sole correct route]. If you have stated the rule in the case of man, who imparts uncleanness when he exerts pressure on an object used for either sitting or lying, and, on which account, he is subject to ostracism, will you say the same rule of utensils, which do not impart uncleanness when they exert pressure on an object used for sitting and lying? [Clearly there is a difference between the uncleanness brought about by a human being from that brought about by an inanimate object, and therefore the rule that applies to the one will not necessarily apply to the other. Logic by itself will not suffice, and, it must follow, the proof of a verse of Scripture alone will suffice to prove the point.]

E.   [No, that objection is not valid, because we can show that the same rule does apply to both an inanimate object and to man, namely] lo, there is the case of the stone affected with a *nega*, which will prove the point. For it does not impart uncleanness when it exerts pressure on an object used for sitting or lying, but it does require ostracism [being sent forth from the camp, a rule that Scripture itself makes explicit].

F.   Therefore do not find it surprising that utensils, even though they in general do not impart uncleanness when they exert pressure on an object used for sitting or lying, are to be sent forth from the camp." [Ishmael's logical proof stands.]

I:VII
3. A.   R. Yosé the Galilean says, "'You shall put out both male and female, putting them outside the camp, that they may not defile their camp, in the midst of which I dwell.'

    B.   "What marks as singular male and female is that they can be turned into a generative source of uncleanness [when they die and are corpses], and, it follows, they are to be sent forth from the camp when they become unclean [even while alive], so anything which can become a generative source of uncleanness will be subject to being sent forth from the camp.

    C.   "What is excluded is a piece of cloth less than three by three fingerbreadths, which in the entire Torah is never subject to becoming a generative source of uncleanness."

I:VII
4. A.   R. Isaac says, "Lo, Scripture states, '[And every person that eats what dies of itself or what is torn by beasts, whether he is a native or a sojourner, shall wash his clothes and bathe himself in water and be unclean until the evening; they he shall be clean.] But if he does not wash them or bathe his flesh, he shall bear his iniquity' (Lev. 17:15-16).

    B.   "It is on account of failure to wash one's body that Scripture has imposed the penalty of extirpation.

    C.   "You maintain that it is on account of failure to wash one's body that Scripture has imposed the penalty of extirpation. But perhaps Scripture has imposed a penalty of extirpation only on account of the failure to launder one's garments.

D.   "Thus you may construct the argument to the contrary [*su eipas*]: if in the case of one who has become unclean on account of corpse-uncleanness, which is a severe source of uncleanness, Scripture has not imposed a penalty merely because of failure to launder one's garments, as to one who eats meat of a beast that has died of itself, which is a minor source of uncleanness, it is a matter of reason that Scripture should not impose a penalty on the account of having failed to launder the garments."

The composition can serve only the document in which it occurs, since we read the verse in a narrow framework: what rule do we derive from the actual language at hand? No. 1 answers the question on the basis of an exegesis of the verse. No. 2 then provides an alternative proof. Aqiba provides yet another reading of the language at hand. Ishmael goes over the possibility of a logical demonstration. I find it difficult to see how Yosé's pericope fits in. It does not seem to me to address the problem at hand. He wants to deal with a separate issue entirely, as specified at C. No. 4 pursues yet another independent question. So Nos. 3, 4 look to be parachuted down. On what basis? No. 3 deals with our base verse. But No. 4 does not. Then what guided the compositors to introduce Nos. 1, 2, 3, and 4? Nos. 1, 2 deal with the exegesis of the limited rule at hand: how do I know to what classifications of persons and objects ostracism applies? No. 1 answers two questions, first, the classifications, then the basis for the rule. No. 2 introduces the second question: on what basis do we make our rule? The answer, as is clear, is Scripture, not unaided reason. Now at that point the issue of utensils emerges. So Yosé the Galilean's interest in the rule governing a utensil – a piece of cloth – leads to the intrusion of his item. And the same theme – the rule governing utensils, garments – accounts for the introduction of I:VII.4 as well. In sum, the redactional principle is clear: treat the verse, then the theme generated by the verse.

V. Sifré to Deuteronomy

My example from this document can have been chosen more or less at random, since, like Sifra, Sifré to Deuteronomy is a formally cogent piece of writing, and a large portion of its contents serves to amplify verses of the book of Deuteronomy. These amplifications may answer philological, theological, or legal questions; they nearly always stay very close to the thematic program of the base verse. I have chosen as my example of writing, the character of which is dictated by the documentary program, a thematic composition, one among many I find strong and well-focused;

Sifré to Deuteronomy Pisqa Three Hundred Thirty-Nine
CCCXXXIX:I

1. A. "You shall die on the mountain that you are about to ascend [and shall be gathered to your kin, as your brother Aaron died on Mount Hor and was gathered to his kin]:"

   B. He said before him, "Lord of the world, Why should I die? Is it not better for people to say, 'Moses is good,' because of what they have personally seen, than that they should say, 'Moses is good,' based on what they have heard? Is it not better that people should say, 'This is that very same Moses, who brought us out of Egypt, split the sea for us, brought down the mana for us, did wonders and acts of might for us,' than that they should say, 'Such and so is what Moses was, such and so is what Moses did'?"

   C. He said to him, "Go your way, Moses, it is a decree of mine that applies to every mortal."

   D. For it is said, "This is the Torah that applies to a mortal: when a person will die in a tent" (Num. 19:14).

   E. And further, "This is the Torah of a mortal, O Lord God" (2 Sam. 7:19).

2. A. The ministering angels said before the Holy One, blessed be he, "Lord of the world, why did the first man die?"

   B. He said to them, "Because he did not carry out my orders."

   C. They said to him, "Lo, Moses did carry out your orders."

   D. He said to them, "It is a decree of mine that applies to every mortal."

   E. For it is said, "This is the Torah that applies to a mortal: when a person dies in a tent" (Num. 19:14).

We have two statements of the same proposition, which is that the death of Moses shows that all mortals die and none can live forever on earth.

Sifré to Deuteronomy Pisqa Three Hundred Thirty-Nine
CCCXXXIX:II

1. A. "...and shall be gathered to your kin:"
   B. to Abraham, Isaac, and Jacob,
   C. to Amram and Kehath,
   D. to Miriam and your brother Aaron.

Sifré to Deuteronomy Pisqa Three Hundred Thirty-Nine
CCCXXXIX:III

1. A. "...as your brother Aaron died on Mount Hor and was gathered to his kin:"
   B. It is the mode of death that you have wanted.

C.   And whence did Moses desire the mode of death that Aaron had received?

D.   When the Holy One, blessed be he, said to him, "Take Aaron and Eleazar his son" (Num. 20:25), "and Aaron removed his garments" (Num. 20:26) – this refers to the garments of the priesthood – and put them on Eleazar, so second, so a third [garment, thus garbing Eleazar in the priestly garments and removing them from Aaron].

E.   He said to him, "Go into the cave." He went in.

F.   "Climb onto the bier." He climbed on.

G.   "Spread out your hands." He spread them out.

H.   "Spread out your legs." He spread them out.

I.   "Close your mouth." He closed it.

J.   "Close your eyes." He closed them.

K.   At that Moment, Moses said, "Happy is anyone who dies in such a way."

L.   That is why God said to Moses, "'...as your brother Aaron died,' the mode of death that you have wanted."

The clarification of the reference to Aaron's death allows the passage to underline the main point, which is that Moses died in a very merciful way.

VI. Genesis Rabbah

The preparation of base-verse/intersecting-verse compositions is surely particular to the concerns of the compositors of a document, e.g., a commentary to Genesis (or, as we see next, Leviticus). No other, non-redactional purpose can be served. The same applies to the preparation of line-for-line commentaries; these are written with the purpose of accomplishing the compilation of a document of commentary. Here is one fine example of writing that serves only the making of Genesis Rabbah.

Genesis Rabbah Parashah One

I:I

1.   A   "In the beginning God created" (Gen. 1:1):

B.   R. Oshaia commenced [discourse by citing the following verse:] "'Then I was beside him like a little child, and I was daily his delight [rejoicing before him always, rejoicing in his inhabited world, and delighting in the sons of men]' (Prov. 8:30-31).

C.   "The word for 'child' uses consonants that may also stand for 'teacher,' 'covered over,' and 'hidden away.'

D.   "Some hold that the word also means 'great.'

E.   "The word means 'teacher,' in line with the following: 'As a teacher carries the suckling child' (Num. 11:12).

F.   "The word means 'covered over,' as in the following: 'Those who were covered over in scarlet' (Lam. 4:5).

G.   "The word means 'hidden,' as in the verse, 'And he hid Hadassah '
       (Est. 2:7).

H.   "The word means 'great,' in line with the verse, 'Are you better
       than No-Ammon?' (Nah. 3:8). This we translate, 'Are you better
       than Alexandria the Great, which is located between rivers.'"

2   A.   Another matter:

    B.   The word means "workman."

    C.   [In the cited verse] the Torah speaks, "I was the work plan of the
           Holy One, blessed be he."

    D.   In the accepted practice of the world, when a mortal king builds a
           palace, he does not build it out of his own head, but he follows a
           work plan.

    E.   And [the one who supplies] the work plan does not build out of his
           own head, but he has designs and diagrams, so as to know how to
           situate the rooms and the doorways.

    F.   Thus the Holy One, blessed be he, consulted the Torah when he
           created the world.

    G.   So the Torah stated, "By means of 'the beginning' [that is to say,
           the Torah] did God create..." (Gen. 1:1).

    H.   And the word for "beginning" refers only to the Torah, as Scripture
           says, "The Lord made me as the beginning of his way" (Prov. 8:22).

I:I.1 begins with the introduction of an intersecting verse, Prov. 8:30,
which will be carefully expounded and only then brought into
relationship to the base verse. No. 1 spells out the several meanings of
the letters used in the word "child," that is, simply explaining the
intersecting verse in its own terms. Then No. 2 interrelates the
intersecting verse with the base verse. How so? The intersecting verse
is made to speak for the Torah, in line with Prov. 8:22. At what point
in the intersecting verse – Prov. 8:30, not Prov. 8:22 – do we then find the
pertinent meaning? I take for granted it is at the first of the meanings
imputed to the word for nursling, namely, tutor or teacher. Thus the
Torah speaks, announcing, "Then I was with him as the tutor" in the
process of the creation of the world. What is curious, then, in No. 2 is
that the original intersecting verse is not cited at the end. I am inclined
to suspect that in the mind of the framer of the passage the cited verse
should then begin with Prov. 8:22 and conclude with Prov. 8:30, so we
have an exceptionally long intersecting verse. Otherwise the
intersecting verse before us makes no sense. There can be no doubt, of
course, that Nos. 1 and 2 form a single statement, since in this way,
without No. 2, No. 1 serves no purpose.

All that has been said assumes that we have an intersecting-
verse/base-verse construction, such as is followed with admirable
formality in Leviticus Rabbah. But what if we have not what is
conventionally called a proem but simply two autonomous

compositions? Then No. 1 deals with the meaning of the letters that may be read as "nurse-maid," "hidden," and the like. No. 2 forms a simple composition on Gen. 1:1, with Prov. 8:22 imputing to the cited verse the message at hand, which is that God looked into the Torah to find out how to lay forth the lines of heaven and earth. Then No. 1 took shape around the philological problem at hand (omitting reference to the original citation of Gen. 1:1. No. 2 was joined to No. 1 as part of the exercise in philology, and the principle of joining Nos. 1 and 2 derived not from an interest in Gen. 1:1 but an interest in the word *amon*. All that suggests otherwise is the opening statement, in which we cite Gen. 1:1 and Oshaia's citation of Prov. 8:30-31. In accord with this second theory of the matter, these elements – the citation of Gen. 1:1 and the introduction of the word " opened" instead of simply "said/says – must be regarded as the contribution of the redactors of our document, who selected the passage and reworked it, on account of the contents of No. 2, for the present purpose. There is no way of settling the question. The sole fact is that the passage at hand does not fall into the classification of intersecting-verse/base-verse construction, such as predominates in Leviticus Rabbah.

Genesis Rabbah Parashah One
I:V

1.   A.   R. Huna in the name of Bar Qappara commenced [discourse by citing the following verse]: "'Let the lying lips be made dumb [which arrogantly speak matters kept secret against the righteous]' (Ps. 31:19).

     B.   "[Translating the Hebrew word for dumb into Aramaic one may use words meaning] 'bound,' 'made dumb,' or ' silenced.'

     C.   "Let [the lying lips] be bound,' as in the following verse: 'For behold, we were binding sheaves' (Gen. 37:7).

     D.   "'Let the lying lips be made dumb,' as in the usage in this verse: 'Or who made a man dumb ' (Ex. 4:11).

     E.   "'Let them be silenced' bears the obvious meaning of the word."

     F.   "Which arrogantly speak matters kept secret against the righteous" (Ps. 31:19):

     G.   "...which speak against the Righteous," the Life of the Ages, matters that he kept secret from his creatures [Freedman: the mysteries of creation].

     H.   "With pride" (Ps. 31:19):

     I.   That is so as to take pride, saying, "I shall expound the work of creation."

     J.   "And contempt" (Ps. 31:19): Such a one treats with contempt the honor owing to me.

     K.   For R. Yosé b. R. Hanina said, "Whoever gains honor through the humiliation of his fellow gains no share in the world to come.

L.   "For one does so through the honor owing to the Holy One, blessed be he, how much the more so!"

M.   And what is written after the cited verse [Ps. 31:19]?

N.   How abundant is your goodness, which you have stored away for those who revere you" (Ps. 31:20).

O.   Rab said, "Let one [who reveals the mysteries of creation] not have any share in your abundant goodness.'

P.   "Under ordinary circumstances, if a mortal king builds a palace in a place where there had been sewers, garbage, and junk, will not whoever may come and say, 'This palace is built on a place where there were sewers, garbage and junk,' give offense? So too, will not whoever comes and says, 'This world was created out of chaos, emptiness, and darkness' give offense?"

Q.   R. Huna in the name of Bar Qappara: "Were the matter not explicitly written in Scripture, it would not be possible to state it at all: 'God created heaven and earth' (Gen. 1:1) – from what? From the following: 'And the earth was chaos' (Gen. 1:2). [Freedman: God first created chaos and emptiness, and out of these he created the world, but this is not to be taught publicly.]"

A new intersecting verse is presented. The pertinent theme of the verse is the notion that there are things about which one must not speak, hence, in the repertoire of meanings attributed to the key word – be dumb – the important one is " silenced." The continuation of the same verse carries forward the same idea, namely that one should not speak arrogantly against the righteous, meaning, God. The combination of the two ideas is then clear. That is, it is arrogant to expound the works of creation, and these are matters about which one must remain silent. J then carries forward the exposition of Prov. 31:20, the matter of contempt. The same point is made over again. There are matters one must not call to mind. Then Huna-Bar Qappara completes the matter and makes the main point. It is stunning and fresh, yet fully prepared: one could not say about creation what Scripture itself says, that is, that the world began unformed and void. Once more it is clear that we deal with a unified and cogent statement, so that A-I and J to the end, while on the surface distinct from one another, are formed to make a single, exceedingly surprising point, which comes only at the end. That I:I and I:V follow a single pattern is quite clear. The exposition of the intersecting verse takes place in stages, with a philological exercise on the meaning of a fundamental word at hand, following by a secondary expansion on the sense of the verse as a whole. That is the point that the base verse enters the frame of reference, and that is not in a philological but in a theological aspect. So if we may characterize the intention of the framers of the two compositions, it is to move from philological to theological issues (using theological in a broad sense).

The philological exercise, moreover, introduces precisely those themes that become important later on, that is, keeping the mouth bound up and closed, not lying, and above all, silence. Then we move on to silence concerning creation, that is, not admitting that what God worked with was garbage.

It is not possible to view the whole as an artificial construct; it seems to me clear that it is a cogent and pointed statement, beginning, middle, and end, even though bits and pieces of available materials may have served the author. If we go back to I:I, moreover, we see that the philological exercise, with its interest in the meanings of tutor, covered over and hidden, moves us right to the direction the author wants us to take   That is, he is interested in making the point that God looked into the Torah and made the world, so the Torah contains the secrets of creation. Then I:V makes the further point, surely deliberate and in the right order, that the secrets of creation, as the Torah contains them, are not to be spelled out.

So before us, thus far, is a remarkably cogent composition, making a single point through the selection and organization of distinct materials. May we say that the things chosen themselves have been written for the present purpose? That question does not carry a self-evident answer. We do not have a verse-by-verse exposition, e.g., such as we find at Sifra. Instead we have discursive essays, taking up such questions as meanings of words and propositions of a philosophical order. So if this is a commentary, it is a different sort of commentary from the sort of verse-by-verse, phrase-by-phrase exercise in exposition, analysis, and secondary expansion, that we might have anticipated. The text finds its meaning in the association of whole units of thought with individual verses, and these units of thought concern themes or topics, not merely meanings of words or phrases (though on the surface the philological interest proves paramount).

Did the compositors of the whole also make up the several units? That we cannot now say. In later passages we shall see strong evidence that the compositors chose from available materials, not making them up, and revising them only in superficial ways. In the present passage it does appear that the one who proposed to put together a sequence of expository passages on the opening verses of Genesis also made up the passages at hand. Why so? Because, despite the original impression of prolixity and diversity, in fact the composition hangs together so cogently as it does only because it depends for sense and deep meaning on the base verse itself (!). Out of contact with the statement, "In the beginning God created...," the two compositions – both I:I and I:V – make little sense. If that reading of the whole is sound, then we are in the hands of remarkably subtle and brilliant authors, not merely redactors, selectors, compositors, and the like. And the nature of the authorship, the mode of creativity – these will not prove at all simple to uncover and define.

VII. Leviticus Rabbah

Leviticus Rabbah Parashah Twenty-Six
XXVI:I

1. A.   "[And the Lord said to Moses,] Speak to the priests, [the sons of Aaron, and say to them]" (Lev. 21:1).

    B.   R. Tanhum b. R. Hanilai opened [discourse by citing the following verse of Scripture]: "'The sayings of the Lord are pure sayings' [Ps. 12:7].

    C.   "[That is to say] the sayings of the Lord are sayings, but the sayings of mortals are not.

    D.   "Under ordinary circumstances when a mortal king comes into a town, and the townsfolk laud him, if their praise pleases him, he says to them, 'Tomorrow I am going to build for you public baths and bathhouses, tomorrow I am going to bring you a water pipe [for fresh water].' But then he goes to sleep and does not awake [in the morning]. So where is he, and where are his sayings?

    E.   "But the Holy One, blessed be he, is not like that.

    F.   "Rather: 'The Lord, God, is truth'" (Jer. 10:10).

    G.   What is the meaning of "truth"?

    H.   Said R. Abin, "It means that he is 'the living God and eternal king'" (Jer. 10:10).

2. A.   "[The sayings of the Lord are] pure" (Ps. 12:7).

    B.   R. Yudan in the name of R. Isaac, R. Berekhiah in the name of R. Eleazar, R. Jacob of Kepar Hanin in the name of R. Joshua b. Levi: "We find that the Scripture rearranged two or three words [as a circumlocution] in the Torah so as not to bring an unseemly word out of [God's] mouth.

    C.   "That is in line with the following verse of Scripture: 'Of every clean beast you will take for yourself seven, male and female, and from every beast that is not clean...' [Gen. 7:2].

    D.   "'And from every unclean beast' is not what is written here, but rather, 'Of every beast that is not clean, two, male and female'" (Gen. 7:2).

    E.   Said R. Yudan b. R. Manasseh, "Even when Scripture came to introduce the signs of unclean beasts, the Scripture commenced only with the signs of clean [beasts], as in the following cases:

    F.   "'The camel, because it does not part the hoof' is not what is written here, but rather, 'Because it chews the cud [but does not...]' [Lev. 11:4].

G.   "'The rockbadger, because it does not part the hoof' is not what is
         written here, but rather, 'Because it chews the cud [but does not...]'
         [Lev. 11:5].

H.   "'The hare, because it does not part the hoof' is not what is written
         here, but rather, 'Because it chews the cud [but does not...]' [Lev.
         11:6].

I.   "'The pig, because it does not chew the cud' is not what is written
         here, but rather, 'Because it parts the hoof [but does not...]'" (Lev.
         11:7).

The intersecting verse uses the word "saying" shared with the base
verse, "*say* to them." The exegete therefore makes two points about the
intersecting verse. First of all, it deals with the principal parts of the
sentence, "The sayings of the Lord are sayings," and explains that what
the Lord says is reliable, while what mortals say are not, because the
Lord is eternal, and mortals are not. No. 2 then deals with the second
matter, the adjective "pure." The point of interest then is standard,
explaining how Scripture avoids ascribing to God sayings that are
inappropriate, for example, in their phrasing or word choice. The
specific context of the base verse has yet – by the end of XXVI:I – to
attract exegetical attention. But the objective clearly is to regain that
base verse, on the strength of which I classify the whole as a
composition formed in response to the requirements of a given document.
But that judgment surely can be challenged, since what follows draws us
no closer to the base verse than anything at hand, and I have classified
XXVI:II within Part V. The following solves the problem quite neatly.

Leviticus Rabbah
XXVI:III

1.   A.   Said R. Tanhum b. R. Hanilai, "There are two passages which
             Moses handed us in writing in the Torah, and they are both [about
             things that are] pure.

      B.   "And on whose account were they given? On account of the tribe
             of Levi, concerning which it is written, 'As silver tried in a furnace
             on the ground' [Ps. 12:7].

      C.   "And it is written, 'And he shall purify the sons of Levi' [Mal. 3:3].

      D.   "Now what are these passages? They are the ones concerning the
             Red Cow [Num. 19:1ff.] and [how the priests are to deal with]
             corpses [Lev. 21:1ff.]: 'And the Lord said to Moses, Speak to the
             priests, [the sons of Aaron, and say to them that none of them
             shall defile himself for the dead among his people']" (Lev. 21:1).

To show how we revert to the base verse, the passage at hand is
essential. The intersecting verse, Ps. 12:7, now decisively joins the base
verse. It turns the whole – Ps. 12:7 in its entirety – into an expansion and
clarification of Lev. 21:1.

VIII. Pesiqta deRab Kahana

The program of Pesiqta deRab Kahana requires the construction of a syllogistic statement of a proposition out of raw materials of exegesis. When we see how this is done, we also realize that the formation of a fair portion of the materials in the document has responded to the program of the document overall; that is the case even though, self-evidently, the bits and pieces of the composition have taken shape on their own and without the plan of Pesiqta deRab Kahana in mind. Here my judgment on the formative power of a document's program rests upon the outcome, but not on the character of the pieces of writing that clearly reached closure prior to their utilization in the document.

Pesiqta deRab Kahana Pisqa Five

[on the base verse, "The Lord said to Moses and Aaron in the land of Egypt,] "This month [shall be for you the beginning of months; it shall be the first month of the year for you]" (Ex. 12:1-2)]

V:I

1. A   *He appointed the moon for [lunar] seasons, yet the sun knows its coming* (Ps. 104:19):

   B   Said R. Yohanan, "Only the orb of the sun was created for the purpose of giving light.

   C.   "*Let there be light* (Gen. 1:14):

   D.   "What is written is *light* [in the singular].

   E.   "If so, why was the moon created? It was for the signification of the seasons, specifically so that, through [regular sightings of the moon, Israelites would] sanctify new months and years.]"

   F.   R. Shila of Kefar Tamarata in the name of R. Yohanan: "Nonetheless: *The sun knows its coming* (Ps. 104:19). On the basis of that statement, we have the following rule: people count the advent of the new moon only once the sun has set."

   G.   [Proving the foregoing proposition,] Yusta, an associate, in the name of R. Berekhiah: "*And they traveled from Raamses in the first month on the fifteenth day of the month* (Num. 33:3). Now if one counts only by the month, up to this point there had been only fourteen [Genesis Rabbah 6:1: thirteen] sunsets. [Freedman, *Genesis Rabbah*, p. 41, n. 4: This is based on the tradition that the Nisan – the first month – in which the Exodus took place fell on a Thursday, while the actual new moon occurred after midday on the preceding Wednesday. It is further assumed that, when this happens, the moon is not visible until the second evening following, i.e., the evening of Friday. Hence if we counted time solely from when the new moon is visible, then by the Thursday on which they left, a fortnight after, there would only have been thirteen sunsets. Since, however, it is called the *fifteenth* of the month, we see that the month was calculated from the first sunset after the new moon.]

H. "One must therefore conclude that one counts the beginning of the month only from sunset."

2. A. R. Azariah in the name of R. Hanina: "Only the orb of the sun was created for the purpose of giving light.

  B. "*Let there be light* (Gen. 1:14):

  C. "What is written is *light* [in the singular].

  D. "If so, why was the moon created at all?

  E. "The Holy One, blessed be he, foresaw that the nations of the world were going to make [the heavenly bodies] into gods. Said the Holy One, blessed be he, 'Now if they are two and contradict one another, and nonetheless, the nations of the world treat them as gods, if they are only one, how much the more so [will the nations of the world find reason to worship the heavenly body]!'"

  F. R. Berekhiah in the name of R. Simon: "Both of them were created in order to give light, as it is said, *And they shall serve for light* (Gen. 1:14)."

3. A. *And they shall serve as lights* (Gen. 1:15). *And God put them in the firmament of the heaven* (Gen. 1:17). *And they shall serve as signs and for seasons* (Gen. 1:14).

  B. *And they shall serve as signs* (Gen. 1:14) refers to Sabbaths, for it is written, *For it is a sign for you* (Ex. 31:13).

  C. *And for seasons* refers to the three pilgrim festivals.

  D. *And for days* refers to new months.

  E. *And years* refers to the sanctification of years.

  F. Indicating in all that the nations of the world will follow a solar calendar, and Israel, a lunar one:

  G. *The Lord said to Moses and Aaron in the land of Egypt, "This month shall be for you the beginning of months; it shall be the first month of the year for you"* (Ex. 12:1-2).

What captures interest in the base verse is the reference to month, that is, new moon, and the stress that it is the new moon that marks the beginning of the months and the years. The further theme, to appear shortly, joins the new moon's appearance to the coming redemption, and further identifies the month of the original redemption, the Exodus, as the month of the final redemption. That, of course, is Nisan, the month in which Passover falls. Accordingly, the first of the two themes at hand – the importance of the lunar calendar – makes its appearance now, and the second, the association of redemption with the new moon of Nisan, will shortly make its appearance. This composition serves at Genesis Rabbah 6:1 and only at the end makes its contribution to the exegesis of Ex. 12:1-2. The intersection is merely thematic; there is no interest in the base verses, which at Genesis Rabbah 6:1 do not occur anyhow. Nos. 1, 2 work out the implications of the intersecting verse, which introduces the view that, while the sun is meant to give light, the moon serves some other purpose. That other purpose is for Israel's calendar, as we see at the end. We see the view, which is Yohanan's, is contradicted at the end by Berekhiah. The force of the intersecting verse is not merely to illuminate the base verse but to propose a syllogism in connection with the theme at hand, which, autonomous of the exegetical task, is subject to discussion and dispute on its own. So the syllogism has been (re)cast in exegetical form. But it remains a syllogistic argument. No. 3 is a narrowly exegetical exercise and the contrast then is probative.

IX. Lamentations Rabbah

The *petihtaot* very commonly are made up with the requirements of a particular document in mind, and that is assuredly the case for those of Lamentations Rabbah. Here is one example among the many that show writing in accord with the documentary protocol.

Lamentations Rabbah Petihta Six
VI.I
1. A   R. Abbah in the name of R. Yosé bar Hanina commenced [by citing the following verse of Scripture]: "'Ephraim shall become a desolation [in the day of punishment among the tribes of Israel I declare what is sure. The princes of Judah have become like those who remove the landmark; upon them I will pour out my wrath like water]' (Hos. 5:9-10).

  B.   "When will this come about?
  C.   "'in the day of punishment.'
  D.   "This is the day on which the Holy One, blessed be he, is destined to enter into litigation with them in court.
  E.   "You find that when the Ten Tribes went into exile, the tribes of Judah and Benjamin did not, so the Ten Tribes were saying, 'How come he has sent us into exile but them he has not sent into exile? It is because they belong to his court. So maybe there's some sort of favoritism in play here!'
  F.   "[He replied to them,] 'God forbid! There is no favoritism, but they have not yet sinned.'
  G.   "When they did sin, he sent them into exile.
  H.   "Said the Ten Tribes, 'Lo, our God! lo, our God! Lo, the mighty one! lo, the mighty one! Lo, the truthful one! lo, the truthful one!
  I.   "'For even to those who belong to his court he did not give preference."

2. A   When they sinned, they went into exile,
  B.   and when they went into exile, Jeremiah began to lament for them: "Alas! Lonely sits the city once great with people!" (Lam. 1:1).

It is difficult to take seriously the proposition that No. 2 belongs in any integral way with No. 1. The exposition of No. 1 is very successful since it is a major exposition of the "rebuke" to which the cited intersecting verse is set forth. It is the Ten Tribes who rebuke God, and the answer is as given. To all this No. 2 is scarcely relevant. What follows is a much better example of writing in accord with a documentary protocol.

Lamentations Rabbah Parashah One to Lamentations 1:1
XXXV:IV

1. A.   Another matter concerning "[How] lonely sits [the city that was full of people]" [now with stress on "sits," in its sense of "sitting in mourning:"]

   B.   Said R. Nahman, "The Holy One, blessed be he, asked the ministering angels, 'A mortal king in mourning – what is fitting for him to do?'

   C.   "They said to him, 'He hangs sacking on his door.'

   D.   "He said to them, 'I too will do so:' 'I clothe the heavens with blackness, and I make sackcloth their covering' (Is. 50:3).'

   E.   "'What else does a mortal king do?'

   F.   "'He turns down the lamps.'

   G.   "I too will do so:' 'The sun and the moon are become black, the stars withdraw their shining' (Joel 4:15).

   H.   "'What else?'

   I.   "'He turns over the couch.'

   J.   "'I too:' 'Until thrones were cast down, and One that was ancient of days did sit' (Dan. 7:9)."

   K.   "It is as though they were overturned [in mourning].

   L.   "'What else?'

   M.   "'He goes barefoot.'

   N.   "'I too:' 'The Lord in the whirlwind and in the storm is his way, and clouds are the dust of his feet' (Nah. 1:5).

   O.   "'What else?'

   P.   "'He tears his purple clothing.'

   Q.   "'I too:' 'The Lord has done that which he devised, he has performed his word' (Lam. 2:17)."

   R.   What is the meaning of "that which he devised"?

   S.   R. Jacob of Kefar Hanan said, "He tore his purple."

   T.   [Continuing from Q:] "'What else?'

   U.   "'He sits in silence.'

   V.   "'I too:' 'He sits alone and keeps silent' (Lam. 3:28).

   W.   "'What else?'

   X.   "'He sits and weeps.'

   Y.   "'I too:' 'How lonely sits....'"

2. A.   Another interpretation of "[How] lonely sits [the city that was full of people]:"

B.   Said R. Yohanan, "Said Jeremiah to the Israelites, 'What value did you ever find in this idolatry, that you yearned for it! Would that it had a mouth, so that we could argue with it!

C.   "'But let us say its [position, that is, evidence that it is valid and powerful], and [God] can say his [position].

D.   "'[The evidence that the idol is powerful is given in the following verse:] "Thus said the Lord, Do not learn to go the way of the heavens, and do not be dismayed by portents in the sky; let the nations be dismayed by them!" (Jer. 10:2).

E.   "'Now [Jeremiah continues,] let us state his position: "For the laws of the nations are delusions, for it is the work of a craftsman's hands. He cuts down a tree in the forest with an ax, he adorns it with silver and gold, he fastens it with nails and hammer, so that it does not totter. They are like a scarecrow in a cucumber path, they cannot speak, they have to be carried, for they cannot walk. Be not afraid of them, for they can do no harm, nor is it in them to do any good" (Jer. 10:3-5).'

F.   "'"Not like these is the Portion of Jacob, for it is he who formed all things, and Israel is his very own tribe, the Lord of hosts is his name" (Jer. 10:16).'"

3. A.   R. Judah and R. Nehemiah:

B.   R. Judah said, "The word 'how' bears the meaning only of rebuke,

C.   "in line with the following usage: 'How shall you say, We are wise' (Jer. 8:8)."

D.   R. Nehemiah said, "The word 'how' bears the meaning only of lamentation,

E.   "in line with the following usage: 'The Lord God said to the man, saying to him, 'Where are you' (Gen. 3:9) [which uses the same letters as the word for 'how.']

F.   "'Where are you' can be read 'woe is you.'"

4. A.   When was the scroll of Lamentations stated?

B.   R. Judah says, "In the time of Jehoiakim it was said."

C.   Said R. Berekhiah, "Do people lament for the deceased before he has died [since the temple had not then been destroyed]?

D.   "But it was written down in the time of Jehoiakim but then recited after the destruction of the house of the sanctuary."

Here is a passage made up to serve the base verse, one that can hardly accomplish any purpose other than the one that it is composed to effect. The systematic application to God of various human rites of mourning is accomplished by appeal to appropriate prooftexts; the effect is to have God the subject of the sense, "how lonely sits...." As to No. 2, I follow Cohen, but then I do not see any connection with the base verse. Buber's text yields a connection through repeated attention to uses of the consonants for the word "solitary." Buber has No. 3 earlier in the unfolding of the passage. It reverts to the opening word and hardly belongs where it now is. No. 4 exhibits the same problem.

X. Esther Rabbah

Esther Rabbah I to Esther 1:15
XXIV:I
1. A   "According to the law:"
    B.   Said R. Isaac, "For this pig it is 'according to law,' but for the holy nation, it is not 'according to the law' but with unprecedented cruelty."
2. A   "to Queen Vashti:"
    B.   How much the more so with a queen who is not Vashti! [Simon, p. 60, n. 5: Probably a reference to God's mercy in that Esther, who entered the king's presence not according to the law (Est. 4:16) was nevertheless pardoned].

The expositions are random but pointed. What makes them exemplary for our purpose is that outside of a commentary to the book of Esther they are simply incomprehensible.

Esther Rabbah I to Esther 1:21
XXX:I
1. A   "The advice pleased the king and the princes, and the king did as Memucan proposed:"
    B.   He made the decree, and he brought in her head on a platter.

Assuming that B refers to the king, then what is underlined is that the king carried out the order of his courtier, as would be the case with Haman later on, and Esther at the end. This entry falls into the same classification as the foregoing, and no further examples are required to register the same point.

XI. Ruth Rabbah

Ruth Rabbah Petihta Three
III:I
1. A   "And it came to pass in the days when the judges ruled, there was a famine in the land:"
    B.   "The way of the guilty man is crooked and strange, but the conduct of the pure is right" (Prov. 21:8):
    C.   This speaks of Esau, who comes crookedly against Israel with harsh decrees:
    D.   "You have stolen!" "We have not stolen."
    E.   "You have murdered!" "We have not murdered."
    F.   "You have not stolen? Then who stole with you?"

G.   "You have not murdered? Then who was your accomplice?"

H.   He fines them on false charges: "Produce your share of the crop, produce your poll tax, produce your state tax."

2. A.   "man:"

B.   this speaks of Esau: "And Esau was a man, a cunning hunter" (Gen. 25:27).

C.   "strange:"

D.   for he estranged himself from circumcision and from the obligations of religious duties.

E.   "the pure:"

F.   this refers to the Holy One, blessed be he,

G.   who behaves toward him in a fair measure and gives him his reward in this world, like a worker who in good faith carries out work for a householder.

3. A.   Another interpretation of the verse, "The way of the guilty man is crooked and strange, but the conduct of the pure is right" (Prov. 21:8):

B.   "The way of the guilty man is crooked:" this speaks of the nations of the world, who come crookedly against Israel with harsh decrees.

C.   "man:" for they derive from Noah, who is called a man.

D.   "strange:"

E.   for they worship alien gods.

F.   "the pure:"

G.   this refers to the Holy One, blessed be he,

H.   who behaves toward him in a fair measure [supply: and gives him his reward in this world, like a worker who in good faith carries out work for a householder].

4. A.   R. Aha said, "'the way...is crooked' refers to the Israelites: 'For they are a crooked generation' (Dt. 32:20).

B.   "'man:' 'Now the men of Israel had sworn' (Judges 21:1).

C.   "'strange:' they alienated themselves from the Holy One, blessed be he: 'They have dealt treacherously against the Lord for they have produced strange children' (Hos. 5:7).

D.   "'but the conduct of the pure is right:' this speaks of the Holy One, blessed be he, who behaves toward him in a fair measure in this world, but gives them the full reward that is coming to them in the world to come,

E.   "like a worker who in good faith carries out work for a householder.

F.   "At that time said the Holy One, blessed be he, 'My children are rebellion. But as to exterminating them, that is not possible, and to bring them back to Egypt is not possible, and to trade them for some other nation is something I cannot do. But this shall I do for them: lo, I shall torment them with suffering and afflict them with famine in the days when the judges judge.'

G.   "That is in line with this verse: 'And it came to pass in the days when the judges ruled, there was a famine in the land.'"

We have yet another absolutely perfect execution of the intersecting-verse/base-verse form. The intersecting verse draws us immediately to Esau, who, of course, stands for Rome. No. 1 then invites us to lament Israel's condition; No. 2, which is continuous, underlines the message. It further explains Rome's present prosperity; they get their reward in this world. No. 3 then broadens the matter to encompass all of the nations of the world. Then No. 4 brings us back to Israel, matching Nos. 1-2 with precision; Israel gets its reward in the world to come, because, through suffering in this world, Israel repents. The picture is then complete, and the famine in the time of the rule of the judges falls into place within the larger program of God for Israel. I cannot imagine a more fully realized and wholly unitary exposition, and the whole surely has been made up for the purpose of the compilers of the document in which the composition now occurs.

Ruth Rabbah Petihta Four
IV:I

1. A.   "The name of the man was Elimelech:"
    B.   Because trouble has come, you forsake them?
    C.   [supply: "and a certain man of Bethlehem in Judah went."]
2. A.   "and a certain man of Bethlehem in Judah went:"
    B.   This is in line with the following verse of Scripture: "[Rabinowitz, p. 9:] Whose leaders are borne with. There is no breach and no going forth [and no outcry]": (Ps. 144:14).
    C.   R. Yohanan said, "What is written here is not 'bear' but 'borne with.'
    D.   "When the young bear with the old, 'there is no breach [and no going forth and no outcry].'
    E.   "That is, there is no breaking forth of plague: 'And the plague broke in upon them' (Ps. 106:29).
    F.   "'and no going forth:' there is no going forth of plague: 'And there came forth fire from before the Lord' (Lev. 10:2).
    G.   "'and no outcry:' there is no outcry on account of plague: 'And all Israel that were round about them fled at the cry of them' (Num. 16:34)."
3. A.   [As to the verse, "Whose leaders are borne with. There is no breach and no going forth and no outcry" (Ps. 144:14)], R. Simeon b. Laqish would transpose the elements as follows:
    B.   "When the elders bear with the youngers, 'there is no breach' into exile: 'And you shall go out at the breaches' (Amos 4:3).
    C.   "'and no going forth:' into exile: 'Cast them out of my sight and let them go forth' (Jer. 15:1).

	D.	"'and no outcry:' of exile: 'Behold, the voice of the cry of the daughter of my people' (Jer. 8:19). 'And the cry of Jerusalem went up.'"
4.	A	[As to the verse, "Whose leaders are borne with. There is no breach and no going forth and no outcry" (Ps. 144:14)], R. Luliani [Julius] said, "When the young listen to the old, but the old do not bear with the young, then 'The Lord will enter into judgment' (Is. 3:14).
	B.	"'The name of the man was Elimelech:' 'Because trouble has come, do you forsake them?'
	C.	"'and a certain man of Bethlehem in Judah went.'"

No. 1 is simply out of place, since it comes at the end and serves to link the intersecting verse, Ps. 144:14, to the base verse, as given. The composition then starts poorly at No. 2, since we should have preferred, "R. Yohanan commenced by citing the following verse" + Ps. 144:14. Then we have three treatments of that same verse, and it is the third that draws us to our goal. For the point is now that Elimelech has betrayed the young by leaving the country, rather than bearing the burdens of the young with him. If that is the point, then the exegete reads "a certain man of Bethlehem went to sojourn," without the remainder: "he and his wife...." At any rate Nos. 2 and 3 are absolutely necessary to complete the symmetry and allow No. 4 to come to its climax. The whole then has been composed to make a complete point in the service of the base verse, with the consequence that the writing of the passage forms part of the compilation of Ruth Rabbah.

Ruth Rabbah to Ruth 1:4
VIII:I

1.	A	"These took Moabite wives:"
	B.	It was taught on Tannaite authority in the name of R. Meir, "They did not convert them nor baptize them nor had the law been taught: 'Amonite male,' but not female, 'Moabite male,' but not female.
	C.	"[Since such a law had not been taught, permitting marriage to a formerly prohibited ethnic group,] they did not escape punishment on that account.
2	A	"the name of the one was Orpah:"
	B.	[The name Orpah and the word back share the same consonants, so] it was because she turned her back on her mother-in-law.
	C.	"and the name of the other Ruth:"
	D.	for she paid attention to the words of her mother-in-law [and the word for see or pay attention and Ruth share the same consonants].
3.	A	R. Bibi in the name of R. Reuben said, "Ruth and Orpah were the daughters of Eglon: 'I have a secret errand for you, O King. And

he said, Keep silence' (Judges 3:19). 'And Ehud came to him...and Ehud said, "I have a message from God for you. And he arose out of his seat' (Judges 3:20).

B. "Said the Holy One, blessed be he, to him, 'You have arisen form your throne in my honor. By your life, I shall raise up from you a son who will sit on the throne of the Lord.'"

4. A. "They lived there about ten years:"

  B. ["about"] as in about thirty, about forty, either less or more.

The composition stays close to the interests of the verse that is elucidated. No. 1 explains why the husbands died. Nos. 2, 3 identify the figures in the base verse, and No. 4 clarifies a point of language. None of this composition would be comprehensible if detached from the base text, with the possible exception of No. 3; but the full weight of that composition is realized only in the present context.

6

Pericopes Framed for the Purposes of a Particular Document but Not of a Type We Now Possess

I. Prologue: Definition

Let us now review the definitions given in Chapter One. The remainder of this chapter, then, sets forth examples of this kind of writing in the classics of Judaism in the third classification. These are writings that can have served well-framed and attested redactional purposes, but that fall outside of the kinds of compilations we now have in hand. I am inclined to see these kinds of writings as earlier in the sedimentary process than the ones catalogued in Part One. To review the definitions now in hand:

Some writings serve not the purposes of the document in which they occur but rather a redactional program of a document, or of a type of document, that we do not now have, but can readily envision.

The second of the four kinds of completed units of thought served a purpose other than that of the authorship of the compilation in which said kind of writing now occurs. It is therefore, as a matter of hypothesis, to be assigned to a stage in the formation of classics prior to the framing of the document in which the writing now occurs; in the context of a given compilation that now contains that writing, it is in a relative sense earlier than a piece of writing that the framers have worked out to serve their own distinctive and particular purposes. It is earlier than a writing that has been made up to serve the document in which it now occurs. But it is also later in its formation than what we find in this third kind of writing classified here. For the third of the four kinds of completed units of thought clearly presupposes a location in a document of a kind we do not have. But the characteristics of a set of such writings permits us to identify and define the kind of writing that can readily have contained, and been well served by, pericopes of this kind.

A piece of writing that serves no where we now know may nonetheless conform to the rules of writing that we can readily imagine and describe in theory. For instance, a propositional composition, that runs through a wide variety of texts to make a point autonomous of all of the texts that are invoked, clearly is intended for a propositional document, one that (like the Mishnah) makes points autonomous of a given prior writing, e.g., a biblical book, but that makes points that for one reason or another cohere quite nicely on their own. Authors of propositional compilations self-evidently can imagine that kind of redaction. We have their writings, but not the books that they intended to be made up of those writings. In all instances, the reason that we can readily imagine a compilation for that will have dictated the indicative traits of a piece of writing will prove self-evident: we have compilations of such a type, if not specific compilations called for by a given composition.

II. Mekhilta

Mekhilta Pisha Chapter One
XV:I
1.   A.   "And the Lord said to Moses and Aaron, 'This is the ordinance of the passover:'"

    B.   There are pericopes in Scripture in which an encompassing principle is stated first of all, then the details are given at the end, and there are pericopes in which the details are given at the outset, with the encompassing principle at the end.

    C.   "You shall be to me a kingdom of priests and a holy nation" (Ex. 19:6) for example constitutes an example of the presentation of details.

    D.   "These are the words that you shall speak to the people of Israel" (Ex. 19:6) forms an instance of an encompassing principle.

    E.   "This is the statute of the Torah" (Num. 19:2) forms an encompassing principle.

    F.   "That they bring to you a red cow, without blemish" (Num. 19:2) is a detail.

    G.   "This is the ordinance of the passover" forms the encompassing principle.

    H.   "No foreigner shall eat of it" is a detail.

    I.   When you have an encompassing principle followed by a detail, then the encompassing principle covers only what is specified by the detail.

No. 1 is not particular to our passage but forms a statement, with examples including our passage, of a general rule of interpretation. The document in which it belongs is one devoted to the general exegetical principles that govern scriptural hermeneutics. We have no such document.

Mekhilta Beshallah Chapter Six
XXIV:I

1.   A.   "And the people of Israel went into the midst of the sea [on dry ground, the waters being a wall to them on their right hand and on their left]:"

      B.   R. Meir presents the matter in one way, R. Judah in another.

      C.   R. Meir says, "When the tribes stood at the sea, this one said, 'I shall go down first into the sea,' and that one said, 'I shall go down first into the sea.'

      D.   "While they were standing there and arguing, the tribe of Benjamin leaped forward and went down into the sea first of all:

      E.   "'There is Benjamin, the youngest, ruling them' (Ps. 68:28). Read the word for 'ruling them' in a different way to produce, 'going down into the sea.'

      F.   "The princes of Judah began throwing stones at them: 'The princes of Judah with their heaps [Lauterbach, p. 232, n. 1: of stones]' (Ps. 68:28).

      G.   "The matter may be compared to the case of a king who had two sons, one adult, one minor.

      H.   "He said to the minor, 'Wake me up at dawn,' and to the adult, 'Wake me up at the third hour [after dawn].'

      I.   "The minor came to wake him up at dawn, but the elder would not let him, saying to him, 'He told me only to wake him up at the third hour.'

      J.   "The minor said to him, 'He told me at dawn.'

      K.   "While they were standing there and arguing, their father got up and said to him, 'My sons, both of you only had in mind the honor that is owing to me anyhow. I won't take it off your reward.'

      L.   "So too, what was the reward that the tribe of Benjamin received for going down into the sea first? The Presence of God took up residence in the share of Benjamin: 'Benjamin is a ravenous wolf [an allusion to the altar of the temple, located in his property]' (Gen. 49:27); 'Of Benjamin he said, 'The beloved of the Lord shall dwell in safety with him' (Dt. 33:12).

      M.   "And what was the reward that the tribe of Judah got? It had the merit of receiving the monarchy: 'The princes of Judah with their royalty [following Lauterbach].' The word translated 'royalty' is shown to have that meaning in the following: 'Then Belshazzar commanded and they clothed Daniel with purple [which shares some of the letters of the word for royalty]' (Dan. 5:29).

N.   "'The princes of Zebulun, the princes of Naphtali: (Ps. 68:28):

O.   "This teaches that just as miracles were done for the Israelites at the sea through the tribes of Judah and Benjamin, so miracles were done for Israel in the days of Deborah and Barak through the tribes of Zebulun and Naphtali:

P.   "'She sent and called Barak, so of Abinoam, out of Kadesh-Naphtali' (Jud. 4:6); 'Zebulun is a people that risked their lives, and Naphtali, upon the high places of the field' (Jud. 5:18)."

2   A.   R. Judah says, "When the Israelites stood at the sea, this one said, 'I am not going to go down first into the sea,' and that one said, 'I am not going to go down first into the sea,'

B.   "for it is said, 'Ephraim surrounds me with lies, and the house of Israel with deceit' (Hos. 12:1).

C.   "While they were standing and taking counsel, Nachshon b. Amminadab leaped forward first into the sea and fell into the waves of the ocean.

D.   "In his connection Scripture says, 'Save me, O God, for the waters have come in even to the soul; I am sunk in deep mire, where there is no standing; I am come into deep waters, and the flood overwhelms me' (Ps. 69:2-3); 'Let not the water-flood overwhelm me, nor let the deep swallow me up; do not let the pit shut her mouth upon me' (Ps. 69:16).

E.   "At that time Moses was standing and protracting a prayer before the Holy One, blessed be he.

F.   "Said to him the Holy One, blessed be he, 'Moses, my friend is sinking into the water, and the sea shuts him off at the fore, and the enemy pursues from behind, and you stand here and protract your prayer before me!'

G.   "He said before him, 'Lord of the world, and just what did you want me to do?'

H.   "He said to him, 'Lift up your rod and stretch out your hand over the sea and divide it, that the people of Israel may go on dry ground through the sea.'

I.   "What did the Israelites say at the sea?

J.   "'The Lord will reign forever and ever' (Ex. 15:18).

K.   "The Holy One, blessed be he, said, 'Him who made me king at the sea will I make king over Israel."

3.   A.   R. Tarfon and elders were in session in the shade of a dovecot in Yavneh, and this question was asked before them [as will be seen presently].

B.   [He said,] "'With their camels bearing spice and balm and laudanum' (Gen. 37:25).

C.   "This tells you the working of the merit of the righteous, showing how much it helps them.

D.   "For if this beloved friend had gone down with Arabs [to Egypt], would they not have simply killed him with the stench of their camels and of the naphtha?

E.   "Accordingly, the Holy One, blessed be he, made arrangements for [them to be carrying] sacks of spices and sweet-smelling balms, so that he would not die from the stench of their camels and naphtha."

F.   [The disciples] said to him, "You have taught us, our master."

G.   They said to him, "Our master, teach us [the law on the following subject:]

H.   "'He who drinks water to quench his thirst – what blessing does he recite?'"

I.   He said to them, "'...who creates many sorts of souls and supplies the things they need.'"

J.   They said to him, "You have taught us, our master."

K.   They said to him, "Our master, teach us: on account of what merit did Judah inherit the monarchy?"

L.   He said to them, "You say."

M.   They said to him, "On account of the merit of having said to his brothers, 'What profit is it if we kill our brother?' (Gen. 37:26)."

N.   He said to them, "It suffices as a reward for the act of saving his life as atonement for the sin of his having sold the brother into slavery."

O.   "So on account of what merit did Judah inherit the monarchy?"

P.   [They said to him,] "It was on account of the merit of his having said, 'And Judah acknowledged them and said, "She is more righteous than I"' (Gen. 38:26)."

Q.   He said to them, "It suffices as a reward for the act of confessing the truth as atonement for the sin of his having had sexual relations with her anyhow."

R.   "If so, it was on account of the merit of his having said, 'Now therefore let your servant, I ask, stay here instead of the boy' (Gen. 44:33)."

S.   He said to them, "The one who guarantees a loan has to pay in the case of default. [He had no reward coming for simply carrying out his obligation; no merit accrues for that.]"

T.   They said to him, "Our master, teach us: on account of what merit did Judah inherit the monarchy?"

U.   He said to them, "When the Israelites stood at the sea, this one said, 'I am not going to go down first into the sea,' and that one said, 'I am not going to go down first into the sea,'

V.   "for it is said, 'Ephraim surrounds me with lies, and the house of Israel with deceit' (Hos. 12:1).

W.   "While they were standing and taking counsel, Nachshon b. Amminadab and his tribe leaped forward first into the sea and fell into the waves of the ocean.

X.   "Therefore he acquired the merit for the monarch to come from his tribe:

Y.   "'When Israel came forth out of Egypt, the house of Jacob from a people of strange language, Judah became his sanctuary,' and therefore, 'Israel was his dominion' (Ps. 114:1-2)."

These three entries are self-contained and not composed for the purposes of the exegesis of the texts that serve to link them to their site in Mekhilta. A document in which they might find a suitable place would focus upon stories that illustrate social virtues in Israel, e.g., pioneering, courage, faith, and the like. Then these would form a tractate in such a treatise.

Mekhilta Beshallah Chapter Six
XXIV:I

7.   A.   "[The Egyptians pursued and went in after them into the midst of the sea, all Pharaoh's horses, his chariots and his horsemen.] And in the morning watch [the Lord in the pillar of fire and of cloud looked down upon the host of the Egyptians]:"

      B.   You find that the prayers of the righteous are listened to in the morning.

      C.   How do we know that concerning the morning of Abraham?

      D.   "And Abraham rose early in the morning" (Gen. 22:3).

      E.   ...of Isaac? "And they went both of them together" (Gen. 22:6), both having risen early in the morning.

      F.   ...of Jacob? "And Jacob rose early in the morning" (Gen. 28:18).

      G.   ...of Moses? "and Moses rose up early in the morning" (Ex. 34:4).

      H.   ...of Joshua? "And Joshua rose up early in the morning and the went off from Shittim" (Josh. 3:1).

      I.   ...of Samuel? "And Samuel rose up early in the morning to meet Saul" (1 Sam. 15:12).

      J.   ...of the prophets who are going to come up in the future? "O Lord, in the morning you will hear my voice, in the morning I will order my prayer to you and will look forward" (Ps. 5:4).

      K.   ...of this world? "They are new every morning, great is your faithfulness" (Lam. 3:23).

      L.   So too you find that the Holy One, blessed be he, is going to exact punishment of the wicked in Gehenna in the age to come only early in the morning: "Morning by morning will I destroy all the wicked of the Lord" (Ps. 101:8).

      M.   So too as to Jerusalem in the age to come, morning by morning the judgment will come forth to light [Lauterbach: And likewise, in the future. He will bring to light Israel's judgment every morning...]: "The Lord who is righteous in the midst of her, he will not do unrighteousness; every morning he brings forth his right to light, it does not fail, but the unrighteous know no shame" (Zeph. 3:5).

The appropriate compilation would constitute a tractate on prayer ("the prayers of the righteous") in a compilation on piety and virtue.

Mekhilta Kaspa 5
LXXX:I

1. A. "The first of the first fruits of your ground you shall bring into the house of the Lord your God:"
   B. Why is this passage set forth?
   C. Since Scripture states, "["It shall come to pass, that when you enter the land that the Lord your God is giving you as a heritage, and you possess it and settle in it,] you shall take some of every first fruit of the soil, [which you harvest from the land that the Lord your God is giving you, put it in a basket, and go to the place where the Lord your God will choose to establish his name. You shall go to the priest in charge at that time and say to him, 'I acknowledge this day before the Lord your God that I have entered the land that the Lord swore to our fathers to assign to us.' And the priest shall take the basket from your hand and set it down in front of the altar of the Lord your God. You shall then recite as follows before the Lord your God: 'My father was a fugitive Aramean. He went down to Egypt with meager numbers and sojourned there; but there he became a great and very populous nation. The Egyptians dealt harshly with us and oppressed us; they imposed heavy labor upon us. We cried to the Lord, the God of our fathers, and the Lord heard our plea and saw our plight, our misery, and our oppression. The Lord freed us from Egypt by a mighty hand, by an outstretched arm and awesome power, and by signs and portents. He brought us to this place and gave us this land, a land flowing with milk and honey. Wherefore I now bring the first fruits of the soil which you, O Lord, have given me.' You shall leave it before the Lord your God and bow low before the Lord your God. And you shall enjoy, together with the Levite and the stranger in your midst, all the bounty that the Lord your God has bestowed upon you and your household" (Dt. 26:1-11)],
   D. I know only that produce belongs as first fruits. What about liquids?
   E. Scripture states, "you shall bring into the house of the Lord your God:"
   F. under all circumstances.
   G. Then what is the difference between the one and the other?
   H. In the case of produce, the farmer brings and makes the required declaration, while in the case of the latter, one brings the liquids but does not make the required declaration.
2. A. "which you harvest from the land:"

B.   this serves to exclude from the rite sharecroppers, those who rent the land, holders of land that has been confiscated and resold, and one who has stolen the land.

3.   A.   "that the Lord your God is giving you:" .

B.   this serves to exclude proselytes and bondservants.

4.   A.   "you:"

B.   this excludes women, those with undefined sexual traits, and those bearing the sexual characteristics of both genders.

5.   A.   Is the implication, then, that they are not to bring and also not to make the required declaration?

B.   Scripture says, "you shall bring:"

C.   under all circumstances.

D.   Then what is the difference between the one and the other?

E.   In the case of the one the farmer brings and makes the required declaration, while in the case of the latter, one brings the first fruits but does not make the required declaration.

The exposition is conventional, beginning with the anticipated question, but then addressing only the counterpart text. The treatment of that text is brief and truncated. This looks more like a fragment of a sustained discourse located in the setting of Deuteronomy's treatment of the same matter, which, of course, it is, as a glance at Sifré Deuteronomy 299 will show.

Mekhilta Kaspa 5
LXXX:II

1.   A.   "You shall not seethe a kid in its mother's milk:"

B.   R. Ishmael says, "On what account is this rule stated in three passages? It corresponds to the three covenants that the Holy One, blessed be he, made with Israel:

C.   "one at Horeb, one in the plains of Moab, one at Mount Gerizim [Ex. 24:7-8, Dt. 29:11, Dt. 28:29, respectively]."

2.   A.   ["You shall not seethe a kid in its mother's milk (Ex. 24:7-8, Dt. 29:11, Dt. 28:29):"]

B.   R. Josiah says, "The first constitutes the initial statement of the matter, and no exegetical work is carried on in connection with the initial statement.

C.   "The second serves to deal with the following argument:

D.   "A clean beast in the classification of carrion imparts uncleanness when it is carried, and an unclean beast in the same classification imparts uncleanness when it is carried.

E.   "If you have derived the rule concerning the one that is clean that it is forbidden to boil its meat in the mother's milk, is it possible to maintain that likewise in the case of the unclean beast it should be forbidden to boil its meat in its mother's milk?

F.   "Scripture states, 'in its mother's milk,'

G.   "not in the milk of an unclean beast.

	H.	"And as to the third usage, it makes the point that it is not forbidden to do so in the milk of a human being."
3.	A.	["You shall not seethe a kid in its mother's milk (Ex. 24:7-8, Dt. 29:11, Dt. 28:29):"]
	B.	R. Jonathan says, "On what account is this matter repeated three times?
	C.	"One applies to a domesticated beast, the second to a wild beast, the third to fowl."
4.	A.	["You shall not seethe a kid in its mother's milk (Ex. 24:7-8, Dt. 29:11, Dt. 28:29):"]
	B.	Abba Hanin in the name of R. Eliezer says, "On what account is this matter repeated three times?
	C.	"One applies to a large beast, one to goats, one to sheep."
5.	A.	["You shall not seethe a kid in its mother's milk (Ex. 24:7-8, Dt. 29:11, Dt. 28:29):"]
	B.	R. Simeon b. Eleazar says, "On what account is this matter repeated three times?
	C.	"One applies to a large beast, one to a small beast, one to a wild beast.
6.	A.	["You shall not seethe a kid in its mother's milk (Ex. 24:7-8, Dt. 29:11, Dt. 28:29):"]
	B.	Simeon b. Yohai says, "On what account is this matter repeated three times?
	C.	"One serves to prohibit eating it, one to derive benefit from it, and the third to cooking with it under any circumstances."
7.	A.	Another treatment of the passage, ["You shall not seethe a kid in its mother's milk (Ex. 24:7-8, Dt. 29:11, Dt. 28:29):"]
	B.	One applies to cooking both in the Land and abroad, one to the period when there is a house [temple], and one afterward. [This is now spelled out.]
	C.	Since Scripture says, "The first of the first fruits of your ground you shall bring into the house of the Lord your God," and we have therefore derived the rule that the law governing first fruits applies, in the place in which the first fruits are brought, but we have not derived the rule that the prohibition of ["seething a kid in its mother's milk"] applies when first fruits do not apply, and to areas in which the first fruits are not brought.
	D.	Scripture states, "You shall not eat anything that dies of itself" (Dt. 14:21), and further, "You shall not seethe a kid in its mother's milk."
	E.	This indicates that just as the prohibition of carrion applies both in the Land and abroad, both when the house is standing and not when the house is standing, so the prohibition of "You shall not seethe a kid in its mother's milk" applies both in the Land and abroad, both when the house is standing and not when the house is standing.

8. A   ["You shall not seethe a kid in its mother's milk (Ex. 24:7-8, Dt. 29:11, Dt. 28:29):"]

    B.   R. Aqiba says, "On what account is this matter repeated three times?

    C.   "One is to encompass, in particular, a domesticated beast, the second a wild beast, the third fowl."

9. A   [Another comment concerning the statement, "You shall not seethe a kid in its mother's milk:"]

    B.   R. Yosé the Galilean says, "Scripture states, 'You shall not eat anything that dies of itself' (Dt. 14:21), and further, 'You shall not seethe a kid in its mother's milk.'

    C.   "The meat of what can be forbidden under the count of carrion falls into the classification of what is forbidden under the count of 'You shall not seethe a kid in its mother's milk.'

    D.   "Then does fowl, the meat of which is forbidden under the count of carrion fall into the classification of what is forbidden under the count of You shall not seethe a kid in its mother's milk'?

    E.   "Scripture says, 'in its mother's milk,' so excluding fowl, the mother of which has no milk.

    F.   "An unclean beast, further, is forbidden whether it is properly slaughtered or carrion."

10. A   "You shall not seethe a kid in its mother's milk:"

    B.   I know only that the prohibition applies to seething. How do I know that it applies also to eating the meat that has been seethed?

    C.   It is an argument *a fortiori:*

    D.   If the passover-offering, which is not subject to an explicit prohibition as to not seething it, is subject to a prohibition against eating it [should it be seethed], meat that has been cooked in milk, which is subject to a specific prohibition against seething, surely should be subject to a prohibition against eating.

    E.   No, if you have invoked that rule in the case of the passover, which may not be cooked with anything, and which therefore also is subject to a prohibition as to being eaten,

    F.   will you say the same of meat in milk? For it is not subject to a prohibition against being cooked in any manner at all, and therefore it should be subject to a prohibition against being eaten.

    G.   R. Aqiba says, "This argument is not the way to go. Rather:

    H.   "If the sinew of the thigh-vein, which is not subject to a prohibition as to being cooked, is subject to a prohibition as to being eaten, the matter of meat in milk, which is subject to a prohibition as to being cooked, surely should be subject to a prohibition as to being eaten.

    I.   "No, if you have invoked that rule in connection with the sinew of the thigh-vein, the prohibition of which comes prior to the giving of the Torah, and therefore it is subject to a prohibition as to being eaten, will you say the same of milk in meat, the prohibition of which does not come prior to the giving of the Torah, and therefore it should not be subject to a prohibition as to being eaten.

J.	"Lo, carrion forms an anomaly that proves the contrary, for its prohibition was not announced prior to the giving of the Torah, yet the prohibition extends to eating it. It will then provide an example for meat in milk, so that, even though the prohibition concerning it was not announced prior to the giving of the Torah, nonetheless it should be subject to a prohibition against being eaten.

K.	"No, if you have invoked the case of carrion, which imparts uncleanness when it is carried, and therefore it also is forbidden as to eating, will you say the same of meat in milk, which does not impart uncleanness when it is carried, and therefore should not be forbidden as to eating.

L.	"Lo, the rule concerning forbidden fat and blood will provide an analogy, for these do not impart uncleanness when they are carried, yet they are forbidden as to being eaten. They then will prove concerning meat in milk, that, even though it does not impart uncleanness when it is carried, it should nonetheless be forbidden as to being eaten.

M.	"No, if you have invoked the case of forbidden fat and blood, on account of eating which one incurs the liability of extirpation, will you say the same of meat in milk, on account of which one does not incur the liability of extirpation, and therefore no prohibition as to eating [but merely as to seething] should apply!

N.	"Accordingly, Scripture states, 'you shall not eat it' (Dt. 12:24), which encompasses meat in milk, indicating that it will be forbidden as to eating."

11. A	[On the same matter of prohibiting not only seething but also eating,] Issi says, "'You shall not eat the life with the flesh' (Dt. 12:23):

B.	"This serves to encompass meat in milk, indicating that it is subject to a prohibition against being eaten."

12. A	[On the same matter of prohibiting not only seething but also eating,] Issi b. Gur Arye says, "Here we find reference to holiness [at Dt. 14:21] and there also we find a reference to holiness [at Ex. 22:30].

B.	"Just as at the one passage the prohibition pertains against eating, so at the other it pertains also to eating."

13. A	I know only that the prohibition extends to [seething and to] eating. How about deriving benefit [from meat cooked in milk]?

B.	You may offer the following argument *a fortiori*:

C.	if produce of fruit trees during the first three years after planting, in which case no transgression has been committed [e.g., by the planting of the orchard], is forbidden both as to eating and as to all other benefit,

D. meat cooked in milk, in which case a transgression already has been committed, surely should be forbidden both as to eating and as to all other benefit!

E. No, if you take that view in the case of produce of fruit trees during the first three years after planting, in which case the produce has never not been subject to a prohibition, and therefore such produce is forbidden both as to eating and as to all other benefit, will you say the same of meat cooked in milk, in which case the meat assuredly has been free of all prohibition [prior to its being cooked in the milk], and therefore it should not be forbidden both as to eating and as to all other benefit.

F. Lo, leaven on Passover forms an anomaly to the rule, for it was once free of all prohibition [prior to Passover], yet it is forbidden both as to eating and as to all other benefit. It therefore provides an appropriate analogy for the case of meat in milk, for even though it was once free of all prohibition, yet it too should be forbidden both as to eating and as to all other benefit.

G. No, if you have invoked the case of leaven on Passover, on account of which one incurs the liability of extirpation, and therefore it is forbidden both as to eating and as to all other benefit, will you say the same of meat in milk, on account of which one does not incur the liability of extirpation, and therefore it should not be forbidden both as to eating and as to all other benefit.

H. Now lo, an anomaly derives from the case of mixed seeds in a vineyard [e.g., wheat sown in a vineyard], for on its account liability to extirpation is not incurred, and yet the crop grown there is prohibited [not only as to eating but also as to] all benefit.

I. That anomaly will then prove concerning the case of meat in milk, that even though one does not on account of eating such meat one will not incur liability to extirpation, nonetheless, a prohibition as to deriving benefit does apply.

J. Rabbi says, "'or you may sell it to a foreigner...you shall not seethe a kid' (Dt. 14:21):

K. "The Torah has said, when you sell it, you may not seethe it and then sell it.

L. "Lo, you have derived the rule that what meat in milk may not be used for any benefit whatsoever."

14. A. "You shall not seethe a kid in its mother's milk:"

B. I know only the prohibition against seething it in the milk of its mother. How about the milk of its sister?

C. You may present the following argument *a fortiori*:

D. if in the case of its mother, with whom the beast may enter the corral for tithing, it is forbidden to seethe the beast with her milk, in the case of its sister, with whom the beast may not enter the corral for tithing, surely it should be forbidden to seethe its meat in her milk.

E.   How about the beast's own milk with its meat?

F.   You may present the following argument *a fortiori:*

G.   if in a case in which the law has permitted use of "produce with produce," e.g., as to slaughter [for one may slaughter them on the same day], the law nonetheless prohibits the offspring with the mother, here, in which the law forbids offspring with offspring [Lauterbach, III, p. 194, n. 11: "The kid and its mother's milk are both the produce of the mother. The animal, so to speak, is the parent of its own milk"], we surely should forbid produce with parent.

H.   How about the milk of goats for use with the meat of lambs?

I.   You may present the following argument *a fortiori:*

J.   if in a case in which the law has permitted offspring with offspring, as in the matter of mating, the law has forbidden offspring with mother, here, in which case the law has prohibited offspring with offspring, as to mating, surely the law should forbid offspring with mother.

K.   The same reasoning applies, moreover, to the use of goat's milk for cooking beef.

L.   Then why does Scripture speak of a kid?

M.   Because its mother produces a lot of milk.

15. A.   ["You shall not seethe a kid in its mother's milk:"]

B.   Rabbi says, "Here we find a reference to 'its mother,' and elsewhere we find 'its mother' (Lev. 22:27).

C.   Just as reference to 'its mother' in the latter passage speaks of the mother of ox, sheep, or goat, so here, 'its mother' encompasses an ox, sheep or goat."

16. A.   "You shall not seethe a kid in its mother's milk:"

B.   It is meat in milk that you are forbidden to seethe, but not all other prohibited things are not so prohibited.

C.   For one might have constructed the following encompassing classification:

D.   if meat in milk, in which case this by itself is permitted, and that by itself is permitted, lo, together they are subject to prohibition as to seething,

E.   all other things in the Torah that are prohibited, in which case this is prohibited on its own and that is prohibited on its own, surely together should be subject to prohibition as to seething.

F.   Scripture is explicit: "You shall not seethe a kid in its mother's milk:"

G.   It is meat in milk that you are forbidden to seethe, but not all other prohibited things are not so prohibited.

17. A.   "You shall not seethe a kid in its mother's milk:"

B.   I know only that the rule applies to ordinary beasts. How do I know that it applies also to beasts that have been consecrated?

C.   You may argue as follows:

D.   If the prohibition applies to unconsecrated beasts, should it not apply also to consecrated beasts?

E.   No, if you have invoked the rule for unconsecrated beasts, which cannot be slaughtered through punching the neck, will you say the same of consecrated beasts, in which case there is no prohibition against slaughter through pinching the neck?

F.   Scripture says, "in the house of the Lord your God you shall not seethe a kid in its mother's milk."

What we have is not exegetical (though the passage includes some exegetical materials) but expository– a well-crafted essay conveying information rather than an argument. In an encyclopaedia built around scriptural materials, this would form an ideal entry on the subject at hand – dietary rules, with special attention to milk and meat and the matter of carrion. This is a classic exposition of a theme, ringing the changes on all the anticipated problems, systematically working through, in particular, the methodical-analytical program of inclusion and exclusion. We begin, No. 1, with the problem of the several passages in which the same rule occurs, and that work, starting with a theological point, works through a variety of inclusionary propositions, Nos. 2-8. The next problem, No. 9, asks about the comparison between this prohibition and the one of carrion. That forms an interlude. The next sequence, beautifully articulated, moves from not seething to not eating, from not eating to not deriving benefit, Nos. 10-13. The next inclusionary problem concerns the origin of the milk – not only the mother, but all other beasts, Nos. 14-15. No. 16 then provides the first exclusion, not a very formidable one, and No. 17, the second and final exclusion. In all, the program is logical, orderly, and so far as I can imagine, complete. It is one of the finest thematic-legal expositions, built upon a well-composed logical structure, in our document, a model for the assessment of all others. As a thematic-legal essay, this piece of writing serves some other sort of document than the exegetical one that is comprised by Mekhilta Attributed to R. Ishmael.

III. Sifra

If the canon of Judaism included a major treatise or compilation on applied logic and practical reason, then a principal tractate, or set of tractates, would be devoted to proving that reason by itself cannot produce reliable results. In that treatise would be a vast and various collection of sustained discussions, which spread themselves across Sifra and Sifré to Deuteronomy, as well as other collections. Here is a sample of how that polemic has imposed itself on the amplification of Lev. 1:2 and transformed treatment of that verse from an exegesis to an example of an overriding proposition. It goes without saying that where we have this type of proof of the priority of Scripture over logic, or of the necessity of Scripture in the defining of generative taxa, the discussion serves a purpose that transcends the case, and on that basis I maintain the proposition that there were types of collections we can readily imagine but that were not made up. In this case, it is, as is clear, a treatise on applied logic, and the general proposition of that treatise is that reliable taxonomy derives only from Scripture.

Sifra Parashat Vayyiqra Dibura Denedabah Parashah Two

III.I

1. A. "Speak to the Israelite people [and say to them, 'When any [Hebrew: Adam] of you presents an offering of cattle to the Lord, he shall choose his offering from the herd or from the flock. If his offering is a burnt-offering from the herd, he shall offer a male without blemish; he shall offer it at the door of the tent of meeting, that he may be accepted before the Lord;] he shall lay [his hand upon the head of the burnt-offering, and it shall be accepted for him to make atonement for him]'" (Lev. 1:2):

   B. "He shall lay his hand:" Israelites lay on hands, gentiles do not lay on hands.

   C. [But is it necessary to prove that proposition on the basis of the cited verse? Is it not to be proven merely by an argument of a logical order, which is now presented?] Now which measure [covering the applicability of a rite] is more abundant, the measure of wavings or the measure of laying on of hands?

   D. The measure of waving [the beast] is greater than the measure of laying on of hands.

   E. For waving [the sacrifice] is done to both something that is animate and something that is not animate, while the laying on of hands applies only to something that is animate.

   F. If gentiles are excluded from the rite of waving the sacrifice, which applies to a variety of sacrifices, should they not be excluded from the rite of laying on of hands, which pertains to fewer sacrifices? [Accordingly, I prove on the basis of reason the rule that is derived at A-B from the verse of Scripture.]

   G. [I shall now show that the premise of the foregoing argument is false:] [You have constructed your argument] from the angle that yields waving as more common and laying on of hands as less common.

   H. But take the other angle, which yields laying on of hands as the more common and waving as the less common.

   I. For the laying on of hands applies to all partners in the ownership of a beast [each one of whom is required to lay hands on the beast before it is slaughtered in behalf of the partnership in ownership of the beast as a whole],

J.   but the waving of a sacrifice is not a requirement that applies to all partners in the ownership of a beast.

K.   Now if I eliminate [gentiles' laying on of hands] in the case of the waving of a beast, which is a requirement applying to fewer cases, should I eliminate them from the requirement of laying on of hands, which applies to a larger number of cases?

L.   Lo, since a rule pertains to the waving of the sacrifice that does not apply to the laying on of hands, and a rule pertains to the laying on of hands that does not apply to the waving of the sacrifice, it is necessary for Scripture to make the statement that it does, specifically:

M.   "He shall lay his hand:" Israelites lay on hands, gentiles do not lay on hands.

The basic premise is that when two comparable actions differ, then the more commonly performed one imposes its rule upon further actions, the rule governing which is unknown. If, then, we show that action A is more commonly performed than action B, other actions of the same classification will follow the rule governing A, not the rule governing B. Then the correct route to overturn such an argument is to show that each of the actions, the rule governing which is known, differs from the other in such a way that neither the one nor the other can be shown to be the more commonly performed. Then the rule governing the further actions is not to be derived from the one governing the two known actions. The powerful instrument of analytical and comparative reasoning proves that diverse traits pertain to the two stages of the rite of sacrifice, the waving, the laying on of hands, which means that a rule pertaining to the one does not necessarily apply to the other. On account of that difference we must evoke the specific ruling of Scripture.

III:II

1.   A   "[Speak to the Israelite people and say to them, 'When any (Hebrew: Adam) of you presents an offering of cattle to the Lord, he shall choose his offering from the herd or from the flock:"

      B.   [The reference to sons of Israel, translated Israelite people, but now understood to mean men, serves to exclude women, with the result:] male Israelites lay on hands, and female Israelites do not lay on hands.

      C.   R. Yosé and R. Simeon say, "As an optional matter women indeed are permitted to lay on hands."

      D.   Said R. Yosé, "Abba Eleazar said to me, 'We had a calf that fell into the classification of a sacrifice of peace-offerings, and we brought it out to the Women's Courtyard, so that the women laid hands on it. Now is there any valid laying on of hands in the

Women's Courtyard? Obviously not. But it was so as to please the women.'"

2. A.   Might one suppose that women should not lay hands on burnt-offerings, for burnt-offerings also do not require waving,

B.   but they may indeed lay hands on peace-offerings, for peace-offerings do require waving?

C.   Scripture says, "...and you will say to them,"

D.   which serves to encompass everything stated in the passage within the fundamental rule, namely,

E.   just as women do not lay hands on burnt-offerings, so they do not lay hands on peace-offerings.

No. 1 makes its own point, and it seems to me that No. 2 stands separate from the foregoing. The exclusion of women is based on the specific statement that the sons, that is, males, do thus and so, understood then to intend the elimination of women. But women in some cases may indeed do the action. No. 2 introduces the distinction between one classification and another of offering, specifically, with reference to the act of waving. That consideration derives directly from III:I, since otherwise, why should anyone have thought to introduce a distinction hardly in evidence in the frame of argument to that point? The distinction between laying on of hands upon the sacrifice and waving the sacrifice plays no role in the present matter, a proposition also demonstrated on an exegetical basis. The order, III:I, II, then is absolutely necessary, since we could not have made the point we wish to make at II were the facts of III:I not in hand. And since the element of the base verse invoked at III:I comes later in the verse than the key element important at III:II, it further follows the the authorship at hand has in mind not a clause-by-clause amplification of the verse at hand. Rather, it has its own logical program in mind, which dictates the order in which the several theorems are taken up. That is further shown when, at III:III, we resume the exposition of the words of the base verse in the order in which those words occur in the verse at hand.

III:III

1. A.   "[Speak to the Israelite people and say to them, 'When] any man [Hebrew: Adam] of you [presents an offering of cattle to the Lord, he shall choose his offering from the herd or from the flock]:"

B.   "Adam" encompasses within the rule proselytes as well.

C.   "...of you" excludes from the rule apostates.

D.   Why have you determined so to read matters that "Adam" encompasses within the rule proselytes as well, while "of you" excludes from the rule apostates? [You could have proven that fact solely on the basis of a principle of logic, spelled out as follows:]

E.   Scripture has first of all imposed an inclusionary statement, in saying "the sons of Israel."

F.   Just as the sons of Israel are those who have accepted the covenant, so proselytes have accepted the covenant.

G.   Accordingly, excluded are apostates, who do not accept the covenant.

H.   [But that reading competes with another, namely] just as Israelites are the sons of those who accept the covenant, so apostates remain sons of those who accept the covenant, then excluding proselytes who by definition are not sons of those who accept the covenant. [So reason by itself can lead to contradictory conclusions.]

I.   Scripture states, "...of you."

J.   Now lo, state matters only as follows: just as Israelites are those who accept the covenant, so proselytes are included within the rule, since they accept the covenant, and apostates are excluded, for they do not accept the covenant.

K.   Lo, Scripture says, "The sacrifice of the wicked is an abomination; how much more when he brings it with evil intent" (Prov. 21:27).

The upshot is that appeal to the principle invoked at D-G fails. Hence the claim that a fixed principle of logic, even one that itself invokes exegetical considerations, is rejected. Rather, we have to rely solely upon exegesis and cannot skip any step or stage in the exegetical process. We note the premise that Adam stands only for Israelite.

III:IV

1. A   ["Speak to the Israelite people and say to them, 'When] any of you presents [an offering of cattle to the Lord, he shall choose his offering from the herd or from the flock:]"

    B.   Might one suppose that it is by decree [that such an offering is presented]?

    C.   Scripture says, "When...presents...," which is only optional [and not obligatory].

2. A   "an offering of cattle to the Lord:"

    B.   "[Since the order of the words is, 'offering,' then, 'to the Lord,' the sense is that one should first undertake the act of sanctification of the beast for the sacrifice, and then offer it up," the words of R. Judah.

3. A   Said R. Simeon, "How on the basis of Scripture do we know that a person should not say, 'For the Lord, a burnt-offering,' 'for the Lord, a meal-offering,' 'for the Lord, peace-offerings,' but rather he should say, 'A burnt-offering for the Lord,' 'a meal-offering for the Lord,' 'peace-offerings for the Lord'?

    B.   "Scripture says, 'an offering [of a given classification] for the Lord.' [The word order then is as follows: such and such a classification of offering applies to the beast at hand, then, 'for the Lord.']

C.   "And lo, this yields an argument *a fortiori:*

D.   "If in the case of one who is going to undertake an act of sanctification of a beast, the Torah has said, 'the name of Heaven should not be treated as profane in connection with the offering,' [but rather, the offering has to be named first, only then the name of Heaven is invoked, as at B],

E.   "how much the more so [are to be condemned] those who make mention of the name of Heaven for any null purpose whatsoever!"

No. 1 makes its own point, that under discussion here are optional and not obligatory-offerings. Nos. 2, 3 make the same point twice. First the classification of offering into which a beast is set is specified, and then the purpose – "for the Lord" – is to be mentioned. No. 2 states the law without amplification, and No. 3 presents matters in a fuller framework and also explains what is at stake in the rule.

III:V

1.   A   R. Yosé says, "Any passage in which 'an offering' is stated along with the divine name, lo, it is so as not to give unbelievers occasion to cavil.

When we make it explicit that an offering is for "the Lord" and not merely for "the divinity," we state that there is only one, particular God, and that is the Lord, so Finkelstein, p. 22. These "unbelievers" then cannot be Christian.

III:VI

1.   A   "...an offering to the Lord, of cattle [he shall choose his offering from the herd or from the flock]"

B.   Might one suppose that the rule applies also to a wild beast, which also falls into the classification of cattle, in line with this verse: "This is the wild beast which you may eat among all the cattle which is upon the earth" (Lev. 11:2) [RSV: "These are the living thing which you may eat among all the beasts that are on the earth"].

C.   Scripture states [so as to exclude that reading,] "from the herd or from the flock [that is, only of domesticated, but not of wild, beasts].

2.   A   Might one suppose that one should not bring an offering of a wild beast, but if one has brought a wild beast as an offering, it is valid?

B.   The matter may be compared to the case of someone whose master said to him, "Go and bring me wheat," and he went and brought him both wheat and barley.

C.   Lo, such a one is in the position of merely having added to the instructions.

D.   Scripture makes it explicit: "he shall choose his offering from the herd or from the flock,"

E.   You have as eligible for an offering among beasts only those of the domesticated herd or flock alone.

F.   Lo, to what may the matter be compared?

G.   To the case of someone whose master said to him, "Go and bring me only wheat."

H.   Lo, if he went and brought him both wheat and barley, lo, such a one is in the position of having violated his master's instructions.

The potential unclarity of the reference to "cattle," which can encompass both wild and domesticated beasts, is cleared up here. First the simple fact is adduced by reference to the qualifying language in context. Then, No. 2, what is at stake is spelled out with enormous power. The instructions are specific and must be carried out as stated.

III:VII

1.   A   "...of cattle:"

     B.   That statement serves to exclude a beast that has had sexual relations with a human being, or one that has been used for an act of bestiality.

     C.   But is that proposition not merely a matter of logic [in which case a verse of Scripture hardly is required to make the matter explicit]?

     D.   If a blemished beast, which has not served for the commission of a transgression, is invalid for use on the altar, a beast that has had sexual relations with a human being, or one that has been used for an act of bestiality, with which a transgression indeed has been committed, surely should be deemed invalid for use on the altar!

     E.   Lo, [to the contrary], a beast that has threshed with an ass [which should not be done by reason of the prohibition against ploughing with beasts of different species] [will prove the contrary], for with such a beast a transgression has been committed, yet, nonetheless, that beast is permitted for use on the altar.

     F.   No, if you have invoked the rule concerning a beast that has threshed with an ass, on which account the beast involved does not incur liability to the death penalty, will you say the same in the case of a beast that has had sexual relations with a human being, or one that has been used for an act of bestiality, in which case the death penalty is invoked [for the beast involved in the act]!

     G.   Now [the case at hand bears traits distinctive to itself, as we shall now see, so you must] examine the very case that you yourself have introduced [for it is not so pertinent as you maintain, specifically:]

     H.   The rule would apply in the case of a beast with which a transgression has been committed, in a case in which there are two valid witnesses to the act.

     I.   But how would you derive the rule governing a case in which a transgression has been committed with a beast, in a circumstance in which there is only a single valid witness, or in which only the owner of the beast himself serves as the witness?

J.   R. Ishmael said, "Lo, I reason as follows:

K.   "If a blemished beast, in which case it is not necessary for two witnesses to come and testify so that it should be rendered impermissible for eating [there being no rules of testimony pertinent to the certification of a disqualifying blemish], if a single witness should testify [as to an invalidating blemish], the beast would be invalided for use for an offering, in the case of a beast that has had sexual relations with a human being, or one that has been used for an act of bestiality, in which instance two witnesses to the fact indeed are required to render such a beast invalid for ordinary consumption, is it not reasonable that the testimony of only a single witness should invalidate such a beast for use on the altar?" [We have now met the objection of F-H by showing, I-K, that a separate process of reasoning covers the objection spelled out at H.]

L.   Said to him R. Aqiba, "No, if you have invoked such a rule in the case of a blemished beast, when the blemish is discernible to the naked eye, will you make the same statement in the case of a beast that has had sexual relations with a human being, or one that has been used for an act of bestiality, in which case the blemish is not immediately visible [for only if there are witnesses can we prove that such an action has in fact taken place]?

M.   "Since the blemish pertaining to a beast that has had sexual relations with a human being, or one that has been used for an act of bestiality is not visible to the naked eye, perhaps the rule should be that they should not be deemed invalid for use on the altar!

N.   "[Accordingly it is necessary for a verse of Scripture to make the rule clear, namely:] '...of cattle:' that statement serves to exclude a beast that has had sexual relations with a human being, or one that has been used for an act of bestiality."

The somewhat meandering argument ends precisely where C wishes to lead it, namely, to proof that a verse of Scripture is the sole source of a valid rule. Reason unaided by Scripture bears no reliable evidence as to the law.

III:VIII

1. A.   "...from the herd [or from the flock]:"

      B.   This reference serves to exclude [from use on the altar] a beast that has been worshipped.

      C.   Is that not a matter of mere logic [to prove, so that an explicit statement by Scripture is hardly required, specifically:]

      D.   if the covering of a beast given in exchange for the services of a whore or for the price of a dog is permitted for use [by a common person], even though such a beast is forbidden for use on the altar, a beast that has been worshipped, the covering of which is forbidden [for use by an ordinary person, but must be destroyed along with the beast], surely should be unfit for use on the altar!

E.   But matters may be turned around as follows:

F.   if the covering of a beast given in exchange for the services of a whore or for the price of a dog, which may not be used on the altar, may itself be used by a common person, the covering of a beast that has been worshipped, which is [for the sake of argument] permitted, surely itself should be permitted?

G.   [By way of reply, I shall show that the premise of your proposed argument is wrong:] Lo, by this argument you have nullified the rule, "You shall not covet the silver and gold that is upon them and take it for yourself" (Dt. 7:25).

H.   Not at all, for I shall carry out the requirement of the rule, "You shall not covet the silver and gold that is upon them and take it for yourself" (Dt. 7:25) by applying it only to something that is not animate. But as to something that is animate, since such a thing itself [again, for the purposes of the proposed argument] is permitted, its covering also is permitted!

I.   [The proposed argument leads in contradictory directions, so only Scripture can settle matters, as it does in the following way:] "...from the herd [or from the flock]:" this reference serves to exclude [from use on the altar] a beast that has been worshipped.

The exercise presents no surprises. We now review an established protocol of items, the beast used for bestiality, the beast that has been worshipped, and, in what follows, the beast suffering a terminal ailment, the beast designated for, but not yet used in, idolatry, and the like. The protocol yields the same argument time after time.

III:IX

1.   A   When Scripture states, "...from the herd," it serves an exclusionary purpose, namely to exclude a beast suffering a terminal ailment. [Such a beast may not be offered on the altar.]

B.   Is that not a matter of a logical inference?

C.   Namely, If a blemished beast, which is permitted for use for ordinary food, is unfit for use on the altar, a beast suffering a terminal ailment, which is forbidden for use for ordinary food, surely should be unfit for use on the altar.

D.   [No, that reasoning does not apply at all, for lo:] forbidden fat and blood will prove to the contrary, for they are forbidden for use as ordinary food, but they are most certainly valid for use on the altar [where they are to be burned up]!

E.   No, if you have stated that rule in the case of forbidden fat and blood, which derive from something that, under ordinary circumstances, is permitted [for use as food, for one may eat fat and make use of blood of a valid beast], will you say the same of the beast suffering from a terminal ailment, the whole of which is forbidden for use on the altar? [So the logical demonstration is a good one, and a verse of Scripture is needless to make the point.]

F.   A fowl that has been strangled [as an offering[will prove to the contrary, for the whole of it is forbidden [for ordinary food[yet [by definition[is is valid for use on the altar.

G.   No, if you have invoked the case of fowl that has been strangled, it is the very fact that it has been sanctified that renders it forbidden for ordinary use.

H.   But will you say the same of a beast suffering a terminal ailment, which is not forbidden by reason of its having been sanctified? Since it is prohibited for reasons other than its having been sanctified, it should not be declared unfit for use on the altar!

I.   Lo, there is your answer to the proof [and there is no argument *a fortiori* to be made].

J.   Thus when Scripture states, "...from the herd," it serves an exclusionary purpose, namely to exclude a beast suffering a terminal ailment. [Such a beast may not be offered on the altar.]

The sense of J is not self-evident, but we need not be detained by the obvious fact that the argument of F stands. The basic intention is consistent throughout.

III:X

1.   A.   "...from the flock:"

     B.   The specification serves to exclude from use on the altar a beast that has been designated for use for idolatrous worship [even though no act of service has taken place with it].

2.   A.   "...from the flock:"

     B.   This serves to exclude a violent beast [one wont to gore]

3.   A.   Said R. Simeon, "A rule pertains to a beast that has had sexual relations with a human being that does not apply to a beast that is wont to gore, and one pertains to a beast that is wont to gore that does not apply to a beast that has committed an act of sexual relations with a human being.

     B.   "In the case of a beast that has had sexual relations with a human being, the law has treated in one and the same way the beast that acts under constraint and the one that performs the act willingly.

     C.   "But as to a beast that is wont to gore, the law does not treat in one and the same way the beast that acts under constraint and the one that performs the act willingly.

     D.   "As to a beast that is wont to gore, the owner has to pay a ransom even after the death of the beast.

     E.   "But in the case of a beast that has committed an act of sexual relations with a human being, the owner does not pay a ransom after death.

F.   "A rule pertains to a beast that has had sexual relations with a human being that does not apply to a beast that has been worshipped for an idolatrous purpose, and a rule pertains to a beast that has been worshipped for an idolatrous purpose that does not apply to a beast that has had sexual relations with a human being.

G.   "The same prohibition applies to a beast that has had sexual relations with a human being whether it belongs to the person who has done the deed or whether it belongs to some other person,

H.   "while in the case of a beast that has been used for idolatrous purposes, if it belongs to the person who has used the beast in such a way, then it is forbidden, but if the beast belongs to some other person than the one who has used it for idolatrous purposes, it is permitted [since the idol-worshipper had no right to use the beast in that way and no control over the status of the beast].

I.   "Further, the covering of a beast that has had sexual relations with a human being is permitted, while the covering of a beast that has been worshipped for an idolatrous purpose is forbidden."

J.   Therefore it was necessary for Scripture to make explicit the rule covering all of these cases [since each of them is differentiated from all the others in one way or another].

The concluding component of the composition is a triumph, since it completes our examination of the conventional list of forbidden beasts, and shows that it is only through Scripture's explicit reference to each of them that we know the rule. The several items on the protocol are *sui generis*, on which account each has its own rule, and Scripture, and Scripture alone, can inform us of that rule. The polemic in favor of Scripture, uniting all of the components of this chapter into a single coherent argument, then insists that there really is no such thing as a genus at all, and Scripture's rules and regulations serve a long list of items, each of them *sui generis*, for discovering rules by the logic of analogy and contrast is simply not possible.

IV. Sifré to Numbers

Numbers 5:1-4

I:I

1. A   "The Lord said to Moses, 'Command the people of Israel that they put out of the camp [every leper and everyone having a discharge, and everyone that is unclean through contact with the dead]'" (Num. 5:1-2).

    B.   For what purpose is this passage presented?

    C.   Because it is said, "But the man who is unclean and does not cleanse himself, [that person shall be cut off from the midst of the assembly, since he has defiled the sanctuary of the Lord, because the water for impurity has not been thrown upon him, he is unclean]" (Num. 19:20).

D. Consequently, we are informed of the penalty [for contaminating the sanctuary]. But where are we informed of the admonition not to do so?

E. Scripture accordingly states, "Command the people of Israel that they put out of the camp every leper and everyone having a discharge, and everyone that is unclean through contact with the dead" (Num. 5:1-2).

F. Lo, here is an admonition that unclean persons not come into the sanctuary ["out of the camp"] in a state of uncleanness. [Consequently, the entire transaction – admonition, then penalty – is laid forth.]

Sifré to Numbers I:II

1. A. "Command" (Num. 5:2):

B. The commandment at hand is meant both to be put into effect immediately and also to apply for generations to come.

C. You maintain that the commandment at hand is meant both to be put into effect immediately and also to apply for generations to come.

D. But perhaps the commandment is meant to apply only after a time [but not right away, at the moment at which it was given].

E. [We shall now prove that the formulation encompasses both generations to come and also the generation to whom the commandment is entrusted.] Scripture states, "The Lord said to Moses, 'Command the people of Israel that they put out [of the camp every leper and everyone having a discharge, and everyone that is unclean through contact with the dead. You shall put out both male and female, putting them outside the camp, that they may not defile their camp, in the midst of which I dwell.'] And the people of Israel did so and drove them outside the camp, as the Lord said to Moses, *so the people of Israel did*" (Gen. 5:1-4). [The verse itself makes explicit the fact that the requirement applied forthwith, not only later on.]

F. Lo, we have learned that the commandment at hand is meant to be put into effect immediately.

G. How then do we derive from Scripture the fact that it applies also for generations to come? [We shall now show that the same word used here, *command*, pertains to generations to come and not only to the generation at hand.]

H. Scripture states, "Command the children of Israel to bring you pure oil from beaten olives [for the lamp, that a light may be kept burning continually outside the veil of the testimony in the tent of meeting, Aaron shall keep it in order from evening to morning before the Lord continually; it shall be a statute for ever throughout your generations]" (Lev. 24:2).

I.   Lo, we here derive evidence that the commandment at hand is meant both to be put into effect immediately and also to apply for generations to come, [based on the framing of the present commandment].

J.   How, then, do we derive evidence that all of the commandments that are contained in the Torah [apply in the same way]? [We wish now to prove that the language, *command*, always bears the meaning imputed to it here.]

K.   R. Ishmael maintained, "Since the bulk of the commandments stated in the Torah are presented without further amplification, while in the case of one of them [namely, the one at hand], Scripture has given explicit details, that commandment [that has been singled out] is meant both to be put into effect immediately and also to apply for generations to come. Accordingly, I apply to all of the other commandments in the Torah the same detail, so that in all cases the commandment is meant both to be put into effect immediately and also to apply for generations to come."

Sifré to Numbers I.III

1.   A   R. Judah b. Beterah says, "The effect of a commandment stated in any context serves only [1] to lend encouragement.

B.   "For it is said, 'But command Joshua and encourage and strengthen him' (Deut. 3:28).

C.   "Accordingly, we derive the lesson that strength is granted only to the strong, and encouragement only to the stout of heart."

D.   R. Simeon b. Yohai says, "The purpose of a commandment in any context is only [2] to deal with the expenditure of money, as it is said, 'Command the children of Israel to bring you pure oil from beaten olives for the lamp, that a light may be kept burning continually outside the veil of the testimony in the tent of meeting, Aaron shall keep it in order from evening to morning before the Lord continually; it shall be a statute for ever throughout your generations' (Lev. 24:2). 'Command the people of Israel that they put out of the camp every leper and everyone having a discharge, and everyone that is unclean through contact with the dead' (Num. 5:1-2). 'Command the children of Israel that they give to the Levites from the inheritance of their possession cities to dwell in, and you shall give to the Levites pasture lands round about the cities' (Num. 35:2). 'Command the people of Israel and say to them, "My offering, my food for my offerings by fire, my pleasing odor you shall take heed to offer to me in its due season"' (Num. 28:2). Lo, we see in all these cases that the purpose of a commandment is solely to bring about the expenditure of money.

E.   "There is one exception, and what is that? It is this verse: 'Command the people of Israel and say to them, "When you enter the land of Canaan, this is the land that shall fall to you for an inheritance, the land of Canaan in its full extent'" (Num. 34:2).

F.   "You must give encouragement to them in the matter of the correct division of the land."

G.   And Rabbi [Judah the Patriarch] says, "The use of the word, 'commandment' in all passages serves only for the purpose of [3] imparting an admonition [not to do a given action], along the lines of the following: 'And the Lord God commanded the man, saying, "You may freely eat of every tree of the garden, but of the tree of the knowledge of good and evil you shall not eat'" (Gen. 2:16)."

At Sifré to Numbers I:I and I:II we have a philological essay. At issue at I:I is the repetition of the same matter, and the solution is to find a distinct purpose for each point at which the rule is expressed. The exegetical focus, then, is on the larger composite of Scripture, rather than on a word-for-word explication of what is at hand. The exegete-compositors want to know how one passage serves a distinct purpose. The pericope is continuous and unitary. This is a fine instance of a passage that can serve in a number of distinct contexts, not only in the one in which it appears. At Sifré to Numbers I:II the point of interest is in the sense of the word, *command,* and the demonstration will focus upon evidence of a variety of verses of Scripture that command refers both for the present instant and for generations to come. No one then can maintain that the commandments apply only in the distant past. The exegesis of the verse at hand hardly forms the focus of interest at all. The same point can have been introduced in the exegesis of any of the prooftexts that are laid before us. Not only so, but the base verse before us does not even come first in the repertoire of prooftexts. So the composition has been worked out in its own terms and only afterward selected for this, among other, positions. The same is so for Ishmael's proof. The upshot is that the purpose of the pericope is to make a point applicable in general, and the passage falls into the classification of a syllogism, not an exegesis of a particular verse. While the passage serves nicely for its current setting, in fact a different sort of compilation altogether – one focusing upon philological propositions and demonstrations – will have served still more appropriately. The same is so for Sifré to Numbers I:III. The three points at hand hardly pertain to our verse in particular. They form general comments on the meaning of the word command, just as in the former case. The reason for the inclusion of this syllogistic discourse is at D, which clearly intersects with our passage. Otherwise I see no reason for inserting the passage here.

V. Sifré to Deuteronomy

Sifré to Deuteronomy Pisqa One

I:I

1. A.   "These are the words that Moses spoke to all Israel in Transjordan, in the wilderness, that is to say in the Arabah, opposite Suph, between Paran on the one side and Tophel, Laban, Hazeroth, and Dizahab, on the other" (Dt. 1:1):

     B.   ["These are the words that Moses spoke" (Dt. 1:1):] Did Moses prophesy only these alone? Did he not write the entire Torah?

     C.   For it is said, "And Moses wrote this Torah" (Dt. 31:9).

     D.   Why then does Scripture say, "These are the words that Moses spoke" (Dt. 1:1)?

     E.   It teaches that [when Scripture speaks of the words that one spoke, it refers in particular to] the words of admonition.

     F.   So it is said [by Moses], "But Jeshurun waxed fat and kicked" (Dt. 32:15).

2. A.   So too you may point to the following:

     B.   "The words of Amos, who was among the herdsmen of Tekoa, which he saw concerning Israel in the days of Uzziah, king of Judah, and in the days of Jeroboam, son of Joash, king of Israel, two years before the earthquake" (Amos 1:1):

     C.   Did Amos prophesy only concerning these [kings] alone? Did he not prophesy concerning a greater number [of kings[] than any other?

     D.   Why then does Scripture say, "These are the words of Amos, [who was among the herdsmen of Tekoa, which he saw concerning Israel in the days of Uzziah, king of Judah, and in the days of Jeroboam, son of Joash, king of Israel, two years before the earthquake]" (Amos 1:1)

     E.   It teaches that [when Scripture speaks of the words that one spoke, it refers in particular to] the words of admonition.

     F.   And how do we know that they were words of admonition?

     G.   As it is said, "Hear this word, you cows of Bashan, who are in the mountain of Samaria, who oppress the poor, crush the needy, and say to their husbands, 'Bring, that we may feast'" (Amos 4:1).

     H.   ["And say to their husbands, 'Bring, that we may feast'"] speaks of their courts.

3. A.   So too you may point to the following:

     B.   "And these are the words that the Lord spoke concerning Israel and Judah" (Jer. 30:4).

     C.   Did Jeremiah prophesy only these alone? Did he not write two [complete] scrolls?

     D.   For it is said, "Thus far are the words of Jeremiah" (Jer. 51:64)

     E.   Why then does Scripture say, "And these are the words [that the Lord spoke concerning Israel and Judah]" (Jer. 30:4)?

F. It teaches that [when the verse says, "And these are the words that the Lord spoke concerning Israel and Judah" (Jer. 30:4)], it speaks in particular of the words of admonition.

G. And how do we know that they were words of admonition?

H. In accord with this verse: "For thus says the Lord, 'We have heard a voice of trembling, of fear and not of peace. Ask you now and see whether a man does labor with a child? Why do I see every man with his hands on his loins, as a woman in labor? and all faces turn pale? Alas, for the day is great, there is none like it, and it is a time of trouble for Jacob, but out of it he shall be saved" (Jer. 30:5-7).

4. A. So too you may point to the following:

B. "And these are the last words of David" (2 Sam. 23:1).

C. And did David prophesy only these alone? And has it furthermore not been said, "The spirit of the Lord spoke through me, and his word was on my tongue" (2 Sam. 23:2)?

D. Why then does it say, "And these are the last words of David" (2 Sam. 23:1)?

E. It teaches that, [when the verse says, "And these are the last words of David" (2 Sam. 23:1)], it refers to words of admonition.

F. And how do we know that they were words of admonition?

G. In accord with this verse: "But the ungodly are as thorns thrust away, all of them, for they cannot be taken with the hand" (2 Sam. 23:6).

5. A. So too you may point to the following:

B. "The words of Qohelet, son of David, king in Jerusalem" (Qoh. 1:1).

C. Now did Solomon prophesy only these words? Did he not write three and a half scrolls of his wisdom in proverbs?

D. Why then does it say, "The words of Qohelet, son of David, king in Jerusalem" (Qoh. 1:1)?

E. It teaches that [when the verse says, "The words of Qohelet, son of David, king in Jerusalem" (Qoh. 1:1)], it refers to words of admonition.

F. And how do we know that they were words of admonition?

G. In accord with this verse: "The sun also rises, and the sun goes down...the wind goes toward the south and turns around to the north, it turns round continually in its circuit, and the wind returns again – that is, east and west to its circuits. All the rivers run into the sea" (Qoh. 1:5-7).

H. [Solomon] calls the wicked sun, moon, and sea, for [the wicked] have no reward [coming back to them].

The focus is upon the exegesis of the opening word of Deuteronomy, "words...." The problem is carefully stated. And yet, without the arrangement within what is going to be a commentary on Deuteronomy, we should have no reason to regard the composition as exegetical at all.

In fact, it is a syllogism, aiming at proving a particular proposition concerning word usages. Standing by itself, what we have is simply a very carefully formalized syllogism that makes a philological point, which is that the word "words of...," bears the sense of "admonition" or "rebuke." Five proofs are offered. We know that we reach the end of the exposition when, at 5.H, there is a minor gloss, breaking the perfect form. That is a common mode of signaling the conclusion of discourse on a given point.

VI. Genesis Rabbah

Genesis Rabbah
I:VII

1. A. R. Isaac commenced [discourse by citing the following verse]: "'The beginning of your word is truth [and all your righteous ordinance endures forever]' (Ps. 119:16)."

   B. Said R. Isaac [about the cited verse], "From the beginning of the creation of the world, 'The beginning of your word was truth.'

   C. "'In the beginning God created' (Gen. 1:1).

   D. ""And the Lord God is truth '(Jer. 10:9).

   E. "Therefore: 'And all your righteous ordinance endures forever' (Ps. 119:16).

   F. "For as to every single decree which you lay down for your creatures, they accept that decree as righteous and receive it in good faith, so that no creature may differ, saying, 'Two powers gave the Torah, two powers created the world.'

   G. "'[Why not?]' Because here it is not written, 'And gods spoke,' but rather, 'And God spoke' (Ex. 20:1).

   H. "'In the beginning [gods] created is not written, but rather, 'in the beginning [God] created' [in the singular]."

What we have is a syllogism, that there are not two gods or two dominions. Our base verse supplies a fact for the proof of that syllogism. Here again the purpose of the intersecting verse is not to conduct an inquiry into the intersecting verse leading to the exposition of the base verse (to state matters negatively). Rather the interest is in a proposition, namely, that matters are so formulated as to give the lie to those who hold there are two powers or dominions. That is proven by a number of verses, e.g., Ex. 20:1, and not only by Gen. 1:1. Therefore the purpose of the construction is to make the theological point that is expressed, namely, to prove that there is only a single dominion. The exposition of Gen. 1:1 is not at the center of interest. It follows that the passage at hand is not to be classified in the same category as I:I and I:V.

We shall now see yet another composition of the same classification, namely, an effort to make a point autonomous of the verse at hand (Gen. 1:1), or, indeed, of any other verse. In this type of composition, the point of interest is in the proposition that is subject to demonstration, the proofs, of course, deriving from verses of Scripture. No one in the passages before us proposes to construct a simple clarification or exposition of one verse in terms of another, that is, of the base verse in terms of the intersecting verse. That is an essentially different mode of construction entirely.

Genesis Rabbah
I:II
1. A   R. Joshua of Sikhnin in the name of R. Levi commenced [discourse by citing the following verse]: "'He has declared to his people the power of his works, in giving them the heritage of the nations' (Ps. 111:6).

    B.   "What is the reason that the Holy One, blessed be he, revealed to Israel what was created on the first day and what on the second?

    C.   "It was on account of the nations of the world. It was so that they should not ridicule the Israelites, saying to them, 'Are you not a nation of robbers [having stolen the land from the Canaanites]?'

    D.   "It allows the Israelites to answer them, 'And as to you, is there no spoil in your hands? For surely: "The Caphtorim, who came forth out of Caphtor, destroyed them and dwelled in their place" (Deut. 2:23)!

    E.   "'The world and everything in it belongs to the Holy One, blessed be he. When he wanted, he gave it to you, and when he wanted, he took it from you and gave it to us.'

    F.   "That is in line with what is written, '...in giving them the heritage of the nations, he has declared to his people the power of his works' (Ps. 111:6). [So as to give them the land, he established his right to do so by informing them that he had created it.]

    G.   "He told them about the beginning: 'In the beginning God created...' (Gen. 1:1)."

The purpose of the passage is to demonstrate Israel's right to the land. The point at hand is that God informed Israel of his power (Ps. 111:6) so as to give them a valid claim on the Land of Israel. Then Gen. 1:1 is cited only to validate the claim at hand, so the joining of Ps. 111:6 to Gen. 1:1 is for the purpose of expounding the principle of divine ownership of the Land – that is, Israel's valid claim – and not the meaning of either verse. For the purposes of an exegetical compilation on the book of Genesis, Gen. 1:1 is essential. It serves to join the syllogism to the present context. But without Gen. 1:1 the passage makes its point quite amply, and its principal verse is Deut. 2:23 aligned with Ps. 111:6. I would therefore be inclined to see Gen. 1:1 as the sole, completely redactional contribution to the whole – that, and, of course, the selection of the completed entry for the present context. The upshot is that these writings serve a document other than that in which they are located; but we can readily envisage the kind of document – a treatise on theology divided into tractates on subsets of that theme – into which both of these entries fit quite comfortably.

VII. Leviticus Rabbah

Leviticus Rabbah
XXVI:VII

1. A   What is written just prior to the present passage? "A man or a woman who is a medium or a wizard shall be put to death" (Lev. 20:27).

    B.   R. Joshua of Sikhnin in the name of R. Levi: "'A man' refers to Saul. 'A woman' refers to a woman who divines by a ghost" (1 Sam. 28:7).

2. A   R. Levi in the name of R. Hama b. R. Hanina: "It would have been better for Saul to consult the Urim and Thumin, which belong to the upper world, and not to inquire through the ghost or familiar spirit, which belong to the lower world.

    B.   "That is in line with what Saul says to his servants, 'Seek out for me a woman who is a medium, that I may go to her and inquire of her'" (1 Sam. 28:7).

    C.   Said R. Simeon b. Laqish, "What was Saul like at that moment? He was like a king who entered a city and made a decree, saying, 'Let all the roosters be slaughtered this night.'

    D.   "He wanted to go out on a journey [and needed to be awakened in the morning]. He said, 'Aren't there any roosters here to crow?'

    E.   "They said to him, 'You are the one who gave orders to have them slaughtered.'

    F.   "So yesterday: 'And Saul had put the mediums and the wizards out [of the land]' [1 Sam. 28:3]. And today: 'Then Saul said to his servants, "Seek out for me a woman who is a medium, [that I may go to her and inquire of her]." And his servants said to him, "Behold, there is a medium at Endor"'" (1 Sam. 28:7).

    G.   "So Saul disguised himself" (1 Sam. 28:8). The word is written with a *shin*, producing the meaning, "He went forth free" from the kingship.

    H.   "He put on other garments" (1 Sam. 28:8): the garments of ordinary folk.

    I.   "And he went, with two men with him" (1 Sam. 28:8): this refers to Abner and Amasa.

J.   Said R. Isaac, "The Torah thereby teaches you rules of proper conduct, that a person should not go off on a trip with less than two others with him.

K.   "For if someone goes forth with less than two others with him, in the end he will be made a servant of servants."

L.   Said R. Aibu, "Two acted properly, Abraham and Saul.

M.   "Abraham: 'And he took two of his servants with him' [Gen. 22:3].

N.   "And Saul: 'And he went with two men with him' [1 Sam. 28:8]. This refers to Abner and Amasa."

O.   "And they came to the woman by night" (1 Sam. 28:8). Now was it actually night? But the verses teach that that hour was as dark for them as night.

P.   "And he said, 'Divine for me by a spirit, and bring up for me whomever I shall name to you.' And the woman said to him, 'Surely you know what Saul has done, [how he has cut off the mediums and the wizards from the land. Why then are you laying a snare for my life to bring about my death?'] But Saul swore to her by the Lord, 'As the Lord lives, no punishment shall come upon you for this thing'" (1 Sam. 28:8-10).

Q.   Said R. Simeon b. Laqish, "What was Saul like at that moment? He was like a woman who was with her lover and took an oath by the life of her husband. So Saul inquired of a familiar spirit and took an oath to her, 'As the Lord lives, no punishment shall come upon you for this thing.'"

R.   "Then the woman said, 'Whom shall I bring up for you?'" (1 Sam. 28:11).

S.   Should it be one of those who said, "Who is the Lord [that I should listen to his voice]" (Ex. 5:2).

T.   [Or] should it be one of those who said, "Who is like you among the gods, O Lord" (Ex. 15:11).

U.   He said to her, "Samuel, master of the prophets, bring up for me."

V.   She did what she did, said what she said, and he came up. When she saw him, she was frightened, as it is said, "When the woman saw Samuel, she cried out with a loud voice, and the woman said to Saul, 'Why have you deceived me? You are Saul'" (1 Sam. 28:12).

W.   How did she know at that moment that he was Saul? It is as they say, [When the ghost comes up], not for an ordinary person does it come up as it does for a king. For an ordinary person it comes up with its head downward and its feet upward. But for a king it comes up with its feet downward and its head upward.

X.   "The king said to her, 'Have no fear. What do you see?' And the woman said to Saul, 'I see gods coming up out of the earth'" (1 Sam. 28:13).

Y.   When he heard the word "gods," he was frightened.

Z.	And there are those who say, "Many elders came up with him at that hour."
AA.	"He said to her, 'What is his appearance?'" (1 Sam. 28:14).
BB.	Did he not know him?
CC.	Three things are stated concerning him who brings up [the dead] by means of necromancy.
DD.	The one who brings him up sees him but does not hear his voice.
EE.	The one who requires him hears his voice but does not see him.
FF.	And the one who does not need him does not hear his voice and does not see him.
GG.	So in the case of Samuel, the woman who brought him up saw him but did not hear his voice.
HH.	Saul, who needed him, heard his voice but did not see him.
II.	Abner and Amasa, who did not need him, did not hear his voice and did not see him.
JJ.	"And she said, 'An old man is coming up, and he is wrapped in a robe'" (1 Sam. 28:14).
KK.	That is in line with the verse, "And his mother made him a little robe" (1 Sam. 2:19).
LL.	At that moment, "Saul knew that it was Samuel, and he bowed with his face to the ground and did obeisance" (1 Sam. 28:14).
MM.	"Then Samuel said to Saul, 'Why have you disturbed me [by bringing me up]?'" (1 Sam. 28:15).

3.

A.	Rabbi would explain the meaning of verses of Scripture. When he came to these verses, he would weep:
B.	"For lo, he who forms the mountains and creates the wind and tells a man his thought" (Amos 4:14). Even things that have no substance whatsoever are written down in a person's record in his notebook.
C.	Who writes them down? "He who makes the morning gloom" (Amos 4:13).
D.	And this verse also: "Seek the Lord, all you humble of the earth, seek righteousness, seek humility, perhaps you will be hidden on the day of the wrath of the Lord" (Zeph. 2:3).
E.	And this verse also: "Hate evil, love good, establish justice in the gate, perhaps the Lord of hosts will show you grace, O remnant of Joseph" (Amos 5:15).
F.	And this verse also: "For God will bring every evil deed unto judgment" (Qoh. 12:14).
G.	And this verse also: "Let him put his mouth in the dust, perhaps there may be hope" (Lam. 3:29).
H.	And this verse also: "Then Samuel said to Saul, Why have you disturbed me" (1 Sam. 28:15).
I.	He said to him, "You should have not disturbed your Creator, but rather me. You have made an idol of me.

J.   "Did you not know that just as they exact punishment from the one who worships [an idol], so they exact punishment from the one who is worshipped as an idol?

K.   "And not only so, but since I thought that it was the Day of Judgment, I brought Moses along with me!"

L.   Now is it not an argument *a fortiori:* If Samuel, the master of the prophets, concerning whom it was written, "Samuel was established to be a prophet of the Lord" (1 Sam. 3:20), was afraid of the day of judgment, all other people all the more so [should be afraid of it]!

4.   A.   "Saul answered, 'I am in great distress, for the Philistines are warring against me [and God has turned away from me and answers me no more, either by prophets or by dreams; therefore I have summoned you to tell me what I shall do]'" (1 Sam. 28:15)

B.   Said R. Isaac b. R. Hiyya, "'The heart knows its own bitterness' [Prov. 14:10]. Why did he not tell him both by the Urim and by the Thummim?

C.   "For if he had so spoken to him by the Urim and the Thummim, he would have said to him, 'You were the one who did evil when you slew Nob, the city of the priests.'"

D.   "And Samuel said, 'Why then do you ask me, since the Lord has turned from you and become your enemy ('RYK)'" (1 Sam. 28:16). It is on account of those concerning him it is written, "And the sons of Aaron, the priests, shall arrange . . . ('RK)" (Lev. 1:8).

E.   "The Lord has done to you as he spoke by me, for the Lord has torn the kingdom out of your hand and has given it to your neighbor, David" (1 Sam. 28:17).

F.   He said to him, "When you were with me, you said to me, 'To your neighbor who is better than you' [1 Sam. 15:28]. But now you say, 'To your neighbor, to David.'"

G.   He said to him, "When I was with you, I was in the world of lies, and I was afraid of you, lest you kill me. So I phrased matters to you in a duplicitous way. But now that I am dwelling in the world of truth, you will hear from me only truth, for I am not afraid of you."

H.   "Moreover the Lord will give Israel also with you into the hand of the Philistines" (1 Sam. 28:19).

I.   He said to him, "Then should I not flee?"

J.   He said to him, "If you flee, you will be saved."

K.   He said to him, "But should I not make preparation for battle?"

L.   He said to him, "If you make preparation for battle, you will be victorious, but if you accept for yourself the rightness of the attribute of justice, tomorrow: 'you and your sons shall be with me'" (1 Sam. 28:19).

M.   What is the meaning of "with me"?

N.   Said R. Yohanan, "With me, within my circle [of righteous men]."

O.   When Saul heard the words of Samuel, he was afraid.

P.   That is in line with the following verse of Scripture: "Then Saul fell at once full length upon the ground, filled with fear, because of the words of Samuel; and there was no strength in him, for he had eaten nothing all day and all night" (1 Sam. 28:20).

Q.   Now when he came back to Abner and Amasa, they said to him, "What did Samuel say to you?"

R.   He said to them, "If you do battle, you will win. Not only so, but your two sons will be appointed generals."

S.   Forthwith he went out to battle and took his three sons with him: Jonathan, Abinadab, and Malkishua.

T.   Said R. Simeon b. Laqish, "At that moment the Holy One, blessed be he, said to the ministering angels, 'Come and see a creature whom I created in my world, the work of art that I have fashioned in my world. Under ordinary circumstances, a man who goes to a celebration does not take his sons with him, on account of the evil eye. But this one goes down to war, and he knows that he will be slain, and yet takes his sons with him, rejoicing that the attribute of justice will overtake him.'"

5. A.   It was for five sins that Saul died:

B.   "And Saul died on account of the sacrilege, which he did against the Lord" (1 Chron. 10:13).

C.   Because he slew Nob, the city of the priests, because he had pity for Agag, king of Amalek.

D.   "On account of the word of the Lord, which he did not keep" (1 Chron. 10:13).

E.   Because he did not listen to Samuel, who said to him, "Seven days you shall wait, until I come to you" (1 Sam. 10:8), but he did not do so.

F.   "And also because he consulted a medium, seeking guidance" (1 Chron. 10:13),

G.   "and he did not seek guidance from the Lord. Therefore the Lord slew him [and turned the kingdom over to David, the son of Jesse]" (1 Chron. 10:14).

6. A.   "And Saul said to the priest, Withdraw your hand" (1 Sam. 14:19).

B.   R. Joshua of Sikhnin in the name of R. Levi said, "This passage teaches that the Holy One, blessed be he, showed to Moses each generation and its sages, each generation and its wise men, each generation and its interpreters, each generation and its judges, each generation and its officers, each generation and its priests, each generation and its Levites, each generation and its kings.

C.   "When he showed him Saul, king of Israel, falling by the sword, he said before him, 'Lord of the world! Is this appropriate respect for your children? Should the king who stands over them fall by the sword first of all!'

D.   "Said to him the Holy One, blessed be he, 'And are you speaking to me? Speak to the priests, the sons of Aaron, for they are drawing up the indictment against him!'"

E.   "And the Lord said to Moses, Speak to the priests" (Lev. 21:1).

The principle that one passage relates to some other, upon which it sheds light, explains the observation at No. 1. As soon as the matter of necromancy enters, thoughts turn immediately to Saul, and No. 2 presents a vast exposition of the verses of Scripture that report Saul's encounter with the witch of Endor. The principle accounting for the layout of the materials is not difficult to discern. What we have is mainly a systematic exposition of successive verses on Saul and the witch of Endor. Inserted materials are self-evident. For instance, No. 4 continues No. 2. Nos. 5 and 6 are added because of their self-evident relevance to the theme at hand. No. 6 shows us how we regain Lev. 21:1 – an unusually circuitous but artful route. But if we did not regain our base verse, we should have a quite coherent exposition on an important subject, serving the interests of a commentary on a scriptural passage.

VIII. Pesiqta deRab Kahana

A treatise on Israel's history will have a tractate on redemption, and in such a treatise, the following nicely composed thematic exercise on the time of redemption – in Nisan – will find a very commodious place. On that basis I take the following to demonstrate that in Pesiqta deRab Kahana we find materials that serve a purpose other than the one guiding the framing of that document, but one that can well serve a document we can envisage.

Pesiqta deRab Kahana
V:IV

1. A.   Judah bar Nahman in the name of R. Simeon b. Laqish opened discourse by citing the following verse of Scripture: "*Oh send out your light and your truth; let them lead me, let them bring me to your holy hill and to your dwelling. [Then I will go to the altar of God, to God my exceeding joy; and I will praise you with the lyre, O God, my God]* (Ps. 43:3-4).

    B.   "*...send out your light* refers to Moses: *And Moses did not know that his face was glistening with beams of light* (Ex. 34:29).

    C.   "*...and your truth* refers to Aaron, *The Torah of truth was in his mouth* (Malachi 2:7).

    D.   "*Your truth and light be with your holy one* (Deut. 33:8)."

    E.   And there are those who reverse matters:'

    F.   "*...send out your light* refers to Aaron: *Your truth and light be with your holy one* (Deut. 33:8).

G.   "*...and your truth* refers to Moses, *Not so is my servant Moses, in all my household the most trustworthy (Num. 12:7)."*

2. A.   Said R. Isaac, "Even at the sea Moses foresaw that he was not going to enter the Land of Israel: *She keeps her eye on the doings of her household* (Prov. 31:27).

   B.   "What is written in the pertinent passage is not, 'you will bring it and plant it,' but rather, *You brought them in and planted them* (Ex. 15:17).

   C.   "Yet it is written: *...let them lead me, let them bring me to your holy hill and to your dwelling.*

   D.   "This refers to the scribes of the Land of Israel, who are as holy as the Land of Israel itself."

3. A.   Another comment on the verse: *Oh send out your light and your truth; [let them lead me, let them bring me to your holy hill and to your dwelling. Then I will go to the altar of God, to God my exceeding joy; and I will praise you with the lyre, O God, my God]* (Ps. 43:3-4).

   B.   *...send out your light* refers to Moses and Aaron, through whom the Holy One, blessed be he, sent light to Israel to redeem them from Israel.

   C.   When did this take place?

   D.   In this month: *This month for you is the first of the months* (Ex. 12:2).

A long sequence of wide-ranging passages about redemption, each ending, "When did this take place? In this month: *This month for you is the first of the months* (Ex. 12:2), now begins. A particular point of contact between the "illustrative" passage and the topic at hand, Ex. 12:2, never is specified. The general theme of redemption in Nisan than accounts for pretty much everything that follows; in no way can we regard the exercise as mainly exegetical. In fact it is a syllogistic exposition, through innumerable examples, of the single fact that redemption takes place "in this month." No. 1 sets the stage for No. 3, with No. 2 a secondary expansion of No. 1. Specifically, we apply the intersecting verse to Moses, then to Aaron, then to both. But how the intersecting verse opens the base verse to a deeper meaning is not self-evident, since, as I said, the reversion to the base verse seems artificial and mechanical. On the basis of this case one could revert to any base verse one wished. The theme, however, is clearly conventional – that is to say, syllogistic: redemption on the first of the months. And that is I believe what has guided the authorship at hand which wishes to read each of the base verses as another instance in the unfolding of Israel's redemption.

The following is an elegant demonstration for a tractate on the fate of Israel, that God's fate and Israel's are one and the same. The document in which this item appears has no important role in the framing of the passage, though formally it can accommodate this kind of writing.

Pesiqta deRab Kahana
V:VI

1. A.   *I sleep but my heart is awake. Listen! My beloved is knocking: "Open to me, my sister, my dearest, my dove, my perfect one, for my head is drenched with dew, my locks with the moisture of the night"* (Song 5:2):

   B.   Said the community of Israel before the Holy One, blessed be he, "While *I am asleep* at the house of the sanctuary [because it is destroyed], *my heart is awake* in the houses of assembly and study.

   C.   "*I am asleep* as to the offerings, but *my heart is awake* as to the religious duties and acts of righteousness.

   D.   "*I am asleep* as to religious duties, but *my heart is nonetheless awake* to carry them out.

   E.   "*I am asleep* as to the end, but *my heart is awake* as to redemption.

   F.   "*I am asleep* as to redemption, but *the heart* of the Holy One, blessed be he, *is awake* to redeem us."

2. A.   Said R. Hiyya bar Abba, "How do we know that the Holy One is called 'the heart of Israel'?

   B.   "On the basis of this verse: *Rock of my heart and my portion is God forever* (Ps. 73:26)."

3. A.   ...*My beloved is knocking* refers to Moses: *And Moses said, Thus said the Lord, At about midnight I shall go out in the midst of Egypt* (Ex. 11:4).

   B.   *Open to me:* said R. Yosé, "Said the Holy One, blessed be he, '*Open to me* [a hole] as small as the eye of a needle, and I shall open to you a gate so large that troops and siege-engines can go through it.'"

   C.   ...*my sister:* [God speaks:] "*My sister* – in Egypt, for they became my kin through two religious duties, the blood of the Passover-offering and the blood of circumcision."

   D.   ...*my dearest* – at the sea, for they showed their love for me at the sea, *And they said, the Lord will reign forever and ever* (Ex. 15:19).

   E.   ...*my dove* – *my dove* at Marah, where through receiving commandments they become distinguished for me like a dove.

   F.   ...*my perfect one* – *My perfect one* at Sinai, for they became pure at Sinai: *And they said, all that the Lord has spoken we shall do and we shall hear* (Ex. 24:7)."

   G.   R. Yannai said, "My twin, for I am not greater than they, nor they than I."

H. R. Joshua of Sikhnin said in the name of R. Levi, "Just as in the case of twins, if one of them gets a headache, the other one feels it, so said the Holy One, blessed be he, '*I am with him in trouble* (Ps. 91:15)."

I. *...for my head is drenched with dew. The heavens dropped dew* (Judges 5:4).

J. *...my locks with the moisture of the night: Yes, the clouds dropped water* (Judges 5:4).

K. When is this the case? In this month: *This month is for you the first of the months* (Ex. 12:2).

The pattern is the same as before: an extended disquisition on a theme remote from our base verse, ending with an artificial and unprepared for introduction of the base verse. The sole relevant point is that the beginning of God's relationship to Israel is with the first of the months. Nothing else pertains. But the proposition, that God and Israel share one and the same destiny, on its own is stunning.

IX. Lamentations Rabbah

Lamentations Rabbah Parashah One to Lamentations 1:1
XXXV:I

1. A. "How lonely sits the city:"

    B. Three prophets made use of the word "how" in stating their prophecies, and these are they: Moses, Isaiah, and Jeremiah.

    C. Moses said, "How can I myself alone bear your burden" (Dt. 1:12).

    D. Isaiah said, "How is the faithful city become a harlot" (Is. 1:21).

    E. Jeremiah said, "How lonely sits the city."

2. A. Said R. Levi, "The matter may be compared to the case of a noble lady who had three representatives of her family at hand. One of them saw her when she was prosperous, one saw her when she was confused, one of them saw her when she was degraded.

    B. "So Moses saw Israel in their prosperity: 'How can I myself bear up under the weight of your prosperity?' (Deut. 1:12).

    C. "Isaiah saw them in their confusion and said, 'Alas, she has become a harlot' (Isaiah 1:21).

    D. "Jeremiah saw them in their utter degradation and said, 'How [lonely sits the city that was full of people! How like a widow has she become, she that was great among the nations! She that was a princess among the cities has become a vassal. She weeps bitterly in the night, tears on her cheeks, among all her lovers she has none to comfort her; all her friends have dealt treacherously with her, they have become her enemies]' (Lamentations 1:1-2).

    E. "'How lonely sits the city....'"

Here is a composition that is arranged to serve Lamentations Rabbah, but that, as to its presentation, can stand entirely independent of any compilation. The opening proposition links the opening word of Lamentations Rabbah to the three prophets, leading to Jeremiah, the author; No. 2 then builds upon the foregoing. No. 2 can stand independent of No. 1, but the two together form a strong statement. The same is so in the following:

Lamentations Rabbah Parashah One to Lamentations 1:1
XXXV:II

1. A.   [As to the meaning of the Hebrew word for "how:"] R. Eleazar and R. Yohanan:
    B.   R. Eleazar said, "The word is made up of two syllables, which read individually mean 'where is the "thus"?'
    C.   "So the 'thus' that God said to Abraham: 'Thus will be your seed' (Gen. 15:5)."
    D.   R. Yohanan said, "The word is made up of two syllables, which read individually mean 'where is the "thus"?'
    E.   "So the 'thus' that God said to Moses: 'So shall you say to the house of Jacob' (Ex. 19:3)."
2. A.   They asked Ben Azzai, "Tell us something concerning the scroll of lamentations."
    B.   He said to them, "The Israelites were sent into exile only after they had denied the Unique One of the world, the Ten Commandments, circumcision, which had been given to the twentieth generation [Abraham], and the Pentateuch.
    C.   "How do we know it? From the word 'how' [the letters of which stand for one, hence the Divine Unity, ten, twenty, and five.]"
3. A.   Said R. Levi, "The Israelites did not go into exile until they had denied the thirty-six laws in the Torah [Cohen, p. 66:] for which the penalty is extirpation.
    B.   "How do we know it? 'How...' [the numerical value of the letters of which add up to thirty-six]."

We have a series of amplifications of the meaning and sense of the word "how." We start with the word and then reduce it to its letters, interpreting each of these, first as standing for other words, then as standing for numerical values. These items can stand well in a philological compilation, justifying the inclusion of this entry in the present catalogue.

Here is another example of a fine composition for some document, but not really for the one at hand. We begin with a proposition, "They did not fully explore the limits of the measure of justice, so the measure of justice did not go to extremes against them," that serves a theological-ethical treatise, not an exegetical one.

Lamentations Rabbah Parashah One
XXV:VI
1.   A.   "How like a widow has she become:"

      B.   Said R. Aibu, "They did not fully explore the limits of the measure of justice, so the measure of justice did not go to extremes against them.

      C.   "They did not fully explore the limits of the measure of justice: 'And the people were like murmurers' (Num. 11:1).

      D.   "What is written is not 'murmurers,' but only, 'like murmurers.'"

      E.   "'The princes of Judah are like those who remove the landmark' (Num. 5:10).

      F.   "What is written is not 'remove,' but 'like those who remove.'

      G.   "'For Israel is like a stubborn heifer' (Hos. 4:16).

      H.   "What is written is not 'a stubborn heifer,' but 'like a stubborn heifer.'

      I.   "What is written here is not 'a widow' but 'like a widow.'

      J.   "She is like a woman waiting for her husband, who has left her and gone on a distant journey.

      K.   "'He has bent his bow like an enemy' (Lam. 2:4).

      L.   "What is written here is not 'an enemy' but 'like an enemy.'"

2.   A.   Another interpretation of the clause, "How like a widow has she become:"

      B.   R.Hama bar Uqba and rabbis:

      C.   R. Hama bar Uqba said, "To what may the Israelites be likened? To a widow who has laid claim for living expenditures but has not laid claim for the payout of her marriage-settlement [upon the death of her husband. By doing so, she has forfeited the latter claim. So Israel has refused to be parted from the Temple (Cohen, p. 72, n. 1).]"

      D.   Rabbis say, "The matter may be compared to the case of a king who grew angry with his wife and wrote out her writ of divorce and handed it over to her, but then went and snatched it back.

      E.   "Whenever she wishes to be married to a third party, he says to her, 'Where is your writ of divorce, proving that I have divorced you?'

      F.   "And whenever she lays claim for her living expenditure, he says to her, 'I've already divorced you.'

      G.   "Thus whenever the Israelites seek to worship an idol, the Holy One, blessed be he, says to them, 'Where is the writ of your mother's divorce from me' (Is. 50:1).

      H.   "And whenever they want him to do a miracle for them, he says to them, 'I have already divorced you.'

      I.   "That is in line with this verse: 'I had put her away and given her a writ of divorce' (Jer. 3:8)."

No. 1 does not fully work out its announced proposition, since the second clause, "so the measure of justice did not go to extremes against them," is not developed. What we have is a quite separate set of prooftexts for the proposition that the prophetic critique of Israel is mitigated by mercy. There is no proof that just as the Israelites did not go to extremes in sinning, so the measure of justice did not do so. But that is the announced proposition. Buber's printed text revises to meet that need by using H-L to prove the counterpart point. No. 2 is well worked out, a successful demonstration that Israel stands in an ambiguous relationship with God, both divorced and not divorced. The clause that is explicated serves only the first of the two positions, however, and that means the passage was made up in its own terms and then inserted here because of its usefulness to the compilers of our document or this passage therein.

X. Esther Rabbah

Esther Rabbah One to Esther 1:11
XX:I

1. A. "to bring Queen Vasti before the king with her royal crown, [in order to show the peoples and the princes her beauty; for she was fair to behold]:"

    B. Said R. Aibu, "The atonement for Israel is this: when the Israelites eat and drink and make merry, they bless and praise and glory in the Holy One, blessed be he.

    C. "But when the nations of the world eat and drink, they get involved in light-headed matters.

    D. "This one says, 'Median women are prettier,' and that one says, 'Persian women are more beautiful.'

    E. "Said to them that idiot, 'The utensil that I use is neither Median nor Persian but Chaledean. Want to see her?'

    F. "They said to him, 'Yes, but only naked.'

    G. "He said to them, 'O.k., naked.'"

    H. R. Phineas and R. Hama bar Guria in the name of Rab said, "She wanted to come in wearing at least a bikini, like a whore, but they wouldn't allow it.'

    I. "He said to them, 'Naked.'

    J. "She said, 'Without a crown?'

    K. "'They will say that she's only a slave-girl.'"

    L. Then why not let her wear her royal garment and come in?

    M. Said R. Huna, "A commoner cannot use royal garments."

While the passage serves Esther in particular, the proposition is suitable without the base verse. The composition therefore is not particular to a commentary on Esther, even though it works well *in situ*. The amplification seizes upon the detail that she is to wear the crown and the framers assume that is all she is to wear. The rest follows.

Esther Rabbah One to Esther 2:20

L:I

1. A. "Now Esther had not made known her kindred or her people, as Mordecai had charged her; [for Esther obeyed Mordecai just as when she was brought up by him]:"

    B. This teaches that she kept silent like Rachel, her ancestor, who kept silent.

    C. All of her great ancestors had kept silent.

    D. Rachel kept silent when she saw her wedding band on the hand of her sister but shut up about it.

    E. Benjamin, her son, kept silent.

    F. You may know that that is so, for the stone that stood for him on the high priest's breastplate was a jasper, indicating that he knew of the sale of Joseph, but he kept silent.

    G. [The word for jasper contains letters that stand for] "there is a mouth," [meaning, he could have told], but he kept silent.

    H. Saul, from whom she descended: "Concerning the matter of the kingdom he did not tell him" (1 Sam. 10:16).

    I. Esther: "Now Esther had not made known her kindred or her people, as Mordecai had charged her."

The effect is to link Esther's conduct to her ancestors, with the upshot that the incident reveals an ongoing law of correct conduct about discretion. Then the proposition is prior to the exegesis of the verse at hand, since, without losing its power, the passage can well serve in a document on proper conduct.

XI. Ruth Rabbah

Ruth Rabbah

III:III

1. A. R. Nehemiah commenced discourse by citing the following verse: "'Your prophets have been like foxes among ruins, O Israel. You have not gone up into the breaches or built up a wall for the house of Israel, that it might stand in battle in the day of the Lord' (Ez. 13:4-5):

    B. "Just as a fox spies out in the ruins for a place to flee when it sees people coming, so 'Your prophets have been like foxes among ruins, O Israel. You have not gone up into the breaches,'

    C. "like Moses.

    D. "To whom may our lord Moses be compared?

    E. "To a faithful shepherd, whose fence collapsed at twilight.

    F. "He went and repaired it on three sides, but a breach remained on the fourth.

    G. "Since he had no time to repair it before dark, he himself stood in the breach.

H.	"Came a lion, and he stood against it.
I.	"Came a wolf, and he stood against it.
J.	"But as for you, 'You have not gone up into the breaches,' like Moses.
K.	"For had you thrust yourselves into the breach like Moses, you would have been able to stand in war on the day of the wrath of the Lord."
L.	[Supply: "And it came to pass in the days when the judges ruled, there was a famine in the land."]

The only way I can make sense of the inclusion in Ruth Rabbah of this entire composition – powerful and well crafted as it is – is by my addition of L at the end. Then the point becomes the failure of the prophets to defend Israel, on account of which, in their watch, the famine came. Otherwise I can see no point in inserting the whole here. And yet the composition without L is quite complete and makes its point with force. It is then a generalized critique of prophecy for its failures, rather than a specific amplification of the situation prevailing in the time of the judges. If so, the preferred location should be in either a compilation on Ezekiel or, more likely, a compilation on the excellence of Moses.

Ruth Rabbah IV:II

[Genesis Rabbah XLII:III.1-6 – Leviticus Rabbah XI:VII]:

1.	A	R. Tanhuma and R. Hiyya the Elder state the following matter, as does R. Berekhiah in the name of R. Eleazar [the Modite], "The following exegetical principle we brought up from the exile.
	B.	"Any passage in which the words, 'And it came to pass' appear is a passage that relates misfortune." [Ruth Rabbah adds here: "R. Hiyya the Elder said, "Where it is said, 'and it came to pass,' it may denote either trouble or rejoicing; if trouble, then unprecedented trouble; if rejoicing, then unprecedented rejoicing."]
	C.	Said R. Samuel bar Nahman, "There are five such passages marked by the words, 'and it came to pass,' that bear the present meaning.
	D.	"'And it came to pass in the days of Amraphel, king of Shinar...these kings made war with Bera, king of Sodom' (Gen. 14:1).
	E.	"The matter [of Abram's defending the local rulers] may be compared to the ally of a king who came to live in a province. On his account the king felt obligated to protect that entire province. Barbarians came and attacked him. Now when the barbarians came and attacked him, the people said, 'Woe, the king is not going to want to protect the province the way he used to [since it has caused him trouble]. That is in line with the following verse of

Scripture, 'And they turned back and came to En Mishpat [source of justice], that is Kadesh [holy] [and subdued all the country of the Amalekites]' (Gen. 14:7)." [This concludes the first of the five illustrations.] [Lev. R. XI:VII.2.E adds: So too, Abraham was the ally of the King, the Holy One, blessed be he, and in his regard it is written, 'And in you shall all the families of the earth be blessed' (Gen. 12:4). So it was on his account that the Holy One, blessed be he, felt obligated to protect the entire world.]

F.   Said R. Aha, "They sought only to attack the orb of the Eye of the world. The eye that had sought to exercise the attribute of justice in the world did they seek to blind: 'That is Kadesh' (Gen. 14:7)."

G.   Said R. Aha, "It is written, 'that is...,' meaning, that is the particular one who has sanctified the name of the Holy One, blessed be he, by going down into the fiery furnace."

H.   [Reverting to the discourse suspended at the end of E:] When the barbarians came and attacked, they began to cry, "Woe, woe!"

I.   "And it came to pass in the days of Amraphel" (Gen. 14:1).

2.   A.   "And it came to pass in the days of Ahaz" (Is. 7:1):

B.   What was the trouble in that case? "The Aramaeans on the east and the Philistines on the west devour Israel with open mouth" (Is. 9:12):

C.   The matter [of Israel's position] may be compared to the case of a king who handed over his son to a tutor, who hated the son. The tutor thought, "If I kill him now, I shall turn out to be liable to the death penalty before the king. So what I'll do is take away his wet-nurse, and he will die on his own."

D.   So thought Ahaz, "If there are no kids, there will be no he-goats. If there are no he-goats, there will be no flock. If there is no flock, there will be no Shepherd, if there is no Shepherd, there will be no world."

E.   So did Ahaz plan, "If there are no children, there will be no adults. If there are no adults, there will be no disciples. If there are no disciples, there will be no sages. If there are no sages, there will be no elders. If there are no elders, there will be no prophets. If there are no prophets, the Holy One, blessed be he, will not allow his presence to come to rest in the world." [Lev. R.: ...Torah. If there is no Torah, there will be no synagogues and schools. If there are no synagogues and schools, then the Holy One, blessed be he, will not allow his presence to come to rest in the world.]

F.   That is in line with the following verse of Scripture: "Bind up the testimony, seal the Torah among my disciples" (Is. 8:16).

G.   R. Huna [Ruth Rabbah: Hanina] in the name of R. Eleazar: "Why was he called Ahaz? Because he seized (ahaz) synagogues and schools."

H.   R. Jacob in the name of R. Aha: "Isaiah said, 'I will wait for the Lord, who is hiding his face from the house of Jacob, and I will hope in him' (Is. 8:17). You have no more trying hour than that moment concerning which it is written, 'And I shall surely hide my face on that day' (Deut. 31:18).

I. "From that hour: 'I will hope in him' (Is. 8:17). For he has said, 'For it will not be forgotten from the mouth of his seed' (Deut. 31:21).

J. "What good did hoping do for Isaiah?

K. "'Behold I and the children whom the Lord has given me are signs and portents in Israel from the Lord of hosts who dwells on Mount Zion' (Is. 8:18). Now were they his children? Were they not his disciples? But this teaches that they were precious to him so that he regarded them as his children."

L. [Reverting to G:] Now since everyone saw that Ahaz had seized the synagogues and schools, they began to cry out, "Woe, woe!" Thus: "And it came to pass [marking the woe] in the days of Ahaz" (Is. 7:1).

3. A. "And it came to pass in the days of Jehoiakim, son of Josiah" (Jer. 1:3).

B. What was the trouble in that case? "I look on the earth and lo, it was waste and void" (Jer. 4:23).

C. The matter may be compared to the case of royal edicts which came into a province. What did the people do? They took the document, tore it up, and burned the bits in fire. That is in line with the following verse of Scripture: "And it came to pass, as Jehudi read three or four columns, that is, three or four verses, the king would cut them off with a penknife and throw them into the fire in the brazier until the entire scroll was consumed in the fire that was in the brazier" (Jer. 36:23).

D. When the people saw all this, they began to cry out, "Woe, woe."

E. "And it came to pass in the days of Jehoiakim" (Jer. 1:3).

4. A. "And it came to pass in the days of Ahasuerus" (Est. 1:1). What was the trouble in that case? "Haman undertook to destroy, to slay, and to annihilate all the Jews, young and old, women and children, in one day" (Est. 3:13).

B. The matter may be compared to the case of a king who had a vineyard, and three of his enemies attacked it. One of them began to clip off the small branches, the next began to take the pendants off the grapeclusters, and the last of them began to uproot the vines altogether.

C. Pharaoh [began by clipping off the small branches]: "Every son that is born will you throw into the river" (Ex. 1:22).

D. Nebuchadnezzar [began to clip off the pendants of the grapeclusters,] deporting the people: "And he carried away captive the craftsmen and smiths, a thousand" (2 Kgs. 24:16).

E. R. Berekhiah in the name of R. Judah and rabbis:

F. R. Berekhiah in the name of R. Judah: "There were a thousand craftsmen and a thousand smiths."

G.   Rabbis say, "This group and that group all together added up to a thousand."

H.   The wicked Haman began to uproot the vines altogether. "To destroy, to slay, and to annihilate all the Jews" (Est. 3:13).

I.   When everybody saw that [Ahasuerus had sold and Haman had bought the Jews], they began to cry, "Woe, woe."

J.   "And it came to pass in the days of Ahasuerus" (Est. 1:1).

5. A.   "And it came to pass in the days in which the judges ruled" (Ruth 1:1). What was the trouble in that case? "There was a famine in the land" (Ruth 1:1).

B.   The matter may be compared to a province which owed taxes in arrears to the king, so the king sent a revenuer to collect. What did the inhabitants of the province do? They went and hung him, hit him, and robbed him. They said, "Woe is us, when the king gets word of these things. What the king's representative wanted to do to us, we have done to him."

C.   So too, woe to the generation that has judged its judges.

D.   "And it came to pass in the days in which the judges themselves were judged" (Ruth 1:1).

6. A.   R. Simeon b. Abba in the name of R. Yohanan: "Any context in which the words, 'And it came to pass...,' appear serves to signify either misfortune or good fortune. If it is a case of misfortune, it is misfortune without parallel. If it is a case of good fortune, it is good fortune without parallel."

B.   R. Samuel b. Nahman came and introduced this distinction: "Any context in which the words, 'And it came to pass...' occur signifies misfortune, and any context in which the words, 'And it shall come to pass...' are used signifies good fortune."

C.   They objected [to this claim], "And God said, 'Let there be light,' and it came to pass that there was light" (Gen. 1:3).

D.   He said to them, "This too does not represent good fortune, for in the end the world did not enjoy the merit of actually making use of that light."

E.   [Gen. R.:] R. Judah [b. R. Simeon] said, "With the light that the Holy One, blessed be he, created on the first day of creation, a person could look and see from one side of the world to the other. When the Holy One, blessed be he, foresaw that there would be wicked people, he hid it away for the [exclusive use of the] righteous. 'But the path of the righteous is as the light of the dawn that shines more and more to the perfect day' (Prov. 4:18)."

F.   They further objected, "And it came to pass that there was evening and morning, one day" (Gen. 1:5).

G.   He said to them, "This too does not signify good fortune. For whatever God created on the first day of creation is destined to be wiped out. That is in line with the following verse of Scripture: 'For the heaven shall vanish away like smoke, and the earth shall wax old like a garment' (Is. 51:6)."

H. They further objected, "And it came to pass that there was evening and it came to pass that there was morning, a second day..., a third day..., a fourth day..., a fifth day..., a sixth day..." (Gen. 1:8, 13, 19, 23, 31).

I. He said to them, "This too does not signify good fortune. For everything which God created on the six days of creation was incomplete and would require further processing. Wheat has to be milled, mustard to be sweetened, [lupine to impart sweetness]."

J. They further objected, "And it came to pass that the Lord was with Joseph, and Joseph was a prosperous man" (Gen. 39:2).

K. He said to them, "This too does not signify good fortune, for on this account that she-bear [Potiphar's wife] came his way."

L. [Gen. R.:] They further objected, "And it came to pass on the eighth day that Moses called Aaron and his sons for consecration in the priesthood" (Lev. 9:1).

M. He said to them, "This too does not signify good fortune, for on that same day Nadab and Abihu died."

N. They further objected, "And it came to pass on the day on which Moses made an end of setting up the tabernacle" (Num. 7:1).

O. He said to them, "This too does not signify good fortune. For on the day on which the Temple was built, the tabernacle was hidden away. Thus: 'And Moses was not able to enter into the tent of meeting' (Ex. 40:35)."

P. They further objected, "And it came to pass that the Lord was with Joshua and his fame was in all the land" (Joshua 6:27).

Q. He said to them, "This too does not signify good fortune, for he still had to tear his garments [on account of the defeat at Ai, Joshua 7:6]."

R. They further objected, "And it came to pass that the king dwelt in his palace, and the Lord gave him rest round about" (2 Sam. 7:1).

S. He said to them, "This too does not signify good fortune. On that very day Nathan the prophet came to him and said, 'You will not build the house' (1 Kgs. 8:19)."

T. They said to him, "We have given our objections, now you give your proofs about good fortune."

U. He said to them, "'And it shall come to pass in that day that living waters shall go out of Jerusalem' (Zech. 14:8). 'And it shall come to pass in that day that a great horn shall be blown' (Is. 27:13). 'And it shall come to pass in that day that a man shall rear a youngling' (Is. 7:21). 'And it shall come to pass in that day that the Lord will set his hand again a second time to recover the remnant of his people' (Is. 11:11). 'And it shall come to pass in that day that the mountains shall drop down sweet wine' (Joel 4:18). [All of these represent good fortune without parallel.]"

V.   They said to him, "'And it shall come to pass on the day on which Jerusalem is taken...' (Jer. 38:28)."

W.   He said to them, "This too does not signify misfortune but good fortune [without parallel], for on that day the Israelites received a full pardon for all their sins.

X.   [Gen. R.:] "That is in line with what R. Samuel b. Nahman said, 'The Israelites received a full pardon for all their sins on the day on which the Temple was destroyed. That is in line with the following verse of Scripture, "The punishment of your iniquity is completed, daughter of Zion, and he will no more take you away into exile" (Lam. 4:22).'"

The fact that this passage serves three documents quite well alerts us to the indicative traits: it fits no document in particular; it is in fact focused on an issue, not on a document, and it makes a philological point, not an exegetical one particular to a given setting or even a given usage of a word. On that basis I point to the composition as a wonderful example of writing for a documentary purpose other than one now realized by a compilation in our hands. I reproduce the version of Genesis Rabbah XLII:III.1-6, noting differences from the other versions. This passage has not been composed to serve any of the documents in which it is included; that is shown by the simple fact that the several base verses are subordinated to the common proposition. Therefore the whole has been compiled to prove the syllogism at hand, and, it must follow, the person who brought together the various pieces had in mind a document in which syllogistic, rather than exegetical, propositions would prevail – a work in this case of both philology and theology. The philological point is clearly stated; the theological one is equally self-evident. The fundamental syllogism, not stated at all, is that Israel's history follows rules that can be learned in Scripture. Nothing is random, all thing connected, and fundamental laws of history dictate the sense and meaning of what happens. These laws are stated in the very language of Scripture. The long discussion obviously is constructed independent of any of the verses used as prooftexts. It serves equally well in any number of contexts, not only here but also at Gen. R. XLII:III and Lev. R. XI:VII, as indicated. The differences in the versions of Gen. R. and Lev. R. are minor and signify nothing of consequence. The fact that our compilation's interests predominate is shown by the placing of our base verse at a subordinate position, No. 5. No. 5 clearly forms the climax, but that is only for the reason of the positioning of the pertinent entry. In fact, as is clear, the whole serves no document we now have, but a document we can imagine, a philological treatise. No. 6 then proceeds in its own direction. Clearly, the version of Gen. R. concludes with an invitation to place the whole in Lam. R. for Lam. 4:22. That none of this serves as a petihta for Ruth Rabbah hardly requires demonstration.

Ruth Rabbah VI:I

1. A.   R. Simon in the name of R. Joshua b. Levi and R. Hama, father of R. Joshua, in the name of Rabbi: "The purpose of the book of Chronicles is only for interpretation [and not for a literal reading, as we shall now see in the following verse [which will be read not literally but as an account of the encounter of the spies and Rahab, leading to the priest-prophets of Israel]:

   B.   "'The sons of Shelah son of Judah: Er father of Lecah, [Laadah father of Mareshah, and the families of the linen factory at Beth-ashbea; and Jokim, and the men of Cozeba and Joash, and Saraph, who married into Moab and Jashubi Lehem (the records are ancient). These are the potters who dwelt at Netaim and Gederah; they dwelt there in the king's service]' (1 Chr. 4:21-23).

   C.   "'father of Lecah:' head of the court of Lecah.

   D.   "'Laadah father of Mareshah:' head of the court of Mareshah.

   E.   "'and the families of the linen factory:' this speaks of Rahab the whore, who hid the spies in linen: 'And she hid them with stalks of flax' (Josh. 2:6)."

   F.   Said R. Judah b. Simon, "Her occupation was in perfumes."

   G.   [Resuming E:] "'at Beth-ashbea:' For she imposed on the spies an oath [a word that uses the same consonants as the word ashbea]: 'Now therefore I pray you swear to me by the Lord' (Josh. 2:12).

   H.   "'and Jokim:' and they carried out the oath for her [the words Jokim and carried out share the same consonants]: 'And the young men, the spies, went in and brought out Rahab [and all her families they also brought out]' (Josh. 6:23)."

   I.   What is the meaning of the phrase, "and all her families they also brought out"?

   J.   R. Simeon b. Yohai taught, "Even if her family were two hundred men and they went and joined two hundred other families, all of them were delivered on account of her merit.

   K.   "What Scripture says is not, 'all her family,' but 'all her families.'"

   L.   [Resuming H:] "'and the men of Cozeba:' for she deceived [the word for deceive and Cozeba sharing the same consonants] the king of Jericho: 'Yes, the men came to me' (Josh. 2:4).

   M.   "'and Joash:' for she despaired of life [the words for despair and Joash sharing the same consonants].

   N.   "'and Saraph:' for she prepared to be burned to death.

   O.   "'who married into Moab:' for she came and joined Israel, and her deeds went up to her father in heaven.

P.	"'and Jashubi Lehem:' she cleaved to Israel, who had accepted the Torah in which it is written, 'against them who fight against me' (Ps. 34:1). [The words for lehem and fight share the same consonants.]"
Q.	"the records are ancient:"
R.	R. Aibu and R. Judah b. R. Simon say, "These words are incomprehensible here but are spelled out elsewhere."
S.	[Reverting to P:] "'These are the potters:' these are the spies: 'And Joshua son of Nun sent out of Shittim two spies secretly saying' (Josh. 2:1) [and the words for secretly and potters share the same consonants]."
T.	R. Judah and R. Nehemiah:
U.	One said, "They had carpenters' tools in hand, since it says, 'spies, saying, "we are carpenters"' [the words for secretly and carpenters share the same consonants]."
V.	The other said, "They had pots in hand, pretending to be potters: 'saying, "we are potters."'"
W.	Taught R. Simeon b. Yohai, "The word 'secretly' is meant literally. Said to them [Joshua], 'Act dumb [using the consonants for the word secretly], and you will master all their secrets.'"
X.	R. Simeon b. Eleazar says, "'If you act dumb, you will master their affairs.'"
Y.	"'who dwelt at Netaim and Gederah' [plantations and hedges]:' they were experts in planting: 'And they cut down from thence a branch' (Num. 13:23).
Z.	"'and hedges:' for she hid them behind a hedge and said to them, 'Go up into the mountain' (Josh. 2:17)."
AA.	Some say, "The Holy Spirit rested upon her before the Israelites came into the land.
BB.	"For how did she know that they would return in three days? Thus the Holy Spirit rested upon her before the Israelites came into the land."
CC.	"they dwelt there in the king's service:"
DD.	In connection with this verse they have said, "Ten priest-prophets descended from Rahab the whore: Jeremiah, Hilkiah, Seraiah, Mahasyah, Hanameel, Shallum, Baruch, Neriah, Ezekial, and Buzzi."
EE.	Some add, "Huldah the prophetess also descended from Rahab the whore."
2 A.	R. Samuel b. Nahman interpreted the passage to speak of David:
B.	"'The sons of Shelah son of Judah: Er father of Lecah, [Laadah father of Mareshah, and the families of the linen factory at Beth-ashbea; and Jokim, and the men of Cozeba and Joash, and Saraph, who married into Moab and Jashubi Lehem (the records are ancient). These are the potters who dwelt at Netaim and Gederah; they dwelt there in the king's service]' (1 Chr. 4:21-23).

C.   "'father of Lecah:' head of the court of Lecah.

D.   "'Laadah father of Mareshah:' head of the court of Mareshah.

E.   "'and the families of the linen factory:' this speaks of David, who took care of the curtain [of the ark (2 Sam. 6)]."

F.   "That is in line with the following verse: 'And Elhanan, son of Jaare-oregim the Bethlehemite, killed Goliath' (2 Sam. 21:19).

G.   "'Elhanan:' this refers to David, to whom God showed grace [using letters that occur in the name Elhanan].

H.   "'son of Jaare:' the son who grew up in a forest [which uses the consonants of the name Jaare].

I.   "'oregim:' [since the word means weavers,] it is because he wove the curtain."

J.   Another reading of "oregim:" they brought problems of law to him and he wove them together.

K.   Another interpretation of "oregim:" it refers to the Sanhedrin, who would weave with him in teachings of the Torah.

L.   [Reverting now to E:] "'at Beth-ashbea:' since the Holy One, blessed be he, took an oath to him: 'I have made a covenant with my chosen one' (Ps. 89:4).

M.   "'and Jokim:' since he kept the oath: 'The Lord swore to David in truth; he will not renege' (Ps. 132:11)."

N.   "and the men of Cozeba:"

O.   R. Azariah and R. Jonathan and R. Isaac Bar Merion, and some say in the name of R. Yosé b. R. Hanina: "The principal part of the Sanhedrin was from Judah.

P.   "What proof from Scripture? 'His eyes shall be red with wine and his teeth white with milk' (Gen. 49:12).

Q.   "[That verse refers to the sanhedrin, which] set forth the law with [the sharpness of] teeth, so that it came out as pure as milk."

R.   [Reverting to M:] "'Joash:' he despaired of life [the words for despair and Joash sharing the same consonants]: 'Let your hand, I pray you, O Lord be against me' (1 Chr. 21:17).

S.   "'and Saraph:' for he called to mind the deed of those who were to be burned to death: 'O Lord, the god of Abraham, of Isaac, and of Israel, our fathers' (1 Chr. 29:18).

T.   "'who married into Moab:' who came from Ruth the Moabite.

U.   "'and Jashubi Lehem:' who came from Beth Lehem in Judah."

V.   "the records are ancient:"

W.   R. Aibu said, "This refers to David and Solomon, who were joined before the Holy One, blessed be he, in building the temple."

X.   R. Judah bar Simon said, "This speaks of Benaiah, son of Jehoiada, who joined efforts with King Solomon in building the temple."

Y.   R. Judah said, "This refers to Jehoiada, high priest, who joined together with Joash in repairing the temple."

Z.   R. Nehemiah said, "This speaks of Jeremiah and Ezekiel, who prayed before the Holy One, blessed be he, not to destroy the temple."

AA.   [Reverting to U:] "'These are the potters:' this refers to Ruth and Boaz [reading 'potter' as 'creator,' which shares the same consonants].

BB.   "'who dwelt at Netaim and Gederah [plantations and hedges]:' plantations refers to Solomon, who in his monarchy was like a planting.

CC.   "'hedges:' this speaks of the Sanhedrin, who hedged him with teachings of the Torah."

DD.   "they dwelt there in the king's service:"

EE.   on this basis they said, "Ruth the Moabite did not die before she saw Solomon, son of her son, in session and trying the case involving the whores.

FF.   "That is in line with this verse: 'And caused a throne to be set for the king's mother' (1 Kgs. 2:19) – Bath Sheba.

GG.   "'And she sat at his right hand' (1 Kgs. 2:19) – that is Ruth the Moabitess."

3. A. R. Menahem b. Abin interpreted the verse to speak of Moses:

B.   "'[The sons of Shelah son of Judah: Er father of Lecah, [Laadah father of Mareshah, and the families of the linen factory at Beth-ashbea;] and Jokim, [and the men of Cozeba and Joash, and Saraph, who married into Moab and Jashubi Lehem (the records are ancient). These are the potters who dwelt at Netaim and Gederah; they dwelt there in the king's service]' (1 Chr. 4:21-23):

C.   "'and Jokim: 'in line with the verse, 'Rise up, O Lord, and let your enemies be scattered' (Num. 10:35). [The word for 'rise up' uses the letters that serve Jokim.]

D.   "'and the men of Cozeba:' for he belied the word of the Holy One, blessed be he: 'Lord, why do you lose your temple against your people' (Ex. 32:11).

E.   "'and Joash:' since he despaired for his life: 'And if not, blot me, I pray you, out of your book which you have written' (Ex. 32:32).

F.   "'and Saraph:' for he called to mind the deed of those who were to be burned to death: 'Remember Abraham, Isaac, and Israel your servants' (Ex. 32:13).

G.   "'who married into Moab:' whose pleasant deeds came and went up before his father in heaven.

H.   "'and Jashubi Lehem:' who ascended on high and captured the Torah: 'You have ascended on high, you have led an exile into captivity' (Ps. 68:19). [The word for 'capture' and Jashubi use the same letters.]

I.   "the records are ancient:"

J.   R. Aibu and R. Judah b. R. Simon and R. Aibu said, "Even matters that had been taken away from them he restored to them: 'Hew two tables of stone' (Ex. 34:1).

K.   "These words were stated concerning the one who move the world: 'And he removed from them' (Gen. 12:8)."

L.   [Supply: "the records are ancient:"]

M.   R. Judah b. R. Simon said, "These words are incomprehensible here but are spelled out in another passage: 'And the Lord said to Moses, write these words, after the manner of the words' (Ex. 34:27)."

N.   "These are the potters:" in line with this verse: "And the Lord formed man" (Gen. 2:7) [since the word for potter and form use the same consonants].

O.   Another reading of "These are the potters:" these are the souls of the righteous, with whom the Holy One, blessed be he, took counsel in creating the world.

P.   "who dwelt at Netaim and Gederah [plants and hedges]:"

Q.   "plants:" in line with this verse: "And the Lord God planted a garden" (Gen. 2:8).

R.   "and hedges:" in line with the following verse: "who have placed the sand for the margin of the sea" (Jer. 5:22).

S.   "they dwelt there in the king's service:" With the King of kings of kings, the Holy One, blessed be he, dwelt the souls of the righteous, with whom he took counsel in creating the world.

4. A.   Another interpretation of "and Jokim:"

B.   this refers to Elimelech.

C.   "and the men of Cozeba:" this speaks of his sons, who were lost [the words for lost and Cozeba use the same consonants].

D.   "and Joash:" they despaired of the land of Israel.

E.   "and Saraph:" they burned the Torah.

F.   R. Menahema in the name of R. Aha: "Did they really burn it? But this serves to teach you that whoever abandons the Torah even in a single matter is as though he had burned it."

G.   "who married into Moab:" they married Moabite women and left [the people of] Israel and joined in the fields of Moab.

H.   "and Jashubi Lehem:" this refers to Naomi: "So Naomi returned, and Ruth the Moabitess her daughter-in-law with her, who returned out of the field of Moab; they came to Bethlehem" (Ruth 1:22).

I.   "the records are ancient:" each of these matters has already been spelled out on its own.

VI:II

1. A.   "The name of the man was Elimelech:"

B.   R. Meir would interpret the meaning of names.

C.   R. Joshua b. Qorhah would interpret the meaning of names.

	D.	"The name of the man was Elimelech:" For he would say, "To me the throne is coming [through David]."
	E.	"and the name of his wife Naomi:" for her actions were all lovely and pleasant.
	F.	"and the names of his two sons were Mahlon and Chilion:"
	G.	"Mahlon:" for they were blotted out from the world [blot out and Manlon use the same consonants].
	H.	"Chilion:" they perished from the world [perish and Chilion use the same letters].
2.	A.	"they were Ephrathites from Bethlehem in Judah:"
	B.	R. Joshua b. Levi says, "Courtiers."
	C.	Rabbi b. R. Nehemiah says, "Aristocrats."
3.	A.	Another interpretation of the name, "Ephrathites:"
	B.	R. Phineas said, "[They held] the entire crown that Ephraim was given by our father, Jacob, when he was dying.
	C.	"He said to him, 'Ephraim, head of the tribe, head of the session, the best and most praiseworthy of my sons will be called by your name.'
	D.	"Thus: 'The son of Tohu, son of Zuph, an Ephraimite' (1 Sam. 1:1); 'And Jeroboam, son of Nebat, an Ephraimite' (1 Kgs. 11:26); 'Now David was the son of an Ephrathite' (1 Sam. 17:12); 'his two sons were Mahlon and Chilion; they were Ephrathites.'"
4.	A.	"They went into the country of Moab and remained there:"
	B.	To begin with, they came to the towns and found them unrestrained in transgression.
	C.	Then they went into the cities and found them short of water.
	D.	So they went back to the towns: "They went into the country of Moab and remained there."

We have a form entirely unlike the intersecting-verse/base-verse construction, since there is no interest whatsoever in reverting to the base verse constituted by Ruth 1:2. The outside verse (now not an intersecting verse, there being nothing with which to intersect) is given a variety of interpretations, one of which involves the theme at hand, namely, Elimelech. But the other readings – Joshua, Moses, David, then Ruth – scarcely demand our consideration of what is of special interest to the compilers of Ruth Rabbah. That seems to me to point to the simple conclusion that the composition has been made up without consideration of the needs of Ruth Rabbah. It then has been taken and inserted whole and complete because, as a matter of fact, it serves those needs quite admirably.

Then what sort of compilation can have been in mind? The obvious answer is, a study of Chronicles – just as is announced at the very outset. But since (out of antiquity) we have no midrash compilation composed with reference to that book, we have to conclude that the authorship that has given us the entire set worked independently of projects in the compilation of midrash exegeses of their own age; or that there was such a project involving Chronicles that did not survive. One might wish to argue that the underlying theme was the acquisition of the land, and that would account for Joshua/the spies and Elimelech. But, as a matter of fact, that theme, while present, hardly predominates and surely cannot explain the massive intrusion of Moses, for one figure, or much that is said about David.

So the purpose of the individual units, which match, has fully carried out the program of the compilers of all four units; but the purpose of the compilers of Ruth Rabbah never intruded in the planning of the authors of the individual passages, Nos. 1-4, or of the compilers of the whole into a single, sustained exercise. Here again we must conclude, I think, that a labor of writing for purposes other than those of producing any of the documents we now have in hand was well underway; and, it goes without saying, the conglomeration of Nos. 1-4, so neatly matched and successful aesthetically, likewise followed a plan for the formation of a document other than any we now can see. But, in the nature of things, we can easily imagine the shape and structure of such a document: Chronicles Rabbah, so to speak. The main indicator that what we have does not serve Ruth Rabbah, then, is that that document's interest is not primary or generative and does not hold together the rather complex and rich presentation at hand.

To show the contrast between this type of composition – for a book we do not have – and writing for a book we do have, which is, a commentary on the book of Ruth in particular, I include the second half of the treatment of the same base verse, which, of course, is now the only verse under discussion. The phrase-by-phrase amplification accomplishes the anticipated task of explaining the deeper meaning of the names. But that is precisely what dominated in the treatment of the passage from Chronicles as well. So the ultimate framers of the whole have given us a somewhat tighter composition than on the face of matters would appear to be the case.

Ruth Rabbah to Ruth 1:3
VII:I

1. A "But Elimelech, the husband of Naomi, died, and she was left with her two sons:"
   B. It has been taught on Tannaite authority:
   C. Everyone is destined for death, and all are going to die.
   D. But happy is the person who leaves this world with a good name.
2. A When a man dies, who feels the loss but his wife: "But Elimelech, the husband of Naomi, died"?

B.   When a woman dies, who feels the loss but her husband: "And as for me, when I came from Paddan, Rachel died to me" (Gen. 48:7).

3. A.   [Supply: "And as for me, when I came from Paddan, Rachel died to me" (Gen. 48:7).]

B.   Said R. Yohanan, "'The death of Rachel is upon me.'

C.   "Said our father, Jacob, 'The death of Rachel is heavier for me to bear than all of the troubles that have come upon me.'"

4. A.   Said R. Yohanan in the name of R. Simeon b. Yehosedeq, "Cohorts in numbers, fellowships in numbers, does the Holy One, blessed be he, bring to the world.

B.   "If one of the members of a cohort dies, let the whole cohort worry, if one associate of the association dies, let the whole association worry."

C.   For R. Samuel b. Abba in the name of R. Yohanan said, "There are specified terms of office, and one of the holders does not enter into the term of office of his fellow by even a hair's breadth."

5. A.   Said R. Yosé b. Halafta, "In my whole life I never called my wife 'my wife,' or my house, 'my house,' but I called my wife 'my house,' and my house 'my wife.'

B.   "Nor did I call my ox 'my ox,' or my field 'my field,' but I called my ox 'my field,' and my field 'my ox.' [Rabinowitz, p. 30, n. 3: "The idea is that the interchangeability of terms shows their close association. The wife is the spirit of the home; the field is useless without the ox."]

6. A.   "and she was left with her two sons:"

B.   Said R. Hanina son of R. Abbahu, "She was equivalent to the residue of meal-offerings."

Nos. 1-5 form an essay on the general theme of death, and the base verse, Ruth 1:3, plays only a subordinated role as a prooftext for the established theme, which is well set forth. The theme is not formed into a proposition; No. 2 makes a point about the same subject as No. 1, but No. 2 has nothing in common with No. 1 except for the topic. So the passage before us serves neither a compilation devoted to the book of Ruth nor a tractate on the good name, on the one side, or death, on the other. But thematic treatises are surely within the range of imaginable compilations. No. 3 complements No. 2. The reason for the inclusion of No. 4 is not because it continues Nos. 2 or 3, but only because it pertains to the general subject. Rabinowitz's explanation for the intrusion of No. 5 is as good as any; but without it, no one would have imagined any sound reason for tacking on such an obviously irrelevant point; if I had to choose a reason, it would be because of No. 2, not No. 4; that is, the importance of the wife, 5.A; 5.B is then irrelevant. No. 6 is the only point pertinent to a sustained amplification of the book of Ruth.

7

Pericopes Framed for Purposes
Not Particular to a Type of
Document Now in Our Hands

I. Free-standing Pericopes Framed Not for Documentary Purposes That Are Now to be Discerned or without Regard to Documentary Requirements at All

As indicated in Chapter One, we turn to free-standing pericopes framed not for documentary purposes that are now to be discerned or without regard to documentary requirements at all. This chapter sets forth examples of this kind of writing in the classics of Judaism in the fourth classification. This kind of writing can have gone on at any time, from the beginning to the end of the sedimentary process that yielded the entire canon and that also omitted from the canon writings of other types than those we now have. To review the definitions offered in the Chapter One:

Some writings stand autonomous of any redactional program we have in an existing compilation or of any we can even imagine on the foundations of said writings.

Compositions of this kind, as a matter of hypothesis, are to be assigned to a stage in the formation of classics prior to the framing of all available documents. For, as a matter of fact, all of our now extant writings adhere to a single program of conglomeration and agglutination, and all are served by composites of one sort, rather than some other. Hence we may suppose that at some point prior to the decision to make writings in the model that we now have but in some other model people also made up completed units of thought to serve these other kinds of writings. These persist, now, in documents that they do not serve at all well. And we can fairly easily identify the kinds of documents that they can and should have served quite nicely indeed. These, then, are the three stages of literary formation in the making of the classics of Judaism.

Of the relative temporal or ordinal position of writings that stand autonomous of any redactional program we have in an existing compilation or of any we can even imagine on the foundations of said writings we can say nothing. These writings prove episodic; they are commonly singletons. They serve equally well everywhere, because they demand no traits of form and redaction in order to endow them with sense and meaning. Why not? Because they are essentially free-standing and episodic, not referential and allusive. They are stories that contain their own point and do not invoke, in the making of that point, a given verse of Scripture. They are sayings that are utterly ad hoc. A variety of materials fall into this – from a redactional perspective – unassigned, and unassignable, type of writing. They do not belong in books at all. By that I mean, whoever made up these pieces of writing did not imagine that what he was forming required a setting beyond the limits of his own piece of writing; the story is not only complete in itself but could stand entirely on its own; the saying spoke for itself and required no nurturing context; the proposition and its associated proofs in no way was meant to draw nourishment from roots penetrating nutriments outside of its own literary limits.

Where we have utterly hermetic writing, able to define its own limits and sustain its point without regard to anything outside itself, we know that here we are in the presence of authorships that had no larger redactional plan in mind, no intent on the making of books out of their little pieces of writing.

We may note that, among the "unimaginable" compilations is not a collection of parables, since parables never stand free and never are inserted for their own sake. Whenever in the rabbinic canon we find a parable, it is meant to serve the purpose of an authorship engaged in making its own point; and the point of a parable is rarely, if ever, left unarticulated. Normally it is put into words, but occasionally the point is made simply by redactional setting. It must follow that, in this canon, the parable cannot have constituted the generative or agglutinative principle of a large-scale compilation. It further follows, so it seems to me, that the parable always takes shape within the framework of a work of composition for the purpose of either a large-scale exposition or, more commonly still, of compilation of a set of expositions into what we should now call the chapter of a book; that is to say, parables link to purposes that transcend the tale that they tell (or even the point that the tale makes). On this basis I exclude from the present catalogue parables of all kinds; none of them is free-standing; none fails to find a place for itself in accord with the purposes of compilers either of documents we now have in hand or of documents we can readily envisage or imagine.

II. Mekhilta

Mekhilta Shabbata Two
LXXXII:I

1. A   "Moses assembled [all the congregation of the people of Israel and said to them, 'These are the things which the Lord has commanded you to do. Six days shall work be done, but on the seventh day you shall have a holy Sabbath of solemn rest to the Lord; whoever does any work on it shall be put to death; you shall kindle no fire in all your habitations on the Sabbath day]:'"

   B.   Why is this passage stated?

   C.   Because Scripture says, "And let them make me a sanctuary" (Ex. 25:10),

   D.   I might infer that this may be both on a week day and on the Sabbath.

   E.   How then shall I interpret the verse, "Those who profane it shall surely be put to death"?

   F.   That pertains to all other acts of labor, except for acts of labor in connection with the sanctuary.

   G.   Perhaps involved are also acts of labor in connection with the sanctuary?

   H.   Then how shall I interpret the statement, "And let them make me a sanctuary" (Ex. 25:10)?

   I.   That applies on all days other than the Sabbath.

   J.   Or might it also encompass the Sabbath?

   K.   The following argument from classification will serve:

   L.   if the temple act of divine service, which is brought about only through the effort of preparations, lo, nonetheless overrides the restrictions of the Sabbath, preparations for the liturgy, out of which alone the temple act of divine service is carried on, surely should override the restrictions of the Sabbath!

   M.   For instance, if the horn of the altar was removed, or the knife was damaged, it would then be permissible to repair them on the Sabbath.

   N.   But Scripture states, "Moses assembled [all the congregation of the people of Israel and said to them, 'These are the things which the Lord has commanded you to do. Six days shall work be done, but on the seventh day you shall have a holy Sabbath of solemn rest to the Lord]."

   O.   That is to say, such work as is just now specified is done on a weekday but not on the Sabbath.

2. A.   "Six days shall work be done:"

    B.   One verse of Scripture says, "Six days shall work be done," while another verse states, "Six days shall you labor and do all your work" (Ex. 20:9).

    C.   How are the two passages to be harmonized?

    D.   When the Israelites do what the Omnipresent wants, "in six days work will be done," in that their work will be done by others, and so Scripture says, "And strangers shall stand and feed your flocks, aliens shall be your plowmen and your vinedressers" (Is. 61:5).

    E.   But when the Israelites do not do what the Omnipresent wants, then "Six days shall you labor and do all your work" Ex. 20:9), in that their work will be done by themselves, and not only so, but even the work of others will be done by them,

    F.   for it is said, "You shall serve your enemy" (Dt. 28:48).

3. A.   "but on the seventh day you shall have a holy Sabbath of solemn rest to the Lord:"

    B.   The Israelites should not say, "Since these acts of labor are permitted in work in the house of the sanctuary, we should be permitted to do these same acts of labor in the provinces."

    C.   Scripture therefore says, "but on the seventh day you shall have a holy Sabbath of solemn rest to the Lord:"

    D.   What is holy for you, but for the Omnipresent it is as if an ordinary day.

4. A.   "whoever does any work on it shall be put to death:"

    B.   "on it" but not on the day alongside.

    C.   Lo, should the Day of Atonement coincide with a Friday and one performed an act of labor at dusk, might I infer that on that account [doing labor on the space of time between the two distinct holy days], one should be liable?

    D.   Scripture states, "whoever does any work on it shall be put to death:"

    E.   "on it" but not on the day alongside.

5. A.   "you shall kindle no fire in all your habitations on the Sabbath day:"

    B.   Since Scripture says, "in plowing time and in harvest you shall rest" (Ex. 34:21),

    C.   one is to refrain from ploughing in harvest time, thus one is not to plow in the sixth year for a crop to grow in the Sabbatical Year.

    D.   I know only that one is to refrain from work in the sixth year that benefits the crop of the seventh year, [i.e., not to plow in the sixth year for a crop to grow in the Sabbatical Year]. Might one suppose that one also is to rest on Friday in connection with work that is done for the Sabbath [in the same way]?

    E.   The following argument on the basis of classification suggests so:

    F.   since the Sabbatical Year is observed for the sake of the Name [of God], and the Sabbath is observed for the Name [of God], if you have derived the rule that one is to refrain from work in the sixth year that benefits the crop of the seventh year, so too one also is to rest on Friday in connection with work that is done for the Sabbath.

G.   And there is yet an argument *a fortiori:*

H.   if as to the observance of the restrictions of the Sabbatical Year, on account of the violation of which one does not incur the penalty of either extirpation or death at the hands of an earthly court, lo, one is to refrain from work in the sixth year that benefits the crop of the seventh year, in regard to the Sabbath itself, in connection with the violation of the laws of which one does incur extirpation or death at the hands of an earthly court, one surely should rest on Friday in connection with work that is done for the Sabbath.

I.   [For example], one should not have the right to kindle a lot for oneself or to keep food warm or to make a fire [on Friday for the Sabbath].

J.   Accordingly, Scripture says, "you shall kindle no fire in all your habitations on the Sabbath day:"

K.   on the Sabbath day you are not to kindle a flame, but you may kindle a flame on Friday for the benefit of the Sabbath.

6. A   Another interpretation of the verse, "you shall kindle no fire in all your habitations on the Sabbath day:"

B.   Since Scripture says, "Fire shall be kept burning on the altar continually" (Lev. 6:6), might I infer that that is both on the weekdays and on the Sabbath?

C.   Then how shall I interpret the verse, "Everyone who profanes it shall surely be put to death" (Ex. 31:14)?

D.   That applies to other acts of labor, except for arranging the altar fires.

E.   But how am I to interpret, "it shall not go out" (Lev. 6:6)?

F.   That pertains to all other days than the Sabbath. [This is an absurd result.]

G.   Accordingly, Scripture says, "you shall kindle no fire in all your habitations on the Sabbath day:"

H.   in your habitations you shall kindle no fire, but you shall kindle fire in the house of the sanctuary.

7. A   Said one of the disciples of R. Ishmael, "Behold, Scripture says, 'you shall kindle no fire in all your habitations on the Sabbath day.'

B.   "Why is this stated? Because Scripture further says, 'And if a man has committed a sin worthy of death' (Dt. 21:22-23), might I infer that the penalty is to be carried out both on weekdays and on the Sabbath?

C.   "Then how shall I apply the rule, 'Everyone who profanes it shall surely be put to death' (Ex. 31:14)?

D.   "That applies to all other forms of the death penalty except for that imposed by the court.

E.   "Or perhaps even the death penalty inflicted by a court is covered as well?

F.   "Then how am I to interpret the verse, 'and you shall hang him on a tree' (Dt. 21:23)?

G.   "That refers to all days except the Sabbath. Perhaps it involves even on the Sabbath?

H.   "Scripture says, 'you shall kindle no fire in all your habitations on the Sabbath day,'

I.   "and that statement allows for the following argument:

J.   "burning was covered by the encompassing rule [against performing labor on the Sabbath] but was singled out to provide the following proposition:

K.   "if burning, which constitutes one of the forms of the death penalty inflicted by a court, does not override the restrictions of the Sabbath, then all other forms of the death penalty likewise should not override the restrictions of the Sabbath."

8. A.   R. Jonathan says, "'you shall kindle no fire in all your habitations on the Sabbath day:'

B.   "Why is this statement made?

C.   "Since Scripture says, 'Moses assembled [all the congregation of the people of Israel and said to them, 'These are the things which the Lord has commanded you to do. Six days shall work be done, but on the seventh day you shall have a holy Sabbath of solemn rest to the Lord; whoever does any work on it shall be put to death; you shall kindle no fire in all your habitations on the Sabbath day],'''

D.   "might I infer that one is liable only if he carries out all thirty-nine prohibited acts of labor?

E.   "Scripture says, 'in plowing time and in harvest you shall rest' (Ex. 34:21).

F.   "Still, I might propose that one is culpable only if he violates the prohibitions against those two acts of work, and if he does not do so, he is not liable.

G.   "Accordingly, Scripture says, 'you shall kindle no fire in all your habitations on the Sabbath day:'

H.   "and you reason as follows:

I.   "burning was covered by the encompassing rule [against performing labor on the Sabbath] but was singled out to provide the following proposition:

J.   "the indicative trait of burning is that it constitutes only one of the thirty-nine generative acts of labor, and yet one is liable for performing that prohibited act of labor on its own,

K.   "so as to all the rest of the thirty-nine generative acts of labor, one is liable for performing each prohibited act of labor on its own."

9. A R. Nathan says, "'you shall kindle no fire in all your habitations on the Sabbath day:'

B. "Why is this verse stated?

C. "Since Scripture says, 'Moses assembled [all the congregation of the people of Israel and said to them, 'These are the things which the Lord has commanded you to do. Six days shall work be done, but on the seventh day you shall have a holy Sabbath of solemn rest to the Lord; whoever does any work on it shall be put to death],'"

D. "might I infer that one should not have the right to light a kindle or to keep food warm or to make a fire [on Friday for use on the Sabbath]?

E. Scripture says, 'you shall kindle no fire in all your habitations on the Sabbath day,'

F. "meaning, on the Sabbath day you are not permitted to kindle a flame, but you are permitted to kindle a flame on the festival day."

The reason I see this piece of writing as not readily located within an existing type of compilation becomes clear only at the end. Let us first review what is before us. The base verse covers a variety of problems, but I see no clear order that dictates to the compilers the sequence of types of problems. No. 1 brings together two conflicting verses, one on the Sabbath, the other on the sanctuary and distinguishes work done in the sanctuary, which is permitted, from work done elsewhere, which is prohibited. No. 2 introduces yet another parallel verse, now seeing a contradiction in the formulation of "work is to be done" as against "do all your work." The passive applies when Israel is in good grace with the Lord, the active when not. No. 3 reverts to the proposition of No. 1. No. 4 has its own problem, the relationship of the sanctity of the Day of Atonement to that of the Sabbath. No. 5 produces yet another distinct problem, now the analogy between the sixth and seventh years of the Sabbatical cycle and the sixth and seventh days of the week. There is none. The upshot is to show the weakness of argument by classification and analogy. Scripture disposes of the proposition. No. 6 reverts to the issue of Nos. 1, 3. The problem of No. 7 is parallel, but the proposition is now other; that proposition will have surprised the authorities who composed the argument that the death penalty indeed may be inflicted on the Sabbath. Nos. 8, 9 form parallel exegeses, but each has its own proposition. This is yet one more mélange of topically-related but propositionally-discrete entries. What makes the composite as a whole difficult to classify, therefore to assign to a given compilation, is the mixture of types of writing: propositional and exegetical;

expository and episodic; so too is the mixture of propositions, which seem to me unrelated. The whole as we have it does not exhibit that kind of consistency that would dictate assigning the passage to one kind of document rather than some other, and on that basis I find here an example of writing beyond existing classes of compilations.

III. Sifra

The issue of the relationship between the Mishnah and Scripture deeply engaged a variety of writers and compilers of documents. Time and again we have evidence of an interest in the scriptural sources of laws, or of greater consequence in the priority of Scripture in taxonomic inquiry. We can show large-scale compositions that will readily have served treatises on these matters. But if I had to point to a single type of writing that is quite commonplace in the compilations we do have, but wholly outside of the repertoire of redactional possibilities we have or can imagine, it must be a sustained piece of writing on the relationship of the Mishnah to Scripture. Such a treatise can have been enormous, not only because, in theory, every line of the Mishnah required attention but also because, in practice, a variety of documents, particularly Sifra, the two Sifrés, and the Talmuds, contain writing of a single kind, meant to amplify the Mishnah by appeal to Scripture (but never to amplify Scripture by appeal to the Mishnah!). It is perfectly clear that no one imagined compiling a commentary to the Mishnah that would consist principally of proofs, of a sustained and well-crafted sort, that the Mishnah in general depends upon Scripture (even though specific and sustained proofs that the principles of taxonomy derive from Scripture are, as I said, susceptible of compilation in such treatises). How do we know that fact? It is because, when people did compile writings in the form of sustained commentaries to the Mishnah, that is to say, the two Talmuds, they did not focus principally upon the scriptural exegesis of the Mishnah; that formed only one interest, and, while an important one, it did not predominate; it certainly did not define the plan and program of the whole; and it certainly did not form a center of redactional labor. It was simply one item on a list of items that would be brought into relationship, where appropriate, with sentences of the Mishnah. And even then, it always was the intersection at the level of sentences, not sustained discourses, let alone with the Mishnah viewed whole and complete.

And yet – and yet if we look into compilations we do have, we find sizable sets of materials that can have been joined together with the Mishnah, paragraph by paragraph, in such a way that Scripture might have been shaped into a commentary to the Mishnah. Let me now give a sustained example of what might have emerged, but never did emerge, in the canonical compilations of Judaism. I draw my case from Sifra, but equivalent materials in other midrash compilations as well as in the two Talmuds in fact are abundant.

Sifra Parashat Behuqotai Parashah Three
CCLXX:I

1. A. ["The Lord said to Moses, Say to the people of Israel, When a man makes a special vow of persons to the Lord at your Valuation, then your Valuation of a male from twenty years old up to sixty years old shall be fifty shekels of silver according to the shekel of the sanctuary. If the person is a female, your Valuation shall be thirty shekels. If the person is from five years old up to twenty years old, your Valuation shall be for a male twenty shekels and for a female ten shekels. If the person is from a month old up to five years old, your Valuation shall be for a male five shekels of silver and for a female your Valuation shall be three shekels of silver. And if the person is sixty years old and upward, then your Valuation for a male shall be fifteen shekels and for a female ten shekels. And if a man is too poor to pay your Valuation, then he shall bring the person before the priest, and the priest shall value him; according to the ability of him who vowed the priest shall value him" (Lev. 27:1-8).]

    B. **"Israelites take vows of Valuation, but gentiles do not take vows of Valuation [M. Ar. 1:2B].**

    C. "Might one suppose they are not subject to vows of Valuation?

    D. "Scripture says, 'a man,'" the words of R. Meir.

    E. Said R. Meir, "After one verse of Scripture makes an inclusionary statement, another makes an exclusionary statement.

    F. "On what account do I say that gentiles are subject to vows of Valuation but may not take vows of Valuation?

    G. **"It is because greater is the applicability of the rule of subject to the pledge of Valuation by others than the applicability of making the pledge of Valuation of others [T. Ar. 1:1A].**

    H. **"For lo, a deaf-mute, idiot, and minor may be subjected to vows of Valuation, but they are not able to take vows of Valuation [M. Ar. 1:1F]."**

    I. **R. Judah says, "Israelites are subject to vows of Valuation, but gentiles are not subject to vows of Valuation [M. Ar. 1:2C].**

    J. "Might one suppose that they may not take vows of Valuation of third parties?

    K. "Scripture says, 'a man.'"

L.   Said R. Judah, "After one verse of Scripture makes an inclusionary statement, another makes an exclusionary statement.

M.   "On what account do I say that gentiles are not subject to vows of Valuation but may take vows of Valuation?

N.   **"It is because greater is the applicability of the rule of pledging the Valuation of others than the applicability of being subject to the pledge of Valuation by others [T. Ar. 1:1C].**

O.   **"For a person of doubtful sexual traits and a person who exhibits traits of both sexes pledge the Valuation of others but are not subjected to the pledge of Valuation to be paid by others" [M. Ar. 1:1D].**

2. A. Since Scripture makes reference to the people of Israel, might I suppose that the pledge of Valuation applies only to home-born Israelites?

B.   How do I know that the law encompasses converts and slaves?

C.   Scripture says, "Say...."

3. A. "a man:"

B.   excluding a minor.

C.   Might I suppose that I should also exclude a minor who is capable of understanding and making a vow?

D.   Scripture says, "When...makes a special vow...." [Hence a minor able to understand such a vow is permitted to make a valid one.]

4. A. "When a man makes a special vow" is stated here,

B.   and "when a man makes a vow" is stated elsewhere [with respect to vowing, Dt. 23:22: "When you make a vow to the Lord your God, do not put off fulfilling it, for the Lord your God will require it of you and you will have incurred guilt; whereas you incur no guilt if you refrain from vowing. You must fulfill what has crossed your lips and perform what you have voluntarily vowed to the Lord your God, having made the promise with your own mouth"].

C.   Just as vow stated here involves making a special vow [so that the statement of the vow must be explicit and clearly uttered],

D.   so the vow stated there involves making the vow explicitly and clearly.

E.   Just as the vow stated elsewhere is subject to the prohibition of not putting off fulfilling the vow, so the vow stated here likewise is subject to the prohibition of not putting off fulfilling the vow.

5. A. "When a man makes a special vow of persons to the Lord at your Valuation:"

B.   The Scripture draws an analogy between vows and pledges of Valuation.

C.   Just as vows are subject to the prohibition of not putting off fulfilling the vow,

D.   so pledges of Valuation are subject to the prohibition of not putting off fulfilling the vow.

6. A.   "your Valuation:"
    B.   this encompasses the Valuation that lacks explicit specification.
7. A.   Another teaching concerning "your Valuation:"
    B.   the Valuation of the whole of a person is what one gives, and one does not give the Valuation only of the limbs by themselves.
    C.   Or might it be the case that I exclude something on which life depends?
    D.   Scripture says, "persons [souls]" –
    E.   "souls," not a corpse. [If someone pledges the Valuation of a part of the body on which life depends, the Valuation is valid.]
    F.   Then I shall exclude a corpse [from the vow of Valuation], but I shall not exclude one who is dying.
    G.   Scripture says, "then he shall bring the person before the priest, and the priest shall value him" –
    H.   one who is subject to being brought is subject to being valuated, and one who is not subject to being brought before the priest [such as a dying man] also is not subject to the pledge of Valuation.
8. A.   Another teaching concerning "persons [souls]:"
    B.   Why does Scripture say, "souls"?
    C.   I know only that the law applies to one who pledged the Valuation of one person. How do I know that if one person pledges the Valuation of a hundred [the vow applies]?
    D.   Scripture says, "souls."
9, A.   Another teaching concerning "persons [souls]:"
    B.   Why does Scripture say, "souls"?
    C.   I know only that the law applies to a man who pledged the Valuation of a woman. How do I know that if a woman pledges the Valuation of a man, [her vow is valid]?
    D.   Scripture says, "souls."
10. A.   Another teaching concerning "persons [souls]:"
    B.   Why does Scripture say, "souls"?
    C.   I might have argued that whoever falls into the category of having worth is subject to the category of vows of Valuation.
    D.   Might one who is ugly, covered with boils, or who otherwise is in no way subject to any sort of value then not be subject to the vow of Valuation?
    E.   Scripture says, "souls."
11. A.   "then [your Valuation of a male from twenty years old up to sixty years old shall be fifty shekels of silver according to the shekel of the sanctuary]:"
    B.   What is Scripture's point here?
    C.   I might have thought that whoever is subject to a vow of Valuation also is in the category of having worth.
    D.   A person of doubtful sexual traits and a person who exhibits traits of both sexes, an infant not a month old, who are not subject to the

pledge of Valuation by others, should not be subject to any sort of value at all.

E. Scripture says, "then" [indicating that such as these do have worth].

12. A. "male:"

B. **not a person of doubtful sexual traits of an androgyne [M. Ar. 1:1D].** [They are not subject to a pledge of Valuation, since we do not know into which category, male or female, they fall.]

C. Might one suppose that while these do not fall into the category of "man," they do fall into the category of "woman"?

D. Scripture says, If the person is a female."

E. Thus one who is undoubtedly male or undoubtedly female, but not a person of doubtful sexual traits of an androgyne.

13. A. And how do we know that the sixtieth year is treated as part of the period prior to that year?

B. Scripture says, "from twenty years old up to sixty years old" –

C. **this teaches that the sixtieth year is treated as part of the period prior to that year.**

D. **I know only that that is the rule governing the status of the sixtieth year. How do I know the rule as to assigning the fifth year, the twentieth year?**

E. **It is a matter of logic:**

F. **Liability is incurred when one is in the sixtieth year, the fifth year, and the twentieth year.**

G. **Just as the sixtieth year is treated as part of the period prior to that year,**

H. **so the fifth and the twentieth years are treated as part of the period prior to that year.**

I. **But if you treat the sixtieth year as part of the prior period, imposing a more stringent law [the Valuation requiring a higher fee before than after sixty],**

J. **shall we treat the fifth year and the twentieth year as part of the period prior to that year, so imposing a more lenient law in such cases [the Valuation being less expensive]?**

K. **Accordingly, Scripture is required to settle the question when it refers repeatedly to "year,"**

L. **thus establishing a single classification for all such cases:**

M. **just as the sixtieth year is treated as part of the prior period, so the fifth and the twentieth years are treated as part of the prior period.**

N. **And that is the rule, whether it produces a more lenient or a more stringent ruling [M. Ar. 4:4M-Q, with somewhat different wording].**

14. A. R. Eliezer says, "How do we know that a month and a day after a month are treated as part of the sixtieth year?

B. "Scripture says, 'up...:'

C. "Here we find reference to 'up...,' and elsewhere we find the same. Just as 'up' used elsewhere means that a month and a day after the month [are included in the prior span of time], so the meaning is the same when used here. **[M. Ar. 4:4R: R. Eleazar says, "The foregoing applies so long as they are a month and a day more than the years which are prescribed."]**

15. A. I know only that this rule applies after sixty. How do I know that the same rule applies after five or twenty?

B. It is a matter of logic:

C. One is liability to pay a pledge of Valuation if the person to be evalued is older than sixty, and one is liable if such a one is older than five or older than twenty.

D. Just as, if one is older than sixty by a month and a day, the person is as though he were sixty years of age, so if the one is after five years or twenty years by a month and a day, lo, these are deemed to be the equivalent of five or twenty years of age.

16. A. "And if a man is too poor to pay your Valuation:"

B. this means, if he is too impoverished to come up with your Valuation.

17. A. "then he shall bring the person before the priest:"

B. this then excludes a dead person.

C. I shall then exclude a corpse but not a dying person?

D. Scripture says, "Scripture says, "then he shall bring the person before the priest, and the priest shall value him" –

E. one who is subject to being brought is subject to being valuated, and one who is not subject to being brought before the priest [such as a dying man] also is not subject to the pledge of Valuation.

18. A. Might one suppose that even if someone said, "The Valuation of Mr. So-and-so is incumbent on me," and he died, the man should be exempt?

B. Scripture says, "and the priest shall value him."

C. That is so even if he is dead.

19. A. "and the priest shall value him:"

B. This means that one pays only in accord with the conditions prevailing at the time of the Valuation.

20. A. "according to the ability of him who vowed the priest shall value him:"

B. It is in accord with the means of the one who takes the vow, not the one concerning whom the vow is taken,

C. whether that is a man, woman or child.

D. In this connection sages have said:

E. **The estimate of ability to pay is made in accord with the status of the one who vows;**

F. **and the estimate of the years of age is made in accord with the status of the one whose Valuation is vowed.**

G.   **And when this is according to the Valuations spelled out in the Torah, it is in accord with the status, as to age and sex, of the one whose Valuation is pledged.**

H.   **And the Valuation is paid in accordance with the rate prescribed at the time of the pledge of Valuation [M. Ar. 4:1A-D].**

21. A   "the priest shall value him:"

B.   This serves as the generative analogy covering all cases of Valuations, indicating that the priest should be in charge.

The program of the Mishnah and the Tosefta predominates throughout, e.g., Nos. 1, 12, 13, 14-15. The second methodical inquiry characteristic of our authorship, involving exclusion and inclusion, accounts for pretty much the rest of this well-crafted discussion, which provides a welcome respite from the this-and-that of the preceding chapters. Now we see a coherent and cogent discussion of a topic in accord with a program applicable to all topics, that trait of our document which so won our admiration. Thus Nos. 2-11, 17-20, involve inclusion, exclusion, or extension by analogy. I should offer this excellent composition as an example of the best our authorship has to give us, and a very impressive intellectual gift at that.

Sifra Parashat Behuqotai Pereq Nine
CCLXXI:I

1. A   ["If it is an animal such as men offer as an offering to the Lord, all of such that any man gives to the Lord is holy. He shall not substitute anything for it or exchange it, a good for a bad or a bad for a good; and if he, in exchanging, makes any exchange of beast for beast, then both it and that for which it is exchanged shall be holy. And if it is an unclean animal such as is not offered as an offering to the Lord, then the man shall bring the animal before the priest, and the priest shall value it as either good or bad; as you, the priest, value it, so it shall be. But if he wishes to redeem it, he shall add a fifth to the valuation" (Lev. 27:9-13)].

B.   "[If] someone said, 'The leg of this beast is a burnt-offering,' might someone suppose that the whole of it is to be a burnt-offering?

C.   "Scripture says, 'all of such that any man gives to the Lord is holy.'

D.   "'of such' but the whole of it is not holy.

E.   "Then might one suppose that the beast should go forth to unconsecrated status?

F.   "Scripture says, 'is holy.'

G.   "What should he then do with the beast [of which he has spoken]?

H.   "The beast should be sold to those who are obligated [e.g., by vow] to bring a burnt-offering, and the proceeds received for the beast are unconsecrated, except for the value of that leg," the words of R. Meir.

I. R. Judah, R. Yosé, and R. Simeon say, "How do we know that even if one has said, 'The leg of this beast is a burnt-offering,' the whole of the beast is deemed a burnt-offering?

J. "Scripture says, 'all of such that any man gives to the Lord is holy.'

K. "'is holy' serves to encompass the whole of the beast [only part of which has been consecrated]."

2. A. Might one suppose that even in connection with what has been consecrated for the upkeep of the house, the law of substitution should apply [so that if something has been consecrated for the upkeep of the temple buildings, and a person said, "That is substituted for this," both items are deemed consecrated, as is the case with a beast for the altar]?

B. Scripture says, "[If it is an animal such as men offer as] an offering [to the Lord],"

C. which then excludes what has been consecrated for the upkeep of the temple building, which does not fall into the category of an offering at all.

D. I shall then exclude what has been consecrated for the upkeep of the temple building, which does not fall into the category of an offering at all, but I shall not exclude **what has been declared a substitute for an offering by action of the community at large [is not substituted, M. Tem. 1:6C].**

E. Scripture says, "*He* [shall not substitute anything for it or] exchange it."

F. I shall exclude what has been declared a substitute for an offering by action of the community at large, but I shall not exclude **what belongs to partners [one of whom has declared the beast a substitute for an already consecrated beast] [M. Tem. 1:6C].**

G. Scripture says, "He shall not substitute anything for it,"

H. an individual thus effects an act of substitution, and neither the community at large or partners can effect an act of substitution.

3. A. Said R. Simeon, "Now is it not the fact that tithe was covered by the law at hand, [prohibiting making substitutions]. When then was it singled out below [when Scripture says, later in this same passage, "And all the tithe of herds and flocks, every tenth animals of all that pass under the herdsman's staff, shall be holy to the Lord. A man shall not inquire whether it is good or bad, neither shall he exchange it; and if he exchanges it, then both it and that for which it is exchanged shall be holy; it shall not be redeemed"]?

B. "It was to establish in its classification a rule that governs other items as well, specifically:

C. "just as a beast designated as tithe is the offering of an individual, so I know that covered by the law of substitution is only the offering of an individual.

D.   "Or might one maintain that, in a matter subjected to reasoning in a single way, one might as well derive conclusions from all of the available ways that are contained therein [so we may draw further comparisons from the rules governing beasts designated as tithe, as follows:]

E.   "just as what is singular to a beast in the status as tithe is that it is consecrated for the altar, applies to the herd and to the flock, and must be eaten in a span of two days, so I encompass under the law of substitution only what bears these same indicative traits.

F.   "How do I know that the law of substitution then encompasses Most Holy Things and Lesser Holy Things that belong to an individual?

G.   "Scripture says, 'if [he makes any exchange of] beast [for beast]....'"

4. A.   "He shall not substitute anything for it:"

B.   What has been consecrated imposes the status of substitute on what has been declared to be its substitution,

C.   but what has been declared a substitute does not impose the status of substitute on yet another beast.

D.   R. Judah says, "The offspring [of a consecrated beast] effects the status of substitute [for any beast that is declared to be in place of the offspring of a consecrated beast, so that the offspring and the substitute both are equally holy]."

E.   They said to him, "What has been consecrated imposes the status of substitute on what has been declared to be its substitution, but neither the offspring of a consecrated beast nor what has been declared a substitute does not impose the status of substitute on yet another beast."

5. A.   **"a good for a bad or a bad for a good:"**

B.   **unblemished beasts for blemished ones, blemished beasts for unblemished ones [M. Tem. 1:2D].**

C.   How do we know that "for bad" refers to a blemished beast?

D.   Scripture says, "You shall not sacrifice to the Lord your God an ox or a sheep in which is a blemish, any bad trait whatever, [for that is an abomination to the Lord your God]" (Dt. 17:1).

6. A.   "and if he, in exchanging, makes any exchange:"

B.   the use of the duplicated verb serves to encompass a woman.

7. A.   "and if he, in exchanging, makes any exchange:"

B.   the use of the duplicated verb serves to encompass an heir.

8. A.   "of beast for beast:"

B.   **one for two, two for one, one for a hundred, a hundred for one.**

C.   **R. Simeon says, "'of beast for beast' – not a beast for beasts."**

D.   **They said to him, "A single beast may be called 'beast,' but many beasts also may be called 'beast'" [M. Tem. 1:2H-J].**

9. A.   "beast for beast:"

B.   not beast for fowl, not fowl for beast,

C.   not beast for meal-offerings, not meal-offerings for beast,

D.   not beast for them [M. Tem. 1:6A].

10. A.   "beast for beast:"

B.   not beast for foetuses, not foetuses for beast,

C.   not limbs for foetuses, not foetuses for limbs,

D.   not limbs for whole beasts, not whole beasts for them.

E.   R. Yosé says, "An act of substitution may be effected between limbs and whole beasts, but not whole beasts for them."

F.   Said R. Yosé, "Is it not the fact that, in the case of consecrated beasts, he who says, 'The leg of this beast is a burnt-offering,' the whole of it is held to be a burnt-offering?

G.   "So here too, he who says, 'The foot of this beast in exchange for that,' –

H.   "the whole of it should be held to have been declared a substitute in its stead [and therefore to have been consecrated]" [M. Tem. 1:3A-E].

11. A.   "then both it and that for which it is exchanged shall be holy:"

B.   [These lines find their context below.] Where does the sanctity apply to it?

C.   In the house of the owner.

D.   Then here too, the sanctity applies to it in the house of the owner [M. Tem. 1:1N-O].

E.   [The foregoing form part of a discussion and are out of place. I supply, following M. Tem. 1:1H-O: Priests do not effect a substitution in the case either of a sin-offering or of a guilt-offering or of a firstling.

F.   Said R. Yohanan b. Nuri, "And on what account do the priests who own firstlings not effect substitution in the case of a firstling?"

G.   Said R. Aqiba, "A sin-offering and a guilt-offering are a gift to the priest, and a firstling is a gift to the priest. Just as in the case of a sin-offering and a guilt-offering, they do not effect a substitution, so in the case of a firstling, they should not effect a substitution."

H.   Said to him R. Yohanan b. Nuri, "What difference does it make to me that one does not effect a substitution in the case of a sin-offering and a guilt-offering? For in the case of these, the priests have no claim to the beasts while the beasts are alive. But will you say the same in the case of the firstling, to which the priests do have a claim while the firstling is still alive?"

I.   Said to him R. Aqiba, "You have responded to the argument based on comparison. But what will you say to Scripture: 'Then both it and that for which it is exchanged shall be holy' (Lev. 27:10)? At what point does sanctity descend onto it? In the house of the owner. So the substitute too becomes holy in the house of the owner. [The substitute and the animal for which it is designated are comparable. The original animal became holy in the owner's house, not in the house of a priest. The priest therefore has no power to effect a substitution for a firstling. If an Israelite exchanged a firstling, the substitute is sacred. If a priest did so, the substituted beast remains unconsecrated.]"

J.   But once the beasts have been given to a priest, neither the owner nor the priest effects an act of substitution [the former because the beast is no longer his, the latter because the beast is not yet in his domain (Hillel)].

12. A   "so it shall be:"

B.   That which has been sanctified has the power to effect substitution [so that if someone says that another beast is a substitute for a beast that has been sanctified, the other beast is in the status of the sanctified beast and so is holy],

C.   but a beast that has attained sanctification merely by being declared a substitute for a sanctified beast does not transmit its status to yet another beast [M. Tem. 1:5E].

D.   Is not the opposite of that proposition a matter of reason?

E.   If a sanctified beast, which is not deemed to be holy if it is blemished with a permanent blemish, effects the status of sanctification for the beast declared to be its substitute,

F.   a beast declared to be a substitute for a sanctified beast, which is deemed to be sanctified even though it bears a permanent blemish, surely should have the power to effect substitution [so that if someone says that another beast is a substitute for a beast that has been sanctified as a substitute, the other beast is in the status of the substituted, now sanctified, beast and so it, too, is holy].

G.   Scripture says, "so it shall be:"

H.   That which has been sanctified has the power to effect substitution [so that if someone says that another beast is a substitute for a beast that has been sanctified, the other beast is in the status of the sanctified beast and so is holy], but a beast that has attained sanctification merely by being declared a substitute for a sanctified beast does not transmit its status to yet another beast.

13. A   "shall be holy:"

B.   **This teaches that sanctified applies to a beast declared a substitute even though it bears a permanent blemish. [M. Tem. 1:2, 2:33F].**

C.   But is not the opposite of that proposition not a matter of logic?

D.   if the beast that is sanctified, which effects substitution in the case of another beast declared holy in its stead, cannot be sanctified if it bears a permanent blemish,

E.   a beast that has been declared a substitute, which does not have the power of effecting substitution should yet another beast be declared a substitute for it, surely should not be deemed sanctified if it bears a permanent blemish!

F.   Scripture says, "shall be holy:"

G.   This teaches that sanctified applies to a beast declared a substitute even though it bears a permanent blemish.

H.   R. Yosé b. R. Judah says, "'shall be holy' serves to indicate that the act of substitution is equally valid when performed inadvertently as when performed deliberately.

As I see it, our exposition of this interesting matter provides little more than a reprise of the language and positions of the parts of the Mishnah's treatment of the same subject. That is the case, clearly, for Nos. 2, 5, and 8-13. A closer look at the propositions, as distinct from the language, would show that the same correspondence is shown by the entire exposition before us. Still, even a brief glance at Mishnah-tractate Temurah shows us how much our authorship has not attempted to replicate or associate with passages of Scripture. It seems to me that only a few of the many important principles of the Mishnah-tractate are drawn upon, and the reason for what is chosen, explaining also what is omitted, then is clear. Our authorship has no task of demonstrating the correspondence of every rule in the Mishnah to a verse of Scripture, because that authorship deems the Mishnah to be a valid source of law on its own; but where our authorship can show that a rule of the Mishnah relates to, or summarizes, or rests upon a statement of Scripture, it will do so. What it tacitly affirms is the validity of the Mishnah's own, enormously rich and speculative reading of the topical program at hand. What is equally interesting is that the established program of our authorship – exclusion, inclusion, for instance – scarcely makes its appearance, e.g., No. 1 is a Mishnah-type problem, concerning the gray area at hand.

Sifra Parashat Behuqotai Pereq Ten
CCLXXIII:I

1.   A   "[When a man dedicates his house to be holy to the Lord,] the priest shall value it as either good or bad; [as the priest values it, so it shall stand. And if he who dedicates it wishes to redeem his

house, he shall add a fifth of the value in money to it, and it shall be his]" (Lev. 27:14-15).

B. **Things that have been consecrated are not redeemed merely by estimating its worth [M. Maaser Sheni 4:2].**

C. "as the priest values it, so it shall stand:"

D. **If the owner says, "Twenty," and any other person says, "Twenty," the owner takes precedence, for in any event he adds the fifth [M. Arakhin 8:23H-I, M. Bekh. 1:7].**

E. **If one said, "Lo, it is mine for twenty-one," the owner pays twenty-six.**

F. **"Twenty-two" – the owner pays twenty-seven.**

G. **"Twenty-three" – the owner pays twenty-eight.**

H. **"Twenty-four" – the owner pays twenty-nine.**

I. **"Twenty-four" – the owner pays thirty.**

J. **For they do not add the fifth to what the other bids more than the owner's bid.**

K. **If one said, "Lo, it is mine for twenty-six" –**

L. **if the owner wants to pay thirty-one and a denar, the owner takes precedence, and if not, they say, "It's yours!" [M. Arakhin 8:3A-I].**

2. A. "And if he who dedicates it wishes to redeem his house:"

   B. This serves to encompass a woman.

3. A. "And if he who dedicates it wishes to redeem his house:"

   B. This serves to encompass an heir.

4. A. "he shall add a fifth of the value in money to it, and it shall be his:"

   B. If he paid the money, lo, it is his.

   C. And if not, it is not his.

No. 1 reverts to the available program on the way in which the added fifth is calculated and its effect upon redeeming the property. Nos. 2-4 are standard.

CCLXXIII:II

1. A. "If a man dedicates to the Lord part of the land which is his by inheritance, [then your valuation shall be according to the seed for it; a sowing of a homer of barley shall be valued at fifty shekels of silver. If he dedicates his field from the Year of Jubilee, it shall stand at your full valuation. But if he dedicates his field after the Jubilee, then the priest shall compute the money value for it according to the years that remain until the Year of Jubilee, and a deduction shall be made from your valuation. And if he who dedicates the field wishes, redeeming, to redeem it, then he shall add a fifth of the valuation in money to it, and it shall remain his. But if he does not wish to redeem the field, or if he has sold the field to another man, it shall not be redeemed any more; but the field, when it is released in the Jubilee, shall be holy to the Lord, as a field that has been devoted; the priest shall be in possession

of it. If he dedicates to the Lord a field which he has bought, which is not a part of his possession by inheritance, then the priest shall compute the valuation for it up to the Year of Jubilee, and the man shall give the amount of the valuation on that day as a holy thing to the Lord. In the Year of Jubilee the field shall return to him from whom it was bought, to whom the land belongs as a possession by inheritance. Every valuation shall be according to the shekel of the sanctuary; twenty gerahs shall make a shekel" (Lev. 27:16-25).]

B. I know only that the law covers a field received by inheritance from one's father.

C. How do I know that it covers also a field received by inheritance from one's mother?

D. Scripture says, "If a man dedicates...."

2. A. "then your valuation shall be according to the seed for it:"

B. not in accord with its dimensions [but rather, its productive capacity].

3. A. "a sowing of a homer of barley shall be valued at fifty shekels of silver:"

B. Lo, this is by decree of the King [without further explanation]:

C. **All the same are he who sanctifies a field in the desert of Mahoz and he who sanctifies a field among the orchards of Sebaste:**

D. **[If he wants to redeem it], he pays fifty shekels of silver for every part of a field that suffices for the sowing of a homer of barley [M. Arakhin 3:2B-C, 7:1].**

4. A. How do we know that a person is not permitted to sanctify his field at the time of the Jubilee, though if one has done so, the field is sanctified?

B. Scripture says, "If he dedicates his field from the Year of Jubilee."

5. A. Why does Scripture say, "his field"?

B. How do you know that, **if in the field were crevices ten handbreadths deep or rocks ten handbreadths high, they are not measured with it [M. Arakhin 7:1G]?**

C. Scripture says, "his field," [and these are not reckoned as part of his field forming domains unto themselves].

6. A. "it shall stand at your full valuation:"

B. **[For a Jubilee of forty-nine years,] one pays forty-nine selas and forty-nine pondions [T. Arakhin 4:10B].**

C. What is the value of this pondion?

D. It is at the rate of exchange of a pondion and some change [Hillel].

7. A. "[But if he dedicates his field] after the Jubilee:"

B. Near the Jubilee.

C. How do we know the rule for the period some time after the Jubilee?

D.   Scripture says, "But if he dedicates his field after the Jubilee."

8.   A.   "his field:"
     B.   What is the point of Scripture here?
     C.   How do you know that, **if in the field were crevices ten handbreadths deep or rocks ten handbreadths high, they are not measured with it [M. Arakhin 7:1G]?**
     D.   Scripture says, "his field," [and these are not reckoned as part of his field forming domains unto themselves].

9.   A.   How do we know that **they do not declare a field of possession sanctified less than two years before the Year of Jubilee nor do they redeem it less than a year after the Year of Jubilee [M. Arakhin 7:1A-B]?**
     B.   **Scripture says, "then the priest shall compute the money value for it according to the years that remain until the Year of Jubilee." [Hence there must be at least two years].**
     C.   **Scripture says, "But if he dedicates his field after the Jubilee, then the priest shall compute the money value for it according to the years that remain until the Year of Jubilee" [T. Arakhin 4:8A-B].**

10. A.   And how do we know that **they do not reckon the months against the sanctuary, but the sanctuary reckons the months to its own advantage [M. Arakhin 7:1C-D]?**
     B.   Scripture says, "But if he dedicates his field after the Jubilee, then the priest shall compute the money value for it according to the years that remain until the Year of Jubilee."

11. A.   And how do we know that **if one said, "Lo, I shall pay for each year as it comes," they do not pay any attention to him, but he pays the whole at once [M. Arakhin 7:1J-K]?**
     B.   Scripture says, "But if he dedicates his field after the Jubilee, then the priest shall compute the money value for it according to the years that remain until the Year of Jubilee."

12. A.   "years that remain:"
     B.   years does one reckon,
     C.   and one does not reckon months.

13. A.   And how do we know that if the sanctuary wanted to treat the months as a year, it may do so?
     B.   Scripture says, "[the priest] shall compute."

14. A.   "until the Year of Jubilee:"
     B.   [But no part of the year of the Jubilee] shall enter the calculation.

15. A.   "and a deduction shall be made from your valuation:"
     B.   even from the sanctuary['s claim,]
     C.   so if the sanctuary had the usufruct for a year or two prior to the Jubilee, or did not exercise the right of usufruct but had access to it [cf. T. Arakhin 4:10B],
     D.   one deducts a sela and a pondion for each year.

16. A   "And if he who dedicates the field wishes, redeeming, to redeem it:"

    B.   the duplicated verb serves to encompass a woman.

17. A   "And if he who dedicates the field wishes, redeeming, to redeem it:"

    B.   the duplicated verb serves to encompass an heir.

18. A   "the field:"

    B.   What is the point of Scripture here?

    C.   One might have thought that subject to the law is only one who sanctifies a field that can take a kor of seed.

    D.   How do I know that if one sanctified a field that can take a letekh of seed, a seah of seed, a qab of seed, the same rule applies?

    E.   Scripture says, "the field."

19. A   "he shall add a fifth of the value in money to it, and it shall be his:"

    B.   If he paid the money, lo, it is his.

    C.   And if not, it is not his.

20. A   "But if he does not wish to redeem the field:"

    B.   this refers to the owner.

21. A   "or if he has sold the field to another man:"

    B.   this refers to the temple treasurer.

22. A   "to another man:"

    B.   and not to his son.

    C.   May one say, "to another man" – and not to his brother?

    D.   When Scripture says, "man," it encompasses his brother.

    E.   How come you include the son but exclude the brother [in the present rule]?

    F.   After Scripture has used inclusionary language, it has gone and used exclusionary language.

    G.   I include the son, who takes the place of his father as to a betrothal of a bondwoman {Ex. 21:9: "And if he designated her for his son, he shall deal with her as is the practice with free maidens"], and as to control of a Hebrew slave [Ex. 21:6: "He shall then remain his slave for life" – but not the slave of his heir, meaning his brother (Hillel)].

    H.   But I exclude the brother, who does not take the place of the deceased brother either as to the betrothal of a bondwoman or as to control of a Hebrew slave.

23. A   "it shall not be redeemed any more:"

    B.   Might one suppose that one may not purchase it from the temple treasurer and it then will enter the status of a field that has been acquired through purchase [not inheritance]?

    C.   Scripture says, ""it shall not be redeemed any more:"

    D.   In its prior status, it will not be redeemed, but one may purchase it from the temple treasurer and it then will enter the status of a field that has been acquired through purchase [not inheritance].

The exposition is inclusionary, Nos. 1, 2. No. 3 begins a long sequence of passages, proceeding through No. 11, drawn from, or dependent upon, the language and the rules of the Mishnah and the Tosefta, as indicated. From No. 12 to the end we work out a familiar type of low-level exegesis, this, not that, or this, and also that.

Sifra Parashat Behuqotai Pereq Eleven
CCLXXIV:I

1.   A   "[But if he does not wish to redeem the field, or if he has sold the field to another man, it shall not be redeemed any more;] but the field, when it is released in the Jubilee, [shall be holy to the Lord, as a field that has been devoted; the priest shall be in possession of it. If he dedicates to the Lord a field which he has bought, which is not a part of his possession by inheritance, then the priest shall compute the valuation for it up to the Year of Jubilee, and the man shall give the amount of the valuation on that day as a holy thing to the Lord. In the Year of Jubilee the field shall return to him from whom it was bought, to whom the land belongs as a possession by inheritance. Every valuation shall be according to the shekel of the sanctuary; twenty gerahs shall make a shekel]:"

     B.   The reference to "when it is released" in the masculine form indicates that the word "field" is masculine.

2.   A   "holy:"

     B.   Just as what is referred to elsewhere [e.g., Lev. 27:14: "If anyone consecrates his house to the Lord...if he who has consecrated his house wishes to redeem it...,"] leaves the status of consecration only through redemption,

     C.   so "holy" in the present context means that what has been consecrated leaves that status only through redemption.

3.   A   "But if he does not wish to redeem the field, or if he has sold the field to another man, it shall not be redeemed any more; but the field, when it is released in the Jubilee, [shall be holy to the Lord, as a field that has been devoted; the priest shall be in possession of it:"]

     B.   **"This teaches that the priests enter into possession of the field and they pay its price," the words of R. Judah.**

     C.   **R. Simeon says, "They enter but they do not pay."**

     D.   **R. Eleazar says, "They neither enter nor pay, but it is called 'an abandoned field' until the second Jubilee. If the second year of the Jubilee came and it was not redeemed, it is called a twice-abandoned field. That is so up to the third Jubilee. The priests under no circumstances enter into possession until another has redeemed it" [M. Arakhin 7:4A-H].**

4.   A   "as a field that has been devoted; the priest shall be in possession of it:"

B. What is the point of Scripture here?

C. In the case of a field that is to go forth into the ownership of the priests in the Jubilee year, which one of the priests redeemed, and lo, it is now in his domain, **might one say, he may say, "Lo, since it goes forth to the priests in the Jubilee, and since, lo, it is now in my domain, then lo, it is mine"?**

D. **How do we know that it goes forth to all his brethren, the priests [M. Arakhin 7:3D-E]?**

E. Scripture says, "shall be holy to the Lord, as a field that has been devoted; the priest shall be in possession of it" –

F. As to field that is to go forth into the ownership of the priests in the Jubilee year, which one of the priests redeemed, and lo, it is now in his domain, this is not his, but **it goes forth to all his brethren, the priests.**

5. A. "If he dedicates to the Lord a field which he has bought, which is not a part of his possession by inheritance:"

B. What is the point of Scripture here?

C. **"He who purchases a field from his father, if his father died and afterward he sanctified it,**

D. **"might one suppose that it is in his possession merely as a field that one has purchased?**

E. **"Scripture says, 'If he dedicates to the Lord a field which he has bought, which is not a part of his possession by inheritance,' – thus excluding this case, since it is indeed a field received by inheritance, [lo, it is deemed a field which one has bought," the words of R. Meir.**

F. **R. Judah and R. Simeon say, "He who purchases a field from his father, then sanctified it, and afterward his father died,**

G. **"might one suppose that it should be in his possession as a field purchased by money?**

H. **"Scripture says, "If he dedicates to the Lord a field which he has bought, which is not a part of his possession by inheritance,' – thus referring to a field which is in no way suitable to being designated as a field that is gained by inheritance,**

I. **"thus excluding the present case, in which the field was suitable to become a field of inheritance" [with variations in the wording, M. Arakhin 7:5A-F].**

J. **A field which has been bought does not go forth to the priests in the Jubilee, for a man does not declare sanctified something is is not his own [M. Arakhin 7:5G-H].**

6. A. "then the priest shall compute the valuation [for it up to the Year of Jubilee, and the man shall give the amount of the valuation on that day as a holy thing to the Lord]:"

B. The meaning of "valuation" is only a calculation of the price.

	C.	This teaches that one pays the worth of the property.
7.	A.	Said R. Eleazar, "Here we find reference to reckoning the value, and in the discussion of the field received by inheritance, we find the same language.
	B.	"Just as in that case, 'then your valuation shall be according to the seed for it; a sowing of a homer of barley shall be valued at fifty shekels of silver,'
	C.	"so in this case, 'then your valuation shall be according to the seed for it; a sowing of a homer of barley shall be valued at fifty shekels of silver.'"
8.	A.	"and the man shall give the amount of the valuation on that day :"
	B.	one should not tarry.
	C.	**For [in the wording of M. Arakhin 6:5F-G] even though if they bring a pearl to a city, it fetches a better price, the sanctuary nonetheless has a claim only in its own place and in its own time.**
9.	A.	"In the Year of Jubilee the field shall return to him from whom it was bought, [to whom the land belongs as a possession by inheritance]:"
	B.	Might one suppose that this refers to the temple treasurer, from whom the field was purchased?
	C.	Scripture says, "to whom the land belongs as a possession by inheritance."
	D.	Why not say only, "to whom the land belongs as a possession by inheritance"? Why then add, "to him from whom it was bought"?
	E.	A field which has gone forth to the priests at the time of the Jubilee, and the priest sold it, and the purchaser sanctified it –
	F.	might one suppose that when the next Jubilee comes, the field returns to its original owner?
	G.	Scripture says, "to him from whom it was bought."
10.	A.	"Every valuation shall be according to the shekel of the sanctuary; twenty gerahs shall make a shekel]:"
	B.	And valuations are never less than a sela.
11.	A.	"according to the shekel of the sanctuary:"
	B.	What is the point of Scripture here?
	C.	Since Scripture says, "and he shall redeem," one might suppose that this may be done even with slaves, bonds, or real estate.
	D.	Scripture says, "according to the shekel of the sanctuary"
	E.	I know only that this is done with selas of the sanctuary. How do I know that the law encompasses movables?
	F.	Scripture says, "and he shall redeem," so encompassing something movable.
	G.	Then why does Scripture say, "according to the shekel of the sanctuary"?
	H.	This is meant to exclude slaves, bonds, and real estate.
12.	A.	"twenty gerahs shall make a shekel:"

	B.	this teaches you how much a sela is.
13.	A	How do we know that if one wanted to use a larger sela than that, he may do so?
	B.	Scripture says, "...shall...."
14.	A	How do we know that if one wanted to use a smaller sela than that [it is not acceptable]?
	B.	Scripture says, "according to...."

After some formalities, No. 3 brings us to the Mishnah's program, which predominates through Nos. 4, 5, 8 as well. The clarifications that follow, Nos. 6, 7, are particular to our topic. The remainder seems to me miscellaneous. But the exclusions and inclusions of Nos. 11-13 are noteworthy.

The point throughout is simple. We know how the compilers of canonical writings produced treatments of the Mishnah. The one thing that they did not do was to create a scriptural commentary to the Mishnah. We see in this sizable sample what might have been done – and therefore we know what at the level of the making of classics in Judaism was not done.

IV. Sifré to Numbers

Our first entry goes over the ground covered just now: the impossibility of composing a scriptural commentary to the Mishnah. That kind of document can readily have been compiled, also, out of materials in Sifré to Numbers.

Sifré to Numbers
I:IX

1.	A	"[You shall put out both male and female, putting them outside the camp,] that they may not defile their camp, [in the midst of which I dwell]:"
	B.	On the basis of this verse, the rule has been formulated:
	C.	**There are three camps, the camp of Israel, the camp of the Levitical priests, and the camp of the Presence of God. From the gate of Jerusalem to the Temple mount is the camp of Israel, from the gate of the Temple mount to the Temple courtyard is the camp of the levitical priesthood, and from the gate of the courtyard and inward is the camp of the Presence of God [T. Kelim 1:12].**

To me this is nothing more than a prooftext joined to a passage of apodictic law deriving from Mishnah-Tosefta (treated as a single document). I see no polemic, simply two statements of the law, the one as given in Scripture, the other as reframed in the Mishnah-mode. I see no polemic of any kind, though the subterranean theme – Scripture, not

Mishnah alone, serves as the basis for reliable judgment – cannot be missed. For reasons given in connection with the entry for Sifra, I regard this item as appropriate for a document that lies outside the (theological and literary) imagination of the compilers of the canonical documents.

There is a different kind of document that can have been compiled; the materials are scattered through a variety of documents; and yet, it is clear, no one imagined making a book out of these ready-made pieces. It is a treatise of hermeneutics. We do have so much material, and material that shows so much intellectual ambition, that we must wonder why, in all, no one bothered to make a book of it. One might wish to suggest that the available materials require the same classification as those on philology and theology: people did not compile entire treatises, or even tractates, devoted to abstractions, and hermeneutics constitutes a primary mode of abstract thought. So we might reasonably claim to deal with pericopes that can have been made into a book but for whatever reason were not so treated. But I am inclined to classify hermeneutical compositions in the same taxon as those that can have yielded a scriptural commentary to the Mishnah. People whose conception of the correct way to utilize for redactional purposes books of Scripture simply cannot have entertained the proposition that all of Scripture can be treated in accord with a single set of principles. For the contrary proposition, – the hermeneutical premise that we can read everything in one way or in some few ways – treats as homogeneous what the framers of commentaries wished to preserve as distinct.

That is to say, if I take for granted each verse of Scripture, each clause, each word, constitutes an irreducible fact, if I resist the conception that I can generalize about Scripture in some way calculated to minimize the distinctiveness of the verses of Scripture, then I can imagine a commentary but not a treatise of hermeneutics. The very conception of hermeneutics violates the fundamental position that each word and phrase must be read as, in some way or other, unique and irreplicable. That is why, it seems to me, the following kinds of discourses cannot have formed so inviting a principal taxon as to yield compilations in the way in which the book of Genesis or of Lamentations or any other biblical book can have set forth, in an exact sense of the words, a categorical imperative.

Sifré to Numbers Two
II:I
2   A   This is the hermeneutic of the Torah:

B. In the case of any pericope stated in a particular location, from which a given matter is left out, when Scripture goes and treats the matter a second time in some other location, the purpose of repeating the matter serves only to cover the item omitted the first time around [in this case, the disposition of the proselyte's intestate estate].

C. R. Aqiba says, "Any passage in which the word, *saying*, occurs, requires exegetical amplification [such as has been given above]."

II:II

1. A. R. Josiah says, "'...a man or a woman....' Why are matters formulated so as to refer to both man and woman?

B. "Since it is said, 'When a man leaves a pit open, or when a man digs a pit...' (Ex. 21:33).

C. "I know only that a man is covered by the law. How do I know that a woman is equally culpable?

D. "Scripture states, '....a man or a woman....'

E. "That statement serves to encompass both a woman and a man in respect to all actions subject to sin-offerings and to all torts that are listed in the Torah."

F. R. Jonathan says, "It is hardly necessary to supply such a proof, for, in that same context, it is stated in any event: 'the *owner* of the pit shall make it good,' and it says, '*the one* that kindled the fire shall make full restitution' (Ex. 22:6). [These formulations encompass both genders.]

G. "Why then does Scripture state, '...a man or a woman...'? Merely to provide yet another occasion for the exercise of learning."

II:III

1. A. "'And the Lord said to Moses, "Say to the people of Israel, 'When a man or woman commits any of the sins that men commit...'"'" (Num. 5:5-10).

B. "Why is this passage stated?

C. "Since it is stated, 'When a man or woman commits any of the sins that men commit by breaking faith with the Lord by deceiving his neighbor in a matter of deposit or security or through robbery, or if he has oppressed his neighbor, or has found what was lost and lied about it....'

D. "I thus know the rule in the case of one who practices deceit against the Lord in the specified cases [of Lev. 6:1ff.] How do I know that one who practices deception against the Lord in any other matter [is culpable]?

E. "Scripture states, 'When a man or woman commits any of the sins that men commit....'"

II:IV

1. A.   ["And the Lord said to Moses, 'Say to the people of Israel, When a man or woman commits any of the sins that men commit] by breaking faith with the Lord ...'" (Num. 5:5-10).

   B.   The word *breaking faith* in all contexts refers to lying, and so Scripture says, "But they broke faith with the God of their fathers and played the harlot after the gods of the peoples of the land" (1 Chr. 5:25).

   C.   So too: "But the people of Israel broke faith in regard to the devoted things" (Josh. 7:1).

   D.   So too: "So Saul died for his unfaithfulness; he was unfaithful to the Lord in that he did not keep the command of the Lord" (1 Chr. 10:13).

   E.   So too with reference to Uzziah: "Go out of the sanctuary, for you have done wrong" (2 Chr. 26:18).

   F.   And it further says, "...by breaking faith with the Lord."

   G.   Lo, the word *breaking faith* in all contexts refers to lying.

The treatment of the base verse begins with the comparison of the present rule to its parallel. The repetition serves a purpose. No. 2 then makes the operative principle articulate. The next pericopes goes over the same base question: Why is this rule given as it is? That accounts for II:I.3 ff. The same exercise goes forward, an interest not in the exegesis of the verse at hand but in the principles of explaining the verse in its larger hermeneutic context. We go over at II:I:III the same question that captured our attention at II:I, II, now explaining the reason that the same matter – false swearing – should come up twice. The passage at II:IV.1 forms part of a larger repertoire of prooftexts for the same proposition. Here too there is no interest in our verse in particular.

V. Sifré to Deuteronomy

One of the persistent issues addressed in this document involves a general issue expressed in very particular cases. The issue is whether the details of a case at hand limits the law, or whether the details are meant to exemplify types of cases covered by the law. That issue then is systematically addressed wherever Scripture expresses a rule through the description of a case. Now a sustained work of hermeneutics, which we do not have and, I have suggested, we cannot imagine within the program of the making of books by our authorships, will assemble a variety of such cases to make a general point. The general point, then, will be that cases exemplify or cases limit or both, and here is how to tell the difference. But such a compilation does not exist, and even the hints of developing generalizations out of innumerable cases do not surface. Here is one example among many of the discussion of whether or not the scriptural case is exemplary or restrictive.

Sifré to Deuteronomy Pisqa One Hundred-One
CI:I
1. A.   "...and any other animal that has true hoofs which are cleft in two [and brings up the cud – such you may eat. But the following, which do bring up the cud or have true hoofs which are cleft through, you may not eat: the camel, hare, and daman, for although they bring up the cud, they have no true hoofs, are unclean for you; also the swine, for although it has true hoofs, it does not bring up the cud, is unclean for you. You shall not eat of their flesh or touch their carcasses]" (Dt. 14:2-8):

    B.   Since we find that Scripture has treated as a paradigm the traits that mark a beast as unacceptable for everyday eating, as *taref*, so extending the matter beyond the specified items on the list,

    C.   should I also treat as a paradigm the traits that mark a beast as unfit [for the altar], so extending the matter also beyond the specified items on the list?

    D.   What would be an instance of such an extension? It would be ploughing with an ox and an ass along with beasts that have been consecrated for the altar. [In such a case, we might treat as unsuitable for eating a beast used for a purpose which makes the beast unsuitable for the altar.]

    E.   Scripture says, "The ox, sheep, goat...you may eat" (Dt. 14:4,6).

    F.   I shall then encompass these, but I still shall not encompass the beast that commits an act of bestiality with a woman, or that is used for an act of bestiality by a man, a beast that has been set aside for an improper purpose in connection with idolatry and one that has been actually used for idolatry, a beast that has served as a harlot's fee and the price of a dog, beasts resulting from the mating of mixed species, a beast suffering a fatal illness, and one that has been produced by caesarean section?

    G.   Scripture states, "The ox, sheep, goat...you may eat" (Dt. 14:4,6).

    H.   I shall encompass these, but still I shall not encompass the beast with which, in the testimony of two valid witnesses, a transgression has been committed but the court trial of which has not yet been concluded.

    I.   Scripture states, "The ox, sheep, goat...you may eat" (Dt. 14:4,6).

    J.   I shall encompass these, all of which were raised in conditions of cleanness [but then made unclean by acts committed by or upon them,] but I shall not encompass the offspring of a valid beast that sucked from a beast suffering from a fatal ailment.

    K.   Scripture states, "The ox, sheep, goat...you may eat" (Dt. 14:4,6).

L.   I shall encompass the offspring of a valid beast that sucked from a beast suffering from a fatal ailment, but I shall not encompass the offspring of a beast suffering a fatal ailment which sucked from a clean beast, [or] a clean beast that sucked from an unclean beast.

M.   Scripture states, "The ox, sheep, goat...you may eat" (Dt. 14:4,6).

N.   That is, from any beast.

2. A.   "The ox, sheep, goat...you may eat" (Dt. 14:4,6):

B.   This serves to encompass, also, the afterbirth [of such a beast, which may be eaten].

C.   Is it possible that that is the case even if only part of it has come forth?

D.   Scripture says, "...it," meaning, "It you may eat."

3. A.   "The ox, sheep, goat...you may eat" (Dt. 14:4,6):

B.   That is subject to eating, but an unclean beast is not subject to eating.

4. A.   I know only that there is a positive commandment involved. How do I know that there also is a negative commandment as well?

B.   Scripture says, "the camel, hare, and daman."

C.   "You shall not eat of their flesh or touch their carcasses."

5. A.   I know only that one may not eat those that are listed by name. How on the basis of Scripture do I encompass all other unclean beasts?

B.   It is a matter of an argument of logic. If these, which exhibit some, though not all, of the indicators of cleanness, lo, they are subject to a negative commandment, all other unclean beasts, which exhibit no other indicators of uncleanness at all, should surely be subject to a negative commandment, prohibiting eating them.

C.   The prohibition of the camel, hare, daman, and swine therefore turn out to derive from the specification of Scripture, and all other unclean beasts are prohibited by reason of the argument *a fortiori* just now given.

D.   It further turns out that the affirmative commandment affecting them derives from Scripture, and the negative from the argument *a fortiori* just now given.

My best sense of the passage is that what we want to know is how beasts not mentioned on the list are covered by the indicators presented by the beasts that are mentioned on the list. The basic issue then is at C, namely, if I know that a beast is unacceptable for the altar, does that fact make a beast of the same sort unacceptable, also, for secular use? Then we are given a variety of possibilities, and at each point, we are told that one may eat oxen, sheep, and goats, and that is without further limitation. The implicit position, as I see it, is that while such beasts as are used for inappropriate purposes for the altar are forbidden to the altar, they nonetheless may be used for secular purposes. That is almost certainly the sense, since many of the items are explicitly permitted by the law for everyday use, e.g., the item that H. Hammer translates, "Since we find that the law of unclean animals has been applied to laymen and not confined to sacred use alone, let me also declare as forbidden for food those that are forbidden to men for other purposes." I find this incomprehensible as worded, though my best sense is that Hammer's basic proposition is the same as mine. Nos. 2, 3, 4, 5 present no problems.

VI. Genesis Rabbah

Here is an instance in which the purposes of narrative predominate, those of exegesis prove subordinate. Yet I cannot imagine the kind of writing that will have required this composition – or, more to the point, one of its type.

Genesis Rabbah
III:IV

1. A. R. Simeon bar Yehosedeq asked R. Samuel bar Nahman, saying to him, "Since I heard that you are a master of lore, [tell me,] from what source was the light created?"
   B. He said to him, "The Holy One, blessed be he, cloaked himself in it as in a cloak, and the splendor of his majesty shown forth from one end of the world to the other."
   C. He had said [this statement] to him in a whisper.
   D. [Simeon] then said to [Samuel], "In point of fact, that is the explicit statement of a verse of Scripture: 'Who covers yourself with light as with a cloak' (Ps. 104:2). Yet you tell it to me in a whisper [as though revealing a hidden doctrine of some sort]!"
   E. He said to him, "Just as I heard it in a whisper, so I repeated it to you in a whisper."
   F. Said R. Berekhiah, "If R. Isaac had not expounded that point, it would not have been possible for us to have said it [anyhow]."
   G. Before this exchange, what in fact had people said about the matter? [That is, what had people thought was the place from which the light was created?]
   H. R. Berekhiah in the name of R. Isaac: "From the place of the holy house [the Temple] light was created. That is in line with the following verse of Scripture: 'And behold the glory of the God of Israel came from the east; and his voice was like the sound of many waters, and the earth shone with his glory' (Ez. 43:2).
   I. "The word 'his glory' refers only to the Temple, in line with this verse of Scripture: 'You throne of glory, on high from the beginning, you place of our sanctuary' (Jer. 17:12)."

This composition serves an exegetical purpose – but the form is extremely odd. For this passage has not been composed with an exegetical treatise in mind. Its narrative purpose is to focus upon the modes of communication, e.g., C, D, E. The narrative is not devoted to the exposition of Gen. 1.3, e.g., through an intersecting verse or through a comment on the word order of the verse, such as we find at III:I-II, and III:III, respectively. Rather we have a composition of a more speculative, abstract character. The issue is the source of light, and that issue in no way draws us back to the base verse at hand.

Another example of writing for a document not in hand and not suggested by any writing we do have in hand involves what we should call today redaction criticism: why are documents as a whole the way they are and not some other way.

Genesis Rabbah
III:V

1. A. Said R. Simon, "The word 'light' is written five times, to match [the five] books of his Torah.

   B. "'And God said, "Let there be light"' (Gen. 1:3) matches the book of Genesis, in which the Holy One, blessed be he, was engaged when he created the world.

   C. "'And there was light' matches the book of Exodus, which begins, 'These are the names,' in which Israel went forth from Egypt, from darkness to light.

   D. "'And God saw the light' matches the book of Leviticus, which is rich in rules.

   E. "'And God divided the light' matches the book of Numbers, in which God divided those who had come forth from Egypt apart from those who would enter the land.

   F. "'And God called the light' matches the book of Deuteronomy, which is rich in many laws."

   G. They objected to him, "But is not the book of Leviticus also filled with many laws?"

   H. He said to them, "[The verse refers only to Deuteronomy, for the verse itself contains] a repetition [just as there is in the book of Deuteronomy]: 'And God called the light day'! Now is not the light the same thing as the day?! [Of course it is.]" [Freedman: Hence it is fitting that this verse should correspond to Deuteronomy, which also contains much repetition of the previous books.]

The point of interpretation yields yet another link between the story of Creation and the larger setting, the Torah as a whole, in which that story is found. So the details of the story correspond to the main frame of the Torah. The result? Creation corresponds to the Torah, and, of greater polemical weight, the Torah corresponds to Creation.

The exposition thus deals not with the verse at hand but with the projected syllogism. The upshot is that the Torah is comparable, in detail, to light. A description of Genesis Rabbah as a verse-by-verse exegesis of the book of Genesis is simply wrong. The present composition bears no resemblance to a verse-by-verse exegesis, since its purpose – to lay forth a syllogism – comes to realization without a close reading of the language of a verse or even of the whole verse.

Finally, here is a mishmash of materials, some of them usable in one kind of writing, some in another; the whole is too miscellaneous to serve a well-crafted piece of writing, such as, in general, the midrash compilations are.

Genesis Rabbah
III:VI

1. A. It has been repeated on Tannaite authority: As to the light that was created in the six days of creation, it is not possible that that light should illuminate the day, for if so, lo, that light would dim the orb of the sun. It also is not possible that that light should illuminate the night, for it was created only to give light, not by night, but by day. So where has it gone?

   B. It has been stored away for the righteous in the age to come, as it is said, "Moreover the light of the moon shall be as the light of the sun, and the light of the sun shall be sevenfold, as the light of the seven days [of creation]" (Is. 30:26).

   C. Seven [days of creation]? But at that point only three [days of creation had already passed]. For were the luminaries not created on the fourth day?

   D. But it may be compared to the case of a man who says, "I am doing so much for the seven days of my wedding-feast [even though in point of fact the food may not last that long]."

   E. R. Nehemiah says, "The reference is to the seven days of mourning for Methuselah, on which the Holy One, blessed be he, lavished much light."

2. A. "And God saw the light" (Gen. 1:3):

   B. R. Zeira son of R. Abbahu gave an exposition in Caesarea: "How do we know that **people may not say a blessing [for the rite of Habdalah, separating the Sabbath from the ordinary week] making use of a light, unless they have actually made use of its light** [M. Ber. 8:5]?

   C. "From the following statement: 'And God saw...then God divided...'[as in saying a blessing to divide the Sabbath from the ordinary week day. So God first made use of the light by looking at it and only then divided it.]"

3. A. [Reading the word "divided" to mean, "set aside," we have the following dispute:] When Scripture says, "He set it aside," R. Judah b. R. Simon said, "It means, he set it aside for himself."

B.   Rabbis say, "He set it aside for the righteous in the age to come."

C.   "The matter may be compared to the case of a king, who had a fine portion [served to himself at a meal] and set it aside for his son."

4. A.   Said R. Berekhiah, "This is how to the two great men of the age, R. Yohanan and R. Simeon b. Laqish, interpreted the matter: 'He divided...' means, he actually did impose a division.

B.   "The matter may be compared to the case of a king who had two generals, one ruling by day, the other ruling by night. The two of them competed with one another. This one would say, 'I shall rule by day,' and that one would say, 'I shall rule by day.'

C.   "The king called the first and said to him, 'General So-and-so, the day will be under your authority.'

D.   "The second he called and said to him, 'General Such-and-such, the night will be under your authority.'

E.   "Thus: 'And God called the light day,' saying to it, 'The day will be your boundary,' and 'the darkness he called night,' saying to it, 'The night will be your boundary.'"

F.   Said R. Yohanan, "That is in line with what the Holy One, blessed be he, said to Job, 'Have you commanded the morning?' (Job 38:12).

G.   "'Have you caused the dayspring to know its place?' (Job 38:12)? Did you inform [the one or the other] of its proper place? [You did none of these things, but God did these things.]"

H.   Said R. Tanhuma, "I shall cite a verse of Scripture that makes the point: 'I form light and create darkness, I make peace' (Is. 45:7). That is to say, once the two of them [light and darkness] were created, God made peace between them."

5. A.   "And God called the light day" (Gen. 1:3):

B.   Said R. Eleazar, "God links his name never with evil but only with good.

C.   "That is in line with the following verse: 'And *God* called the light day.' But the passage does not go on to say, 'And the darkness God called night.' Rather what it says is merely: 'And the darkness he called night' (Gen. 1:3)."

Like the foregoing, the discourse of No. 1 aims at a thematic observation, not at the exposition of the base verse. The point has to do with the character of the remarkable light created at the beginning, and the upshot is to set out yet another bridge to the eschatological theme present throughout. Here we say that that remarkable light has been hidden away and preserved for the righteous in the world to come, so that, at the foundations, creation corresponds to the eschatological age. Then the story of creation matches the contents of revelation and the age of redemption, all together. I cannot think of a more powerful polemic about the character of the cosmos as Israel is to find it in Scripture: harmonious, cogent, uniform, beginning to end, from perfect creation to perfect redemption through Sinai. No. 2 draws us back from the theme to the language of the verse at hand, taking aim at the statement that God first saw and then divided the law. This yields the stated proposition. The verse is not unpacked but itself serves to prove the desired proposition. The passage – lifted whole from its appropriate context as an exposition of M. Ber. 8:5 – bears no clear relationship at all to the exposition of the verse at hand. Rather the cited verse serves as a prooftext for the validity of a rule in the Mishnah. Nos. 3 and 4 take up the exposition of the meaning of the word "divided," with two interesting points. (One could claim that No. 2 is inserted because of the same point of interest.) No. 3 simply finds another occasion for recovering the eschatological dimension of the tale. No. 4 underlines the divine greatness involved in dividing day from night, the plan leading to perfection. No. 5 then underlines the same point, namely, God's perfect goodness, by pointing out, on the basis of the peculiar formulation of the verse, the proposition at hand. It would be difficult to imagine a set of propositions of a more fundamental and wide-ranging character. Nor can I conceive a piece of writing less suitable for a document that follows a well-crafted program.

VII. Leviticus Rabbah

What follows is a miscellany so lacking in any center or focus that I see the whole, and its components, as worked out for no particular document we now have, or, so far as I can tell, can even imagine. The reason, then, that I cannot imagine the canonical authorships' making such a writing is that all of the writings they have compiled make some sort of sense, appeal to a principle of cogency of one kind or another. But what will a large-scale compilation of materials of the following sort have yielded? Something we cannot call a document at all. And that type of compilation, as a matter of fact, falls entirely outside of the frame of imagination of our authorships, who have given us, in the end, nothing that we may classify as a (mere) scrapbook of this and that. At worst, they have given us collages. But at best – and most of what we have is their best – they have produced documents, one after another, of remarkable cogency, given their various contents.

Leviticus Rabbah Parashah Twenty-Six
XXVI:II

1. A   R. Yosé of Malehayya and R. Joshua of Sikhnin, in the name of R. Levi: "Children in David's time, before they had tasted the taste of sin [reached sexual maturity], were able to expound the Torah

in forty-nine different ways to reach a decision on uncleanness, and in forty-nine different ways to reach a decision on cleanness.

B. "And David prayed for them: 'You, O Lord, protect them' [Ps. 12:7].

C. "Preserve their learning in their heart.

D. "'Protect them forever from this generation'" (Ps. 12:7).

E. "From the generation that deserves destruction."

2 A. After all this glory, [that generation of disciples] went out to war and fell.

B. It was because there were renegades among them.

C. That is in line with what David says, "My soul is in the midst of lions. I lie down among them that are aflame, sons of men whose teeth are spears and arrows, their tongues sharp swords" (Ps. 57:4).

D. "My soul is in the midst of lions" refers to Abner and Amasa, who were lions in the Torah.

E. "I lie down among them that are aflame" refers to Doeg and Ahitophel, who were burning with gossip.

F. "Sons of men whose teeth are spears and arrows" refers to the men of Keilah: "Will the men of Keilah hand me over?" (1 Sam. 32:11).

G. "Their tongues are sharp swords" refers to the Ziphites: "When the Ziphites came and said to Saul, 'Does David not hide himself with us?'" (1 Sam. 23:19).

H. At that moment said David, "Now what is the Presence of God doing in the world? 'Be exalted, O God, above the heavens' [Ps. 57:5]. Remove your Presence from their midst!"

I. But the generation of Ahab was made up of idolators. But because there were no renegades among them, they would go out to war and win.

J. That is in line with what Obadiah said to Elijah: "Has it not been told my lord what I did when Jezebel killed the prophets of the Lord, how I hid a hundred men of the Lord's prophets by fifties in a cave and fed them with bread and water?" (1 Kgs. 18:13).

K. If bread, why water? But this teaches that it was harder to bring the water than the bread.

L. Elijah proclaimed on Mount Carmel, saying, "And I alone remain as a prophet to the Lord" (1 Kgs. 18:22).

M. Now the entire people were well informed [that there were other prophets who had survived], but they did not reveal it to the king.

3. A. Said R. Samuel b. Nahman, "They said to the snake, 'On what account are you commonly found among fences?'

B. "He said to them, 'Because I broke down the fence of the world [causing man to sin].'

C. "On what account do you go along with your tongue on the ground?

D. "He said to them, 'Because my tongue made [it happen] to me.'

	E.	"They said to him, 'Now what pleasure do you have [from it all]? A lion tramples but also devours [the prey], a wolf tears but also devours, while you bite and kill [but do not devour what you kill].'
	F.	"He said to them, 'Does the snake bite without a charm?' [Qoh. 10:11] Is it possible that I do anything that was not commanded me from on high?"
	G.	"'And on what account do you bite a single limb, but all the limbs feel it?'
	H.	"He said to them, 'Now are you saying that to me? Speak to the slanderer, who says something here and kills [his victim] in Rome, says something in Rome and kills [his victim] at the other end of the world.'"
4.	A.	And why is [the slanderer] called "the third party"?
	B.	It is because he kills three: the one who speaks [slander], the one who receives it, and the one about whom it is said].
	C.	But in the time of Saul, [slander] killed four: Doeg, who said it, Saul who received it, Abimelech, about whom it was said, and Abner.
	D.	And why was Abner killed?
	E.	R. Joshua b. Levi said, "Because he made a joke out of the shedding of the blood of young men.
	F.	"That is in line with the following verse of Scripture: 'And Abner said to Joab, "Let the young men get up and play before us"'" (1 Sam. 2:14).
	G.	R. Simeon b. Laqish said, "Because he put his name before David's name."
	H.	"That is in line with the following verse of Scripture: 'And Abner sent messengers to David right away, saying, Whose is the land?' (2 Sam. 3:12).
	I.	"He wrote, 'From Abner to David.'"
	J.	And rabbis say, "It was because he did not wait for Saul to become reconciled with David.
	K.	"That is in line with the following verse of Scripture: 'Moreover, my father, see, yes, see the skirt of your robe in my hand' [1 Sam. 24:11]. Abner said to him, 'What do you want of this man's boasting! The [cloth] was caught in a thornbush.'
	L.	"When they came within the barricade, he said to him, 'Will you not answer, Abner?' [1 Sam. 26:14]? Concerning the piece of the cloak you said that it was caught in a thornbush. 'Have the spear and the water jar also been caught in the thornbush?'"
	M.	And there are those who say, "It was because he had the power to protest against Saul in regard to Nob, the city of priests, and he did not do so."

Margulies sees No. 1 as an exposition of the notion that God's words are pure, thus 1.A. But this is farfetched, because if we did not have the passage in the location in the document in which it now occurs, we should never have imagined that at stake was the base verse of Leviticus Rabbah Parahshah XXVI! The "silver refined in the furnace on the ground purified seven times" of Ps. 12:6 yields the figure of forty-nine, important at 1.A. The focus is so vague that we have no way of predicting where the framers will carry us next. Then the exposition moves right on to Ps. 12:7, "Do you, O Lord, protect us, guard us ever from this generation." While No. 2 appears to carry forward the thought of No. 1, that is only at 2.A-B. At that point the power of the renegade is subject to systematic exposition, 2.A-B, as against 2.1. The remainder of the passage at hand explores the secondary materials introduced at 2.C. The upshot is to contrast God's pure speech with humanity's gossip, but I am not inclined to see that as the purpose of the composition. No 3 plays on the theme of impure speech, gossip; it is inserted whole, because it allows for 4.A-B to preface 4.C, and that passage clearly is in close relationship to No. 2. The remainder of No. 4 then works out further materials important to No. 2. All of this is so run-on as to make implausible the conception that the formation of the individual units and the conglomeration of them all into what is before us have responded to a redactional plan or program such as we know from extant writings or even writings we can imagine.

VIII. Pesiqta deRab Kahana

The criterion of whether a composite is miscellaneous or purposeful applies to my sample from Pesiqta deRab Kahana. Purposefulness in this document comes to expression in the forming of all things to yield or demonstrate a proposition. The syllogistic intent of the framers, then, is realized in the effect of the whole. In the following, I see a clear-cut reversion to a base verse from an intersecting verse. But the intervening materials are of such a strikingly miscellaneous character that I have to regard the whole as nothing more than a scrapbook. Among materials of the sort that follows, no documentary interest comes to expression; we cannot imagine the kind of document that can have been served by the distinct and discrete items forming the mélange that follows.

Pesiqta deRab Kahana
V:III
1.   A   *Hope deferred makes the heart sick, [but a desire fulfilled is a tree of life. He who despises the word brings destruction on himself, but he who respects the commandments will be rewarded. The teaching of the wise is a fountain of life, that one may avoid the snares of death] (Prov. 13:12-14):*

	B.	R. Hiyya bar Ba opened discourse by citing the verse: "*Hope deferred makes the heart sick* – this refers to one who betrothes a woman and takes her as his wife only after delay.
	C.	"*...but a desire fulfilled is a tree of life* – this refers to one who betrothes a woman and takes her as his wife right away."
2.	A.	Another interpretation: "*Hope deferred makes the heart sick* – this refers to David, who was anointed and then ruled only after two years had passed.
	B.	"*...but a desire fulfilled is a tree of life* – this refers to Saul, who was anointed and then ruled right away.
	C.	On account of what merit [did Saul have that good fortune]?
	D.	On account of the merit accruing for the good deeds which were to his credit, for he was humble and modest.
	E.	For he ate his ordinary food [not deriving from his share of an animal sacrificed in the Temple, for example] in a state of cultic cleanness [as if he were eating holy food deriving from his share of an offering made in the Temple].
	F.	And, further, he would spend his own funds so as to protect the funds of Israel.
	G.	And he treated as equal the honor owing to his servant with the honor owing to himself.
	H.	Judah bar Nahman in the name of R. Simeon b. Laqish: "For he was one who was subject to study of the Torah: *By me [the Torah speaks] princes rule* (Prov. 18:16). *By me kings rule* [and Saul ruled through his study of the Torah] (Prov. 8:15)."
3.	A.	R. Ishmael taught on Tannaite authority, "Before a man has sinned, people pay him reverence and awe. Once he has sinned, they impose on him reverence and awe.
	B.	"Thus, before the first man had sinned, he would hear [God's] voice in a workaday way. After he had sinned, he heard the same voice as something strange. Before he had sinned, the first man heard God's voice and would stand on his feet: *And they heard the sound of God walking in the garden in the heat of the day* (Gen. 3:8). After he had sinned, he heard the voice of God and hid: *And man and his wife hid* (Gen. 3:8)."
	C.	Said R. Aibu, "At that moment the height of the first Man was cut down and he became a hundred cubits high."
	D.	[Ishmael continues:] "Before the Israelites sinned, what is written in their regard? *And the appearance of the glory of the Lord was like a consuming fire on the top of the mountain before the eyes of the children of Israel* (Ex. 24:17)."
	E.	Said R. Abba bar Kahana, "There were seven veils of fire, one covering the next, and the Israelites gazed and did not fear or take fright."

F.   "But when they had sinned, even on the face of the intercessor [Moses] they could not look: *And Aaron and all the children of Israel feared...to come near* (Ex. 34:40)."

4.   A.   R. Phineas bar Abun in the name of R. Hanin: "Also the intercessor felt the sin: *Kings of hosts do flee, do flee* (Ps. 68:13)." [This is now explained.]

B.   R. Yudan in the name of R. Aibu says, "'Angels of hosts' is not what is written here, but what is written is *Kings of hosts,* the kings of the angels, even Michael, even Gabriel, were not able to look upon the face of Moses.

C.   "But after the Israelites had sinned, even on the faces of lesser angels Moses could not gaze: *For I was in dread of anger and hot wrath* (Deut. 9:19)."

5.   A.   Before the deed of David [with Bath Sheba] took place, what is written? *For David: The Lord is my light and my salvation, of whom shall I be afraid?* (Ps. 27:1).

B.   But after that deed took place, what is written? *I will come upon him while he is weary and weak-handed* (2 Sam. 17:2).

6.   A.   Before Solomon sinned, he could rule over demons and demonesses: *I got for myself...Adam's progeny, demons and demonesses* (Qoh. 2:8).

B.   What is the sense of *demons and demonesses*? For he ruled over demons and demonesses.

C.   But after he had sinned, he brought sixty mighty men to guard his bed: *Lo, the bed of Solomon, with sixty mighty men around it, all of them holding a sword and veterans of war* (Song 3:7-8).

7.   A.   Before Saul had sinned, what is written concerning him? *And when Saul had taken dominion over Israel, he fought against all his enemies on every side, against Moab, against the Ammonites, against Edom, against the kings of Zobah, and against the Philistines; wherever he turned he put them to the worse* (1 Sam. 14:47).

B.   After he had sinned what is written concerning him? *And Saul saw the camp of the Philistines and was afraid* (1 Sam. 28:5).

8.   A.   Another interpretation of the verse "*Hope deferred makes the heart sick:*

B.   Said R. Hiyya bar Abba, "This refers to the Israelites before they were redeemed.

C.   "You find that when Moses came to the Israelites and said to them, 'The Holy One blessed be he has said to me, *Go, say to Israel, I have surely remembered you,* (Ex. 3:16), they said to him, 'Moses, our lord, it is still a mere remembering! *What is my strength, that I should wait? And what is my end, that I should be patient? Is my strength the strength of stones, or is my flesh bronze? [In truth I have no help in me, and any resources is driven from me]* (Job 6:11-13).

D.   "'Is our strength the strength of stones? Is our flesh made of bronze?'

E.   "But when he said to him, 'This month you will be redeemed,' they said, 'That is a good sign.'

F.   "*...but a desire fulfilled is a tree of life: This month shall be for you the beginning of months; it shall be the first month of the year for you*" (Ex. 12:1-2)

The extensive treatment of the intersecting verse does not prepare us for the final clarification of the base verse at No. 8, and that is because the composite bears a heavy and inappropriate accretion of useless material. The point is that when Moses made his announcement that in the cited month of Nisan, the Israelites would be redeemed, that marked the end of hope deferred and the beginning of the desire fulfilled. But nothing has prepared us for that excellent conclusion. No. 1 gives a straightforward application of the verse. No. 2 brings us to David and Saul. The intrusion of Nos. 3-7 is not easy to explain, except as a secondary amplification on the theme of Saul. The first Man, the Israelites, Moses, David, Saul all are examples of the effect of sin, which takes a proud person and humbles him. We see, therefore, a vast insertion of irrelevant materials. No. 8, then, brings us back to the point at issue, and we have to regard the rest of the composite as a rather mindless amplification of a minor point – the mere mention of Saul! The basic intent, however, in introducing the intersecting verse is striking and well executed at the end. But that does not save the whole from falling into the classification of an utter miscellany. Most of the items before us can have fit equally well – or poorly – in any document; they are not framed with documentary interests, either demonstrated or imaginable, in anyone's mind.

IX. Lamentations Rabbah

No. 2 in what follows is parachuted down, but serves no material redactional purpose. It can appear more or less anywhere. The contrast between that entry and the next explains why I catalogue No. 2 as an item made up for purposes autonomous of any document we now have in hand or can envisage (so far as I can tell). Perhaps some book of stories about how traders do business can have found the item appropriate; but then such a book is out of phase with the whole of the canonical literature. The same judgment as to classification applies to No. 4, but for different reasons.

Lamentations Rabbah Parashah One to Lamentations 1:1
XXXV:V
1.   A   ["How lonely sits] the city that was full of people:"

B.   R. Samuel taught on Tannaite authority, "There were twenty-four main streets in Jerusalem. Cohen, p. 69:] Each thoroughfare had twenty-four side-turnings; each side-turning twenty-four roads; each road twenty-four streets; each street twenty-four courts; each court twenty-four houses; and each court residents double the number of those who came out of Egypt.

C.   [Following Buber:] "This illustrates the statement: 'Judah and Israel are as numerous as the sand on the sea shore' (1 Kgs. 4:20).

D.   "That is the sense of the verse, 'the city that was full of people.'"

2. A.   Said R. Eleazar, "There was a case involving a caravan in which there was a merchant who was leading three hundred camels bearing pepper.

B.   "He came by Tyre and found a certain tailor, sitting at the gate. He said to him, 'What are you selling?'

C.   "He said to him, 'Pepper.'

D.   "He said to him, 'Sell me a little.'

E.   "He said to him, 'No, for all of it is for one [purchaser].'

F.   "He said to him, "You are going to sell it only to the Jewish town.'

G.   "He came to the Jewish town and found another tailor sitting at the gate. He said to him, 'What are your camels carrying?'

H.   "He said to him, 'Keep cutting.'

I.   "He said to him again, 'What are you selling?'

J.   "He said to him, 'Keep sewing.'

K.   "He said to him, 'Tell me what you are carrying, and if I can, I shall buy it, and if not, I shall bring you to someone who will buy it all.'

L.   "He said to him, 'Pepper.'

M.   "He took him to a house, and showed him a pile of coins, saying to them, "Look at this money. Does it circulate in your land?' [The other was satisfied and made the sale,] and he took his leave and went off in peace.

N.   "After he had left, he went out to walk in the marketplace. He met one of his friends, who said to him, 'What are you bringing here?'

O.   "He said to him, 'Pepper.'

P.   "He said to him, 'If you have a little, sell it to me for a hundred dinars, for I have a party to give.'

Q.   "He said to him, 'I have already sold it to a certain tailor, but I'll tell him to give you a little of it.'

R.   [Following Cohen, p. 70:] "He went and found the house full of buyers, so that those who were in the first room secured an ounce each, and those in the second room half an ounce each, while those in the third received no attention at all."

S.   "That is the sense of the verse, 'the city that was full of people.'"

3. A.   [Cohen, p. 70:] If you wish to know how many multitudes there were in Jerusalem, you can ascertain it from the priests.

B.   R. Joshua of Sikhnin in the name of R. Levi said, "To what may the matter be compared?

C. "To a large heap that stood in the marketplace, and no one could estimate its volume. There was a smart man there, who said to them, 'If you want to come to an estimate of its volume, you may come to an estimate based on the amount of priestly ration that is separated from it.'

D. "So if you want to estimate the population of the Israelites you make an estimate based on the priesthood.

E. "That is in line with this verse: 'And Solomon offered for the sacrifice of peace-offerings, which he offered to the Lord, twenty-two thousand oxen and a hundred and twenty-thousand sheep' (I Kgs. 8:63)."

4. A. And we have learned: A bull was offered by twenty-four priests and a ram by eleven.

B. That applies in the first Temple, but as to the second:

C. Agrippa wanted to know how many multitudes there were in Jerusalem.

D. "He said to the priests, "Set aside for me one kidney from each passover-offering."

E. They set aside for him 600,000 pairs of kidneys, double the number of those who left Egypt,

F. not counting those who were unclean or on a distant journey [who would celebrate later],

G. and there was not a single passover-offering that was shared by less than ten people.

H. R. Hiyya repeated on Tannaite authority, "Even forty, even fifty."

I. Bar Kappara taught, "Even a hundred."

J. And that Passover they entered the Temple mount, but it could not hold them.

K. That was called the Passover of the crushed.

My text for No. 1 follows Cohen for B, then I include the prooftexts given in Buber, which seem to me to tie the whole to our larger context. But this admittedly is a fabricated text. No. 2 seems to me a rather pointless story, like the first illustrating in a general way the numerous population of Jerusalem. No. 3 is explicit in making its point, that Jerusalem had had an enormous population, and No. 4 goes over the same ground; its materials are autonomous of any exegetical compilation.

X. Esther Rabbah

I present an entire composition, even though only part of it belongs in the rubric of free-standing compositions, utterly out of phase with any available, or conceivable, documentary program. In my comment I shall point to the components that seem to me to belong within the present framework.

Esther Rabbah Petihta One

I:I

1. A.   Rab commenced by introducing the following verse of Scripture: "And your life shall hang in doubt before you; [night and day you shall be in dread, and have no assurance of your life. In the morning, you shall say, 'Would it were evening!' and at evening you shall say, 'Would it were morning!' because of the dread which your heart shall fear and the sights which your eyes shall see. And the Lord will bring you back in ships to Egypt, a journey which I promise that you should never make again; and there you shall offer yourselves for sale to your enemies as male and female slaves, but no man will buy you]" (Dt. 28:66-68).

    B.   Rabbis and R. Berekhiah:

    C.   Rabbis say, "'And your life shall hang in doubt before you:' this is one who buys wheat for a year [rather than raising his own].

    D.   "'night and day you shall be in dread:' this is one who buys wheat in the market [a week at a time].

    E.   "'and have no assurance of your life:' this is one who buys wheat from the baker [for a day or two at a time]."

    F.   R. Berekhiah said, "'And your life shall hang in doubt before you:' this is one who buys wheat for three years.

    G.   "'night and day you shall be in dread:' this is one who buys wheat for a year.

    H.   "'and have no assurance of your life:' this is one who buys wheat in the market."

    I.   Rabbis reply to R. Berekhiah, "What is the rule as to one who buys bread from a baker?"

    J.   He said to them, "The Torah does not speak of corpses."

2. A.   Another interpretation of the verse "And your life shall hang in doubt before you; night and day you shall be in dread, and have no assurance of your life:"

    B.   "And your life shall hang in doubt before you:" this is one who is in prison in Caesarea.

    C.   "night and day you shall be in dread:" this is one who is taken out for trial.

    D.   "and have no assurance of your life:" this is one who is taken out to be executed.

3. A.   [Another interpretation of the verse "And your life shall hang in doubt before you; night and day you shall be in dread, and have no assurance of your life:"]

    B.   Rab interpreted the verse to speak of the time of Haman.

    C.   "'And your life shall hang in doubt before you:' this speaks of the twenty-four hours from the removal of the ring.

    D.   "'night and day you shall be in dread:' this speaks of the time that the letters were sent forth.

	E.	"'and have no assurance of your life:' this was when [the enemies of the Jews were told to be 'ready against that day' (Est. 3:14)."
4.	A.	"In the morning, you shall say, 'Would it were evening!' and at evening you shall say, 'Would it were morning!' :"
	B.	"In the morning," of Babylonia, "you shall say, 'Would it were evening!'"
	C.	"In the morning," of Media, "you shall say, 'Would it were evening!'"
	D.	"In the morning," of Greece, "you shall say, 'Would it were evening!'"
	E.	"In the morning," of Edom, "you shall say, 'Would it were evening!'"
5.	A.	Another interpretation of the verse: "In the morning, you shall say, 'Would it were evening!' and at evening you shall say, 'Would it were morning!':"
	B.	"In the morning," of Babylonia, "you shall say, 'Would it were the evening of Media!'"
	C.	"In the morning," of Media, "you shall say, 'Would it were evening of Greece!'"
	D.	"In the morning," of Greece, "you shall say, 'Would it were evening of Edom!'"
	E.	Why so? "because of the dread which your heart shall fear and the sights which your eyes shall see."
6.	A.	"And the Lord will bring you back in ships to Egypt:"
	B.	Said R. Isaac, "'in ships' [spelled not with the silent alef but with the silent ayin can be read] by reason of poverty and good deeds."
7.	A.	["And the Lord will bring you back in ships to Egypt:"]
	B.	Why Egypt?
	C.	Because it is ugly and wicked for a slave to return to his original master.
8.	A.	Said R. Simeon b. Yohai, "In three passages God warned the Israelites not to go back to Egypt:
	B.	"'For since you have seen the Egyptians today, you shall see them again no more' (Ex. 14:13).
	C.	"'The Lord has said to you, You shall not return any more by that way' (Dt. 17:16).
	D.	"'And the Lord will bring you back in ships to Egypt, a journey which I promise that you should never make again.'
	E.	"They disobeyed all three and were punished on three counts:
	F.	"in the days of Sennacherib: 'Woe to them who go down to Egypt for help' (Is. 31:1). Then: 'Now the Egyptians are men and not God' (Is. 31:3).
	G.	"in the days of Yohanan b. Koreah: 'Then it shall come to pass that the sword which you fear shall overtake you there in the land of Egypt' (Jer. 42:16).

H.   "The third time in the days of Trajan, may his bones be pulverized.'"

9.   A.   The wife of Trajan – may his bones be pulverized – gave birth to a child on the ninth of Ab, while the Jews were observing rites of mourning, and the child died on Hanukkah.

B.   They said to one another, "What shall we do? Shall we kindle the Hanukkah lights or not?"

C.   They said, "Let us light them, and what will be will be."

D.   They went and slandered the Jews to him, saying to his wife, "When your son was born, these Jews went into mourning, and when he died, they lit their lamps."

E.   She sent and said to her husband, "Instead of conquering the barbarians, come and conquer these Jews, who have rebelled against you.

F.   He had made a calculation that the trip would take ten days but the winds carried him and brought him in five days.

G.   He came into the synagogue and found the Jews occupied with this verse of Scripture: "The Lord will bring a nation against you from afar, from the end of the earth, as the vulture swoops down" (Dt. 28:49).

H.   He said to them, "I am the vulture who expected the trip to last ten days but who was brought by the fair wind in five."

I.   He surrounded them with his legions and slaughtered them.

10.   A.   "[there you shall offer yourselves for sale to your enemies as male and female slaves], but no man will buy you. [These are the words of the covenant which the Lord commanded Moses to make with the people of Israel (Dt. 28:69/29:1)]:"

B.   Why is there none to buy?

C.   Rab said, "Because you did not acquire the words of the covenant ['These are the words of the covenant']; none among you purchased the words of the five books of the Torah, and the letters of the word for buy has the numerical value of five."

D.   Said R. Samuel b. Nahman, "Because I made the rounds of all the nations of the world, and none among them would buy the words of Torah as you do ['These are the words of the covenant']."

E.   Said R. Simeon b. Yohai, "You can acquire rights of ownership to members of the nations of the world, as it says, 'Moreover of the children of the strangers that sojourn among you, of them may you buy' (Lev. 25:45),

F.   "but they cannot acquire rights of ownership to you. Why not? Because you acquired 'these the words of the covenant.' And the nations? They did not acquire 'these the words of the covenant' ['These are the words of the covenant']."

G.   Said R. Jonathan, "Because you have patrons, and what are they? 'These are the words of the covenant.'

H.   "You are [Simon, p. 4:] crown property. If a man buys a slave from crown property, is not his life forfeit?

I.   "So said Ahasuerus to his wife, 'Behold, I have given Esther the house of Haman' (Est. 8:7)."

J.   On this matter said R. Judah b. R. Simon, "This was the penalty for having laid hands on the crown property."

11. A   Said R. Isaac, "There was a precedent in Pruspiah of a woman who would ransom captives. A captive woman came and she ransomed her, so too a second. When she ran out of money and could not buy any more, soldiers forthwith surrounded her and killed her.

B.   Why so?

C.   To [Simon:] warn bandits in the future [not to kidnap Jews, since no one would buy them; hence this curse is in a way a blessing in disguise, so Simon, p. 5, n. 1].

12. A   [Another comment on the verse, "there you shall offer yourselves for sale to your enemies as male and female slaves, but no man will buy you:"]

B.   R. Levi and R. Isaac:

C.   R. Levi says, "Who will will buy a companion for himself knowing that on the next day he is going to be put to death? Who is going to take a woman and on the next day she is going to be put to death?"

D.   R. Isaac said, "For slave-boys and slave-girls you will not be purchased, but you will be purchased 'to be destroyed, to be slain, and to perish.'

E.   "For that is what Esther said to Ahasuerus: 'For we are sold...to be destroyed, to be slain, and to perish. But if we had been sold for bondmen and bondwomen, I would have held my peace' (Est. 7:4).

F.   "For so did our master, Moses, write for us in the Torah: 'there you shall offer yourselves for sale to your enemies as male and female slaves, but no man will buy you.' Did he intend to say, 'You shall sell yourselves 'to be destroyed, to be slain, and to perish'? [Surely not.]"

13. A   ["Now it came to pass in the days of Ahasuerus, the Ahasuerus who reigned from India to Ethiopia over one hundred and twenty-seven provinces:"]

B.   When they saw this, they all began to cry, "Woe!"

C.   "Now it came to pass" [since the word in Hebrew for "now it came to pass" can yield the word "woe," hence the sense of the words, 'Now it came to pass in the days of Ahasuerus' is this:] "Woe for that which was in the days of Ahasuerus" (Est. 1:1).

This mélange contains materials that have no strong claim on location in Esther Rabbah, even though, overall, the composition legitimately falls into the classification of the *petihta*, hence of writing in accord with a documentary program and protocol. No. 9 is a story that is told entirely in its own terms; it is connected to the present context in a suitable manner, but as a matter of fact, the story can find its natural place only in a compilation of *Märchen* about Roman emperors and the Jews. There is no such compilation, of course, and the possibility of forming one seems to me to fall outside of the frame of reference of any authorship in the canonical circles. I give that item in the context of its *petihta* to show how out of place it is. The rest, as we see, can find a natural place either as writing prepared for our document in particular (e.g., exegesis of verses in Esther Rabbah or in connection with a *petihta* for Esther Rabbah) or at least writing for a document of a propositional order within the range of imaginable possibilities, hence either my first or my second rubrics. Nos. 1, 2 have no bearing upon our base verse but work only on the intersecting verse, as expected. No. 3 then interprets the intersecting verse in light of Esther 3:10, 14, explicitly citing 3:14. The whole has no bearing upon the base verse before us. The exposition of the intersecting verse goes forward in Nos. 4, 5. No. 6 returns us to the next clause in the intersecting verse, the return to Egypt. No. 7 focuses also on the components of that verse. No. 8 then appeals to the same verse now as part of a proposition about not going back to Egypt and the consequences of doing so. Then comes the utterly free-standing item. The inclusion of No. 9 is only because of 8.H, and, obviously, the composition of No. 9 in no way responds to the redactional purpose in including the item.. No. 10 then returns us to our base verse, now adding the following one, which is Dt. 28:69/29:1 (Hebrew/English). The union of the successive clauses yields the theme of Torah, now with special interest in the fact that Jews may not be taken captive. No. 11 is tacked on for thematic reasons. No. 12 underlines the established proposition of No. 10, explaining why the Jews will not be purchased. And that is the point at which we revert to the book of Esther, but not to our base verse, rather to Est. 7:4. No. 13, then, is the sole point of reversion to the base verse, and, we see, as with Lam. 1:1 spread through the *petihtaot* of Lamentations Rabbah, so here, Est. 1:1 can be tacked on for pretty much any reason and in any context.

Here is another example of materials that are framed to serve no redactional purpose, either the one in which they occur, or any other that falls in the realm of the possible, so it seems to me.

Esther Rabbah I to Esther 1:4
XIII:I
10. A   There is the following case:
     B.   There was a man named Bar Buhin.

C.   Our masters went to him in connection with the fund for support of sages. They heard his son say to him, "What are we going to eat today?"

D.   He said to him, "Raw vegetables."

E.   He said to him, "One bushel to the mina or two to the mina?"

F.   He said to him, "Two to the mina. These are withered, so are cheap."

G.   They said to one another, "How are we going to go to that man. Let's do our business in town and then come to him."

H.   They went and did their business in town, and then came to him. They said to him, "Give us what is required for the religious duty [of supporting sages]."

I.   He said to them, "Go to the lady of the house, and she will give you a basket of denars."

J.   They went to his wife and said to her, "You husband says to give us a contribution of a basket of denars."

K.   She said to them, "Heaped up or level?"

L.   They said to her, "He said simply, a basket."

M.   She said to them, "I will give it to you heaped up, and if he doesn't like it, I'll tell him I gave the extra from my dowry."

N.   They said to her, "May your Creator make up whatever you may lose."

O.   He said to them, "And how did she hand it over to you, heaped up or smooth?"

P.   They said to him, "We said simply a basket, and she said to us, 'I will give it to you heaped up, and if he doesn't like it, I'll tell him I gave the extra from my dowry.'"

Q.   He said to them, "Well, that was my plan all along. But why didn't you come to me first?"

R.   They said to him, "We heard your servant say to you, 'What are we going to eat today?' And you said to him, 'Raw vegetables.' And he said to you, 'One bushel to the mina or two to the mina?' And you said to him, 'Two to the mina. These are withered, so are cheap.'

S.   "So we said to ourselves, 'Imagine someone with all that money eating raw vegetables bought at the rate of two bushels to the mina'!"

T.   He said to them, "True enough, with myself I'm cheap, but with the religious duty of my Creator, I'm not cheap and I'm not stingy at all."

11. A.   Bar Lufini was marrying off his daughter in Sepphoris to someone from Acco, so he put up stalls selling wine from Sepphoris to Acco, with golden lamps strung from the one town to the other.

B.   They said, "They did not leave that place before he had sunk to giving them beans from the threshing floor and wine from the vat."

	C.	Said R. Abin, "And they served it in smoky jars."
12.	A	But here, by contrast, ["a hundred and eighty days:"]
	B.	the last day was like the first day.
13.	A	R. Hiyya had a friend in Ashna.
	B.	He made a banquet for him and fed him everything that was created on the six days of Creation.
	C.	He said to him, "What your God is going to do for you is more than this!"
	D.	He said to him, "Your meal has a limit, but the meal of our God, which he is going to make for the righteous in the age to come, has no limit: 'Eye has not seen, O God, besides you what he shall do for him who waits for him' (Is. 64:3)."
14.	A	R. Simeon b. Yohai had a friend who lived nearby in Tyre.
	B.	One day he came to him. He heard his servant saying to him, "What are we going to eat today, thin lentil soup or thick lentil soup?"
	C.	He said to him, "Thin."
	D.	He began talking with him, and the friend noticed [and realized he had overheard the conversation. Therefore] he sent word to his household: "Get out for him all those silver dishes."
	E.	He said to him, "Will my Lord pay me the honor of drinking with me today?"
	F.	He said to him, "Yes."
	G.	When he went into his house, he saw all the silver dishes and was surprised. He said to him, "Will someone who has all this money eat thin lentil soup?"
	H.	He said to him, "Indeed so, my lord. As for you, your Torah-learning wins you honor, but as for us, the only honor we have is money. Without it no one honors us."
15.	A	Bar Yohania wanted to make a banquet for the aristocrats of Rome. R. Eliezer b. R. Yosé was there. He said, "Let us consult someone from our home-town."
	B.	He came to him, and he said to him, "If you want to invite twenty, make enough for twenty-five, and if you want to invite twenty-five, make enough for thirty."
	C.	He went and made enough for twenty-four and invited twenty-five.
	D.	The upshot was that they lacked one dish.
	E.	Some say it was artichokes, some, date-berries.
	F.	He took out a gold dish and set it before him, and he took it and threw it in his face, saying to him, "Now am I going to eat gold? And do I want your gold?"
	G.	He went to R. Eliezar b. R. Yosé and told him the story.
	H.	He said to him, "By your life, my lord, I should not tell you this, for you gave me advice on what to do and I didn't do it. But why I tell you is simply: I want to know whether God has revealed to you

sages the secrets only of the Torah, or perhaps also the secrets of being a good host too [literally: a banquet]?"

I.   He said to him, "True enough, he has also shown us the secrets of being a good host."

J.   He said to him, "How do you know them?"

K.   He said to him, "From David: 'So Abner came to David to Hebron, with twenty men with him. And David made a feast for Abner and the men that were with him' (2 Sam. 3:20).

L.   "What Scripture says is not, 'he made a feast,' but 'and for the men that were with him a feast.'"

16. A   ["a hundred and eighty days:"]

    B.   But here, by contrast, the last day was like the first day.

No. 9 sets off a sequence of stories about wealth, great wealth, stinginess with oneself and generosity with sages, and the like. The only reason the entire set is tacked on is No. 9, repeated thereafter with little cause. The several stories are not parallel to one another and do not make the same point. They would serve better a collection of stories on how the Torah teaches people proper conduct, how people should spend their money to support sages, and the like. In this context the entire composition is wildly out of place, since, after all, the base verse has to do with Ahasuerus's party; Ahasuerus was not a pious Jew, and the guests were not sages. On that basis I am inclined to dismiss everything beyond No. 9 as essentially out of place.

XI. Ruth Rabbah

I present an entire passage of Ruth Rabbah, so that the indicative traits of free-standing compositions may be seen with great clarity. For here is a classic set of pericopes framed for the purposes of a proposition or purpose not particular to a type of document now in our hands. Each item is autonomous and not framed for documentary purposes that are not to be discerned; my sense is that the several items that are designated are formed without regard to documentary requirements at all. By presenting the whole of the passage, I make the distinctive traits of the free-standing items transparent.

Ruth Rabbah to Ruth 1:17

XXI:I

1. A   "where you die I will die:"

    B.   this refers to the four modes of inflicting the death penalty that a court uses: stoning, burning, slaying, and strangulation.

2. A   "and there will I be buried:"

    B.   this refers to the two burial grounds that are provided for the use of the court,

	C.	one for those who are stoned and burned, the other for the use of those who are slain or strangled.
3.	A.	May the Lord do so to me and more also [if even death parts me from you]:"
	B.	She said to her, "My daughter, whatever you can accomplish in the way of religious duties and acts of righteousness in this world, accomplish.
	C.	"Truly in the age to come, 'death parts me from you.'"
4.	A.	This [proposition that after death one cannot repent (Rabinowitz, p. 41, n. 1)] is in line with the following verse: "The small and great are there alike, and the servant is free from his master" (Job 3:19).
	B.	Said R. Simon, "This is one of four scriptural verses that are alike [in presenting the same message]:
	C.	"'The small and great are there alike:' In this world one who is small can become great, and one who is great can become small, but in the world to come, one who is small cannot become great, and one who is great cannot become small.
	D.	"'and the servant is free from his master:' this is one who carries out the will of his creator and angers his evil impulse. When he dies, he goes forth into freedom: 'and the servant is free from his master.'"
5.	A.	R. Miaha son of the son of R. Joshua fell unconscious from illness from three days, and then three days later he regained consciousness.
	B.	His father said to him, "What did you see?"
	C.	He said to him, "In a world that was mixed up I found myself."
	D.	He said to him, "And what did you see there?"
	E.	He said to him, "Many people I saw who here are held in honor and there in contempt."
	F.	When R. Yohanan and R. Simeon b. Laqish heard, they came in to visit him. The father said to them, "Did you hear what this boy said?"
	G.	They said to him, "What?"
	H.	He told them the incident.
	I.	R. Simeon b. Laqish said, "And is this not an explicit verse of Scripture? 'Thus says the Lord God, the mitre shall be removed, and the crown taken off; this shall be no more the same; that which is low shall be exalted, and that which is high abased' (Ezek. 21:31)."
	J.	Said R. Yohanan, "Had I come here only to hear this matter, it would have sufficed."
6.	A.	R. Huna the exilarch asked R. Hisdai, "What is the meaning of this verse: 'Thus says the Lord God, the mitre shall be removed, and the crown taken off; this shall be no more the same; that which is low shall be exalted, and that which is high abased' (Ezek 21:31)?"

	B.	He said to him, "The mitre shall be taken away from our rabbis, and the crown shall be taken away from the gentile nations."
	C.	He said to him, "Your name is Hisdai [loving kindness] and what you say is full of *hesed* [grace]."
7.	A.	It is written, "For to him who is joined to all living there is hope; for a living dog is better than a dead lion" (Qoh. 9:4):
	B.	It has been taught on Tannaite authority there:
	C.	One who sees an idol – what should he say? Blessed is he who is patient with those who violate his will.
	D.	**[One who sees a place in which miracles were performed for Israel says, "Blessed is he who performed miracles for our fathers in this place.] One who sees a place from which idolatry has been uprooted says, "Blessed is he who uprooted idolatry from our land" [M. Ber. 9:1A-B].**
	E.	"And so may it be pleasing to you, Lord our God, that you uproot it from all places and restore the heart of those who worship idolatry to worship you with a whole heart."
	F.	But does he not then turn out to pray for wicked people?
	G.	Said R. Yohanan, "What is written [at Qoh. 9:4] is [not 'joined'] but 'chosen.'
	H.	"Even those who laid hands on the Temple have hope.
	I.	"To resurrect them is not possible, for they have indeed laid hands on the Temple.
	J.	"But to exterminate them is not possible, for they have already repented.
	K.	"To them the following verse refers: 'They shall sleep a perpetual sleep and not awake' (Jer. 51:39)."
8.	A.	It has been taught on Tannaite authority:
	B.	Minor gentiles and the armies of Nebuchadnezzar are not going to be either resurrected or punished.
	C.	To them the following verse refers: "They shall sleep a perpetual sleep and not awake" (Jer. 51:39).
9.	A.	"For to him who is joined to all living there is hope; for a living dog is better than a dead lion" (Qoh. 9:4):
	B.	In this world one who is a dog can be made into a lion, and he who is a lion can be made into a dog.
	C.	But in the world to come, a lion cannot become a dog, nor a dog a lion.
10.	A.	Hadrian – may his bones rot! – asked R. Joshua b. Hananiah, saying to him, "I am better off than your lord, Moses."
	B.	He said to him, "Why?"
	C.	"Because I am alive and he is dead, and it is written, 'For to him who is joined to all living there is hope; for a living dog is better than a dead lion' (Qoh. 9:4)."
	D.	He said to him, "Can you make a decree that no one kindle a fire for three days?"

	E.	He said to him, "Yes."
	F.	At evening the two of them went up to the roof of the palace. They saw smoke ascending from a distance.
	G.	He said to him, "What is this?"
	H.	He said to him, "It is a sick noble. The physician came to him and told him he will be healed only if he drinks hot water."
	I.	He said to him, "May your spirit go forth [drop dead]! While you are still alive, your decree is null.
	J.	"But from the time that our lord, Moses, made the decree for us, 'You shall not burn a fire in your dwelling place on the Sabbath day' (Ex. 35:3), no Jew has ever kindled a flame on the Sabbath, and even to the present day, the decree has not been nullified.
	K.	"And you say you are better off than he is?"
11.	A.	"Tell me, O Lord, what my term is, what is the measure of my days; I would know how fleeting my life is. [You have made my life just handbreadths long; its span is as nothing in your sight; no man endures longer than a breath. Man walks about as a mere shadow; mere futility is his hustle and bustle, amassing and not knowing who will gather in]" (Ps. 39:5-7):
	B.	Said David before the Holy One, blessed be he, "Lord of the world, tell me when I shall die."
	C.	He said to him, "It is a secret that is not to be revealed to a mortal, and it is not possible for me to tell you."
	D.	He said to him, "...what is the measure of my days."
	E.	He said to him, "Seventy years."
	F.	He said to him, "'I would know how fleeting my life is.' Tell me on what die I am going to die."
	G.	He said to him, "On the Sabbath."
	H.	He said to him, "Take off one day [not on the Sabbath, since on that day the body cannot be tended].
	I.	He said to him, "No."
	J.	He said to him, "Why?"
	K.	He said to him, "More precious to me is a single prayer that you stand and recite to me than a thousand whole-offerings that your son, Solomon, is going to offer before me: 'A thousand burnt-offerings did Solomon offer on that altar' (1 Kgs. 3:4)."
	L.	He said to him, "Add one day for me."
	M	He said to him, "No."
	N.	He said to him, "Why?"
	O.	He said to him, "The term of your son is at hand."
	P.	For R. Simeon b. Abba said in the name of R. Yohanan, "Terms of office are defined in advance, and one does not overlap the other even to the extent of a hair's breadth."
12.	A.	He died on a Pentecost that coincided with the Sabbath.
	B.	The Sanhedrin went in to greet Solomon.
	C.	He said to them, "Move him from one place to another."

D. They said to him, "And is it not a statement of the Mishnah: **One may anoint and wash the corpse, so long as it is not moved [M. Shab. 23:5]**?"

E. He said to them, "The dogs of father's house are hungry."

F. They said to him, "And is it not a statement of the Mishnah: **They may cut up pumpkins on the Sabbath for an animal and a carcass for dogs [M. Shab. 24:4]**?"

G. What did he then do?

H. He took a spread and spread it over the body, so that the sun should not beat down on him.

I. Some say, he called the eagles and they spread their wings over him, so that the sun should not beat down on him.

13. A It is said, "A twisted thing cannot be made straight, a lack cannot be made good" (Qoh. 1:15):

B. In this world one who is twisted can be straightened out, and one who is straight can become a crook.

C. But in the world to come, one who is twisted cannot be straightened out, and one who is straight cannot become a crook.

14. A "a lack cannot be made good" (Qoh. 1:15):

B. There are among the wicked those who were partners with one another in this world.

C. But one of them repented before his death and the other did not.

D. It turns out that this one stands in the company of the righteous, while that one stands in the company of the wicked.

E. The one sees the other and says, "Woe! Is it possible that there is favoritism in this matter? Both of us stole, both of us murdered together. Yet this one stands in the company of the righteous, while I stand in the company of the wicked."

F. And they answer him, saying, "Fool! World-class idiot! You were despicable after you died and lay for three days, and did they not grag you to your grave with ropes? 'The maggot is spread under you, the worms cover you' (Is. 14:11).

G. "But your partner understood this and reverted from that path, while you had the chance to repent and did not do it."

H. He said to them, "Give me a chance to go and repent."

I. They reply to him, saying, "World-class idiot! Don't you know that this world is like the Sabbath, while the world from which you have come is like the eve of the Sabbath? If someone does not prepare on the eve of the Sabbath, what will one eat on the Sabbath?

J. "And furthermore, this world is like the sea, while the world from which you have come is like the dry land. If someone does not prepare on dry land, what is that person going to eat when out at sea?

K. "And furthermore, this world is like the wilderness, while the world from which you have come is like the cultivated land. If someone does not prepare in the cultivated land, what is that person going to eat when out in the wilderness?"

L.   So what does he do?

M.   He folds his hands and chomps on his own flesh: "The fool folds his hands together and eats his own flesh" (Qoh. 4:5).

N.   And he says, "Let me at least see my partner in all his glory!"

O.   They answer and say to him, "World-class idiot! We have been commanded on the authority of the Almighty that the wicked will not stand beside the righteous, nor the righteous by the wicked, the clean with the unclean, nor the unclean with the unclean.

P.   "And on what are we commanded? Concerning this gate: 'This is the gate of the Lord. The righteous [alone] shall enter into it' (Ps. 118:20)."

15. A.   There is the following story.

B.   On the eve of Passover (and some say it was on the eve of the Great Fast [of the Day of Atonement]), R. Hiyya the Elder and R. Simeon b. Halafta were in session and studying the Torah in the major school house of Tiberias.

C.   They heard the noise of the crowd murmuring.

D.   One said to the other, "As to these people, what are they doing?"

E.   He said to him, "The one who has is buying, the one who doesn't have is going to his master to make him give to him."

F.   He said to him, "If so, I too will go to my lord to make him give me."

G.   He went out and prayed in the Ilsis of Tiberias [Rabinowitz, p. 46, n. 1: the famous grotto], and he saw a hand holding out a pearl to him.

H.   He went and brought it to our master [Judah the patriarch], who said to him, "Where did you get it? It is priceless. Take these three denars and go and do what you have to for the honor of the day, and after the festival, we shall announce the matter in the lost and found, and whatever price we get for it you will get."

I.   He took the three denars and went and bought what he needed to buy and went home.

J.   Said his wife to him, "Simeon, have you turned into a thief? Your whole estate is not a hundred manehs, and where did you have the money for all these purchases?"

K.   He told her the story.

L.   She said to him, "What do you want? That your canopy should be lacking by one pearl less than that of your fellow in the world to come?"

M.   He said to her, "What shall we do?"

N.   She said to him, "Go and return what you have purchased to the shopkeepers and the money to its owner and the pearl to its owner."

O.   When our master heard about this, he was upset. He sent and summoned her.

P.   He said to her, "All this suffering you have brought upon this righteous man!"

Q.   She said to him, "Do you want his canopy should be lacking by one pearl less than yours in the world to come?"

R.   He said to her, "And if it does lack, can't we make it up?"

S.   She said to him, "My lord, in this world we have the merit of seeing your face. But has not R. Simeon b. Laqish said, 'Every righteous man has his own chamber'?"

T.   And he conceded her point.

U.   [Continuing S:] "'And not only so, but it is the way of the beings of the upper world to give, but it is not their way to take back.'"

V.   [Reverting to T:] [Rabinowitz: "Nevertheless the pearl was returned"] and this latter miracle was greater than the former one.

W.   When [Simeon] took it, his hand was below, but when he gave it back, his hand was on top,

X.   like a man who lends to his fellow. [Rabinowitz, p. 47, n. 1: When R. Simeon took the pearl, it was as one receiving a gift, but when he returned it, it was as one giving a gift, in that the hand which received it was below his.]

The theme that becoming an Israelite involves special obligations and liabilities is continued at Nos. 1, 2. No. 3 completes the exposition of what is involved at 3.B. I cannot quite grasp 3.C. Rabinowitz translates, "...acquire in this world, for in the world to come, 'death shall part you and me.'" This seems to bear the message that whatever good one can do must be done in this world. That point is then illustrated in the series of stories from No. 4 to the end. But the stories wander far from the point at hand, in no way respond unanimously to the concerns of that point, and in fact are worked out one by one for purposes that can be discerned wholly within the limits of the successive tales. But I cannot conceive of some other document, other than a biographical one, in which stories of this kind will have served a redactional purpose we can identify with the program of the canonical redaction now in hand. These are free-standing stories; they serve indifferently in any context, but have been worked out without a documentary stimulus I can imagine.

8

What Is at Stake: The Three Stages of Literary Formation

I. Hermeneutics and Literary History

Once we recognize, as I have shown we must, that the rabbinic documents constitute texts, not merely scrapbooks or random compilations of ad hoc and episodic materials, both the hermeneutics and the (theoretical) history of the texts are recast. For our criteria for interpreting a passage is now the program of the document. Our interest in philology – meanings of words scattered over a variety of documents – correspondingly diminishes. The context now predominates; meanings of words and phrases, while interesting, move away from center-stage. And the texts now are seen to have histories – the texts, that is, the completed documents, and not merely the materials that the texts happen, adventitiously, to contain. And yet, we recognize, within these same thirteen well-crafted documents, sizable selections of materials did circulate from one document to another. The documentary hypothesis affects the itinerant compositions, for it identifies what writings are extra-documentary and non-documentary and imposes upon the hermeneutics and history of these writings a set of distinctive considerations too. For these writings serve the purposes not of compilers (or authors or authorships) of distinct compilations, but those of a variety of compilers; that means some writings are particular to a document and immediately express the purposes of a distinct authorship or group of compilers, while other writings work well for two or more documents. In terms of the immediately preceding chapters, the materials collected in Chapter Seven form an entity unto themselves, requiring their own hermeneutics, deriving from their own theory of literary history.

Let me expand on this point, since the movement of materials from compilation to compilation has always enjoyed prominence in such literary history and theory as have been shaped for the canon before us. By definition, according to the results of the present experiment, these other writings have been made up not with a given document's requirements in mind, but within a different theory altogether of the purpose and meaning of writing. Not only so, but, as we saw in Chapter Six, there is a class of writings, associated with the kind in Chapter Seven in its independence of existing documentary compilations, that clearly serves the purposes of compilers of a document – but not the document(s) in which these writings now find their place. Writings of this class permit us to speculate on the existence of compilations now no longer in our hands, or, more to the point, *types* of compilations we no longer possess.

II. The Priority of Documentary Hermeneutics

Before proceeding, let me restate the premise of the whole. The analysis of the types of compositions of which rabbinic compilations are made up rests upon one fundamental premise. It is that rabbinic documents are texts and not scrap-books,[1] that we moreover may identify the traits that characterize one piece of compilation and distinguish those traits from the ones that mark another compilation within the canon of the Judaism of the Dual Torah. My argument in favor of the documentary integrity of rabbinic compilations can stand reiteration.

In my study of Leviticus Rabbah I proposed to demonstrate in the case of that compilation of exegeses of Scripture that a rabbinic document constitutes a text, not merely a scrapbook or a random compilation of episodic materials. A text is a document with a purpose, one that exhibits the traits of the integrity of the parts to the whole and the fundamental autonomy of the whole from other texts. I showed

---

[1]But it must be said that some of the compilations, e.g., Leviticus Rabbah and Genesis Rabbah and Sifra, exhibit much more cogency than do others, e.g., Lamentations Rabbah and Esther Rabbah. However, I am not inclined to dismiss even Lamentations Rabbah, Esther Rabbah, and Ruth Rabbah as no more than scrapbooks. There is considerable attention among their compilers devoted to formal patterns, for one thing, and a well-crafted propositional program emerges in each of these compilations, for another. I find them admirable in their documentary cogency, but it is a different kind of coherence from that exhibited in the great Sifra or the two Sifrés. And, I hasten to add, formally we do not deal with the decadence of the form defined by Genesis Rabbah and Leviticus Rabbah, but in a revision of that form.

that the document at hand therefore falls into the classification of a cogent composition, put together with purpose and intended as a whole and in the aggregate to bear a meaning and state a message.

I therefore disproved the claim, for the case before us, that a rabbinic document serves merely as an anthology or miscellany or is to be compared only to a scrapbook, made up of this and that. In that exemplary instance I pointed to the improbability that a document has been brought together merely to join discrete and ready-made bits and pieces of episodic discourse. A document in the canon of Judaism thus does not merely define a context for the aggregation of such already completed and mutually distinct materials. Rather, I proved, that document constitutes a text. So at issue in my study of Leviticus Rabbah is what makes a text a text, that is, the textuality of a document. At stake is how we may know when a document constitutes a text and when it is merely an anthology or a scrapbook.

The importance of that issue for the correct method of comparison is clear. If we can show that a document is a miscellany, then traits of the document have no bearing on the contents of the document – things that just happen to be preserved there, rather than somewhere else. If, by contrast, the text possesses its own integrity, then everything in the text must first of all be interpreted in the context of the text, then in the context of the canon of which the text forms a constituent. Hence my stress on the comparison of whole documents, prior to the comparison of the results of exegesis contained within those documents, rests upon the result of the study of Leviticus Rabbah. Two principal issues frame the case. The first is what makes a text a text. The textuality of a text concerns whether a given piece of writing hangs together and is to be read on its own. The second is what makes a group of texts into a canon, a cogent statement all together. At issue is the relationship of two or more texts of a single, interrelated literature to the world-view and way of life of a religious tradition viewed whole.

Now it may be claimed by proponents of the view that redactional, hence documentary, considerations are of negligible importance and that powerful evidence contradicts my emphasis on the documentary origin of much writing now located in midrash compilations.[2] They point to the fact that stories and exegeses move from document to document. The travels of a given saying or story or exegesis of Scripture from one document to another validate comparing what travels quite

---

[2]These proponents are not fictive; we already have attended at length to the thought of one of them, David Weiss Halivni, who concentrates on sayings and their solitary journeys through various pericopes, scarcely attending to the traits of documents at all.

apart from what stays home. And that is precisely what comparing exegeses of the same verse of Scripture occurring in different settings does. Traveling materials enjoy their own integrity, apart from the texts – the documents – that quite adventitiously give them a temporary home. The problem of *integrity* therefore is whether or not a rabbinic document stands by itself or right at the outset forms a scarcely differentiated segment of a larger and uniform canon, one made up of materials that travel everywhere and take up residence indifferent to the traits of their temporary abode.

The reason one might suppose that, in the case of the formative age of Judaism, a document does not exhibit integrity and is not autonomous is simple. The several writings of the rabbinic canon of late antiquity, formed from the Mishnah, ca. A.D. 200, through the Talmud of Babylonia, ca. A.D. 600, with numerous items in between, do share materials – sayings, tales, protracted discussions. Some of these shared materials derive from explicitly cited documents. For instance, passages of Scripture or of the Mishnah or of the Tosefta, cited verbatim, will find their way into the two Talmuds. But sayings, stories, and sizable compositions not identified with a given, earlier text and exhibiting that text's distinctive traits will float from one document to the next.

That fact has so impressed students of the rabbinic canon as to produce a firm consensus of fifteen hundred years' standing. It is that one cannot legitimately study one document in isolation from others, describing its rhetorical, logical, literary, and conceptual traits and system all by themselves. To the contrary, all documents contribute to a common literature, or, more accurately, religion – Judaism. In the investigation of matters of rhetoric, logic, literature, and conception, whether of law or of theology, all writings join equally to given testimony to the whole. For the study of the formative history of Judaism, the issue transcends what appears to be the simple, merely literary question at hand: when is a text a text? In the context of this book: when do the interests of the framers of a text participate in the writing of their text? and when do they merely compile from ready-made materials whatever suits their purpose? In the larger context of that question we return to the issue of the peripatetic sayings, stories, and exegeses.

III. The Three Stages of Literary Formation

When I frame matters of literary theory, including literary history ("the three stages of literary formation") in terms of the problem of the rabbinic document, I ask what defines a document as such, the text-ness, the textuality, of a text. How do we know that a given book in the canon of Judaism is something other than a scrapbook? The choices are clear. One theory is that a document serves solely as a convenient repository of prior sayings and stories, available materials that will have served equally well (or poorly) wherever they took up their final location. In accord with that theory it is quite proper in ignorance of all questions of circumstance and documentary or canonical context to (to take the example of comparative midrash as presently performed) compare the exegesis of a verse of Scripture in one document with the exegesis of that verse of Scripture found in some other document.

The other theory is that a composition exhibits a viewpoint, a purpose of authorship distinctive to its framers or collectors and arrangers. Such a characteristic literary purpose – by this other theory – is so powerfully particular to one authorship that nearly everything at hand can be shown to have been (re)shaped for the ultimate purpose of the authorship at hand, that is, collectors and arrangers who demand the title of authors. In accord with this other theory context and circumstance form the prior condition of inquiry, the result, in exegetical terms, the contingent one. To resort again to a less than felicitous neologism, I thus ask what signifies or defines the "document-ness" of a document and what makes a book a book. I therefore wonder whether there are specific texts in the canonical context of Judaism or whether all texts are merely contextual. In framing the question as I have, I of course lay forth the mode of answering it. We have to confront a single rabbinic composition, and ask about its definitive traits and viewpoint.

IV. Itinerancy and Documentary Integrity: The Problem of the Peripatetic Composition

But we have also to confront the issue of the traveling sayings, the sources upon which the redactors of a given document have drawn. For there are sayings that do travel from one document to another without exhibiting much wear from the journey, and, as I shall show in Part Three, there also are sources that are equally at home everywhere because they belong nowhere. And such sources call into question the documentary theory of the making of the classics in Judaism that I present in this book. So let us turn to the matter of what is called "the sources."[3]

---

[3]This is defined at great length in my treatment of Halivni's theory of sources and traditions given above. As is clear, I have now redefined "sources" and "traditions" at the end, in terms that I think far more suitable.

By "sources" I mean (for the purposes of argument here) simply passages in a given book that occur, also, in some other rabbinic book. Such sources – by definition prior to the books in which they appear – fall into the classification of materials general to two or more compositions and by definition not distinctive and particular to any one of them. The word "source" therefore serves as an analogy to convey the notion that two or more sets of authors have made use of a single, available item. About whether the shared item is prior to them both or borrowed by one from the other at this stage we cannot speculate.[4]

Let me now summarize this phase of the argument. We ask about the textuality of a document – is it a composition or a scrapbook? – so as to determine the appropriate foundations for comparison, the correct classifications for comparative study. We seek to determine the correct context of comparison, hence the appropriate classification. My claim is simple: once we know what is unique to a document, we can investigate the traits that characterize all the document's unique and so definitive materials. We ask about whether the materials unique to a document also cohere, or whether they prove merely miscellaneous. If they do cohere, we may conclude that the framers of the document have followed a single plan and a program. That would in my view justify the claim that the framers carried out a labor not only of conglomeration, arrangement, and selection, but also of genuine authorship or composition in the narrow and strict sense of the word. If so, the document emerges from authors, not merely arrangers and compositors. For the same purpose, therefore, we also take up and analyze the items shared between that document and some other or among several documents. We ask about the traits of those items, one by one and all in the aggregate. In these stages we may solve for the

---

[4]To state the consequences for comparative midrash, which has received attention in its own terms: These shared items, transcending two or more documents and even two or more complete systems or groups, if paramount and preponderant, would surely justify the claim that we may compare [3] exegeses of verses of Scripture without attention to [2] context. Why? Because there is no context defined by the limits of a given document and its characteristic plan and program. All the documents do is collect and arrange available materials. The document does not define the context of its contents. If that can be shown, then *comparative midrash* may quite properly ignore the contextual dimension imparted to sayings, including exegeses of Scripture, by their occurrence in one document rather than some other. In this connection, see my *Comparative Midrash: The Plan and Program of Genesis Rabbah and Leviticus Rabbah.* Atlanta, 1986: Scholars Press for Brown Judaic Studies. *Comparative Midrash* II. *The Plan and Program of Lamentations Rabbah, Esther Rabbah, Ruth Rabbah, and Song of Songs Rabbah* is planned.

case at hand the problem of the rabbinic document: do we deal with a scrapbook or a cogent composition? A text or merely a literary expression, random and essentially promiscuous, of a larger theological context? That is the choice at hand.

Since we have reached a matter of fact, let me state the facts as they are. To begin with, I describe the relationships among the principal components of the literature with which we deal. The several documents that make up the canon of Judaism in late antiquity relate to one another in three important ways.

First, all of them refer to the same basic writing, the Hebrew Scriptures. Many of them draw upon the Mishnah and quote it. So the components of the canon join at their foundations.

Second, as the documents reached closure in sequence, the later authorship can be shown to have drawn upon earlier, completed documents. So the writings of the rabbis of the talmudic corpus accumulate and build from layer to layer.

Third, as I have already hinted, among two or more documents some completed units of discourse (and many brief, discrete sayings) circulated, for instance, sentences or episodic homilies or fixed apophthegms of various kinds. So in some (indeterminate) measure the several documents draw not only upon one another, as we can show, but also upon a common corpus of materials that might serve diverse editorial and redactional purposes.

The extent of this common corpus can never be fully known. Chapters Five and Six of this book present what can have formed a common corpus. But we know only what we have, not what we do not have. So we cannot say what has been omitted, or whether sayings that occur in only one document derive from materials available to the editors or compilers of some or all other documents. That is something we never can know. We can describe only what is in our hands and interpret only the data before us. Of indeterminates and endless speculative possibilities we need take no account. In taking up documents one by one, do we not obscure their larger context and their points in common?

In fact, shared materials proved for Leviticus Rabbah not many and not definitive. They form an infinitesimal proportion of Genesis Rabbah, under 3-5 percent of the volume of the *parashiyyot* for which I conducted probes.[5]. Materials that occur in both Leviticus Rabbah and

---

[5]There were two kinds of exceptions. First, entire *parashiyyot* occur in both Leviticus Rabbah and, verbatim, in Pesiqta deRab Kahana. Second, Genesis Rabbah and Leviticus Rabbah share sizable compositions. The former sort always conform to the formal program of Leviticus Rabbah. They in no way

some other document prove formally miscellaneous and share no single viewpoint or program; they are random and brief. What is unique to Leviticus Rabbah and exhibits that document's characteristic formal traits also predominates and bears the message of the whole. So much for the issue of the peripatetic exegesis. To date I have taken up the issue of homogeneity of "sources," in a limited and mainly formal setting, for the matter of how sayings and stories travel episodically from one document to the next.[6] The real issue is not the traveling, but the unique, materials: the documents, and not what is shared among them. The variable – what moves – is subject to analysis only against the constant: the document itself.

V. Theology and Hermeneutics:
The Unacknowledged Participant in the Debate

To describe and analyze documents one by one violates the lines of order and system that have characterized all earlier studies of these same documents. Until now, just as people compared exegeses among different groups of a given verse of Scripture without contrasting one circumstance to another, so they tended to treat all of the canonical texts as uniform in context, that is, as testimonies to a single system and structure, that is, to Judaism. What sort of testimonies texts provide varies according to the interest of those who study them. That is why, without regard to the source of the two expositions of the same verse, people would compare one *midrash*, meaning the interpretation of a given verse of Scripture, with another *midrash* on the same verse of Scripture. True enough, philologians look for meanings of words and phrases, better versions of a text. For them all canonical documents equally serve as a treasury of philological facts and variant readings. Theologians study all texts equally, looking for God's will and finding testimonies to God in each component of the Torah of Moses our Rabbi. Why so? Because all texts ordinarily are taken to form a common statement, "Torah" in the mythic setting, "Judaism" in the theological one.

But comparison cannot be properly carried out on such a basis. The hermeneutical issue dictated by the system overall defines the result of description, analysis, and interpretation. Let me give a single

---

stand separate from the larger definitive and distinctive traits of the document. The latter sort fit quite comfortably, both formally and programmatically, into both Genesis Rabbah and Leviticus Rabbah, because those two documents themselves constitute species of a single genus.

[6]*The Peripatetic Saying. The Problem of the Thrice-Told Tale in Talmudic Literature* (Chico, 1985).

probative example. From the classical perspective of the theology of Judaism the entire canon of Judaism ("the one whole Torah of Moses, our rabbi") equally and at every point testifies to the entirety of Judaism. Why so? Because all documents in the end form components of a single system. Each makes its contribution to the whole. If, therefore, we wish to know what "Judaism" or, more accurately, "the Torah," teaches on any subject, we are able to draw freely on sayings relevant to that subject wherever they occur in the entire canon of Judaism. Guided only by the taste and judgment of the great sages of the Torah, as they have addressed the question at hand, we thereby describe "Judaism." And that same theological conviction explains why we may rip a passage out of its redactional context and compare it with another passage, also seized from its redactional setting. It goes without saying that the theological *apologia* for doing so has yet to reach expression; and there can be no other than a theological *apologia*. In logic I see none; epistemologically there never was one. The presence of a theological premise has yet to be acknowledged, or even recognized, by exponents of the anti-documentary hermeneutic and theory of literary history alike.

VI. Autonomy, Connection, Continuity

In fact documents stand in three relationships to one another and to the system of which they form part, that is, to Judaism, as a whole. The specification of these relationships constitutes the principal premise of this inquiry and validates the approach to the formation of compositions and composites that I offer here.

[1] Each document is to be seen all by itself, that is, as autonomous of all others.

[2] Each document is to be examined for its relationships with other documents universally regarded as falling into the same classification, as Torah.

[3] And, finally, in the theology of Judaism (or, in another context, of Christianity) each document is to be allowed to take its place as part of the undifferentiated aggregation of documents that, all together, constitute the canon of, in the case of Judaism, the "one whole Torah revealed by God to Moses at Mount Sinai."

Simple logic makes self-evident the proposition that, if a document comes down to us within its own framework, as a complete book with a beginning, middle, and end, in preserving that book, the canon presents us with a document on its own and not solely as part of a larger composition or construct. So we too see the document as it reaches us, that is, as autonomous.

If, second, a document contains materials shared verbatim or in substantial content with other documents of its classification, or if one document refers to the contents of other documents, then the several documents that clearly wish to engage in conversation with one another have to address one another. That is to say, we have to seek for the marks of connectedness, asking for the meaning of those connections. It is at this level of connectedness that we labor. For the purpose of comparison is to tell us what is like something else, what is unlike something else. To begin with, we can declare something unlike something else only if we know that it is like that other thing. Otherwise the original judgment bears no sense whatsoever. So, once more, canon defines context, or, in descriptive language, the first classification for comparative study is the document, brought into juxtaposition with, and contrast to, another document.

Finally, since the community of the faithful of Judaism, in all of the contemporary expressions of Judaism, concur that documents held to be authoritative constitute one whole, seamless "Torah," that is, a complete and exhaustive statement of God's will for Israel and humanity, we take as a further appropriate task, if one not to be done here, the description of the whole out of the undifferentiated testimony of all of its parts. These components in the theological context are viewed, as is clear, as equally authoritative for the composition of the whole: one, continuous system. In taking up such a question, we address a problem not of theology alone, though it is a correct theological conviction, but one of description, analysis, and interpretation of an entirely historical order.

In my view the various documents of the canon of Judaism produced in late antiquity demand a hermeneutic altogether different from the one of homogenization and harmonization, the ahistorical and anti-contextual one definitive for the prevailing hermeneutic and theory of literary history. It is one that does not harmonize but that differentiates. It is a hermeneutic shaped to teach us how to read the compilations of exegeses first of all one by one and in a particular context, and second, in comparison with one another.

Let me review in this context out the method I applied to both Rabbah compilations[7] and plan to apply to the four final Rabbah compilations later on: Lamentations Rabbah, Esther Rabbah, Ruth Rabbah, and Song of Songs Rabbah.[8] It is not complicated and rests

---

[7]Reference is made to *The Integrity of Leviticus Rabbah* (Chico, 1985), and *Comparative Midrash: The Program and Plan of Genesis Rabbah and Leviticus Rabbah* (Atlanta, 1985).
[8]This will be *Comparative Midrash II*.

upon what seem to me self-evident premises. I have to prove that the document at hand rests upon clear-cut choices of formal and rhetorical preference, so it is, from the viewpoint of form and mode of expression, cogent. I have to demonstrate that these formal choices prove uniform and paramount. So for the several compilations I have analyzed large *parashiyyot* (systematic and sustained compositions of exegeses) to show their recurrent structures. These I categorize. Then, I proceed to survey all *parashiyyot* of each of the complete compilations and find out whether or not every *parashah* of the entire document finds within a single cogent taxonomic structure suitable classifications for its diverse units of discourse. If one taxonomy serves all and encompasses the bulk of the units of discourse at hand, I may fairly claim that Leviticus Rabbah or Genesis Rabbah, or Lamentations Rabbah, Esther Rabbah, and Ruth Rabbah, respectively, do constitute a cogent formal structure, based upon patterns of rhetoric uniform and characteristic throughout.

My next step, for the several probes and documents, is to ask whether the framers of the document preserved a fixed order in arranging types of units of discourse, differentiated in accord with the forms I identified. In both documents I am able to show that, in ordering materials, the framers or redactors paid much attention to the formal traits of their units of discourse. They chose materials of one formal type for beginning their sustained exercises of argument or syllogism, then chose another formal type for the end of their sustained exercises of syllogistic exposition. This seems to me to show that the framers or redactors followed a set of rules which we are able to discern. Finally, in the case of the several documents, I outline the program and show the main points of emphasis and interest presented in each. In this way I characterize the program as systematically as I described the plan. In this way I answer the question, for the documents under study, of whether or not we deal with a text, exhibiting traits of composition, deliberation, proportion, and so delivering a message on its own. Since we do, then Leviticus Rabbah or Genesis Rabbah, on the one side, and Lamentation Rabbah, Esther Rabbah, Ruth Rabbah, and Song of Songs Rabbah, on the other, do demand description, analysis, and interpretation first of all each compilation on its own, as an autonomous statement. It then requires comparison and contrast with other compositions of its species of the rabbinic genus, that is to say, it demands to be brought into connection with, relationship to, other rabbinic compositions.[9]

---

[9]The quite separate question of the use and meaning of Scripture in Judaism is addressed in my *Judaism and Scripture: The Evidence of Leviticus Rabbah*

VII. The Next Stage

My "three stages" in ordinal sequence correspond, as a matter of fact, to three types of writing. The first – and last in assumed temporal order – is writing carried out in the context of the making, or compilation, of a classic. That writing responds to the redactional program and plan of the authorship of a classic. The second, penultimate in order, is writing that can appear in a given document but better serves a document other than the one in which it (singularly) occurs. This kind of writing seems to me not to fall within the same period of redaction as the first. For while it is a type of writing under the identical conditions, it also is writing that presupposes redactional programs in no way in play in the ultimate, and definitive, period of the formation of the canon: when people did things this way, and not in some other. That is why I think it is a kind of writing that was done prior to the period in which people limited their redactional work and associated labor of composition to the program that yielded the books we now have.

The upshot is simple: whether the classification of writing be given a temporal or merely taxonomic valence, the issue is the same: have these writers done their work with documentary considerations in mind? I believe I have shown that they have not. Then where did they expect their work to makes its way? Anywhere it might, because, so they assumed, fitting in no where in particular, it found a suitable locus everywhere it turned up. But I think temporal, not merely taxonomic, considerations pertain. Let me say why.

The third kind of writing seems to me to originate in a period prior to the other two. It is carried on in a manner independent of all redactional considerations such as are known to us. Then it should derive from a time when redactional considerations played no paramount role in the making of compositions. A brief essay, rather than a sustained composition, was then the dominant mode of writing. My hypothesis is that people can have written both long and short compositions – compositions and composites, in my language – at one and the same time. But writing that does not presuppose a secondary labor of redaction, e.g., in a composite, probably originated when authors or authorships did not anticipate any fate for their writing beyond their labor of composition itself.

(Chicago, 1986: University of Chicago Press). The beginning of my theological path is marked by *Writing with Scripture: The Authority and Uses of the Hebrew Bible in the Torah of Formative Judaism* (Minneapolis, 1989: Fortress Press) [with William Scott Green].

Along these same lines of argument, this writing may or may not travel from one document to another. What that means is that the author or authorship does not imagine a future for his writing. What fits anywhere is composed to go nowhere in particular. Accordingly, what matters is not whether a writing fits one document or another, but whether, as the author or authorship has composed a piece of writing, that writing meets the requirements of any document we now have or can even imagine. If it does not, then we deal with a literary period in which the main kind of writing was ad hoc and episodic, not sustained and documentary.

Now this second and third kind of writing – the kind richly exemplified in Chapters Six and Seven – seems to me to derive from either [1] a period prior to the work of the making of midrash compilations and the two Talmuds alike; or [2] a labor of composition not subject to the rules and considerations that operated in the work of the making of midrash compilations and the two Talmuds. As a matter of hypothesis, I should guess that what is in Chapter Seven comes prior to making any kind of documents of consequence, and what is in Chapter Six comes prior to the period in which the specific documents we now have were subject to formation. That is to say, writing that can fit anywhere or nowhere is prior to writing that can fit somewhere but does not fit anywhere now accessible to us, and both kinds of writing are prior to the kind that fits only in what documents in which it is now located.

And given the documentary propositions and theses that we can locate in all of our compilations, we can only assume that the non-documentary writings enjoyed, and were assumed to enjoy, ecumenical acceptance. That means, very simply, when we wish to know the consensus of the entire canonical community – I mean simply the people, anywhere and any time, responsible for everything we now have – we turn not to the distinctive perspective of documents, but the (apparently universally acceptable) perspective of the extra-documentary compositions. That is the point at which we should look for the propositions everywhere accepted but nowhere advanced in a distinctive way, the "Judaism beyond the texts" – or behind them.

Do I place a priority, in the framing of a hypothesis, on taxonomy or temporal order? Indeed I do, as the title of this book suggests. I could have spoken of three types of writing, rather than speaking of the sequence in which these types of writing took shape. Accordingly, I am inclined to suppose that non-documentary compositions took shape not only separated from, but in time before, the documentary ones did. My reason for thinking so is worth rehearsing, even though it is not yet compelling. The kinds of non-documentary writing I have assembled in

Chapter Seven (and, I hasten to add, a good case can be made for the inclusion of the non-extant documentary writing in Chapter Six!) focus on matters of very general interest.

These matters may be assembled into two very large rubrics: virtue, on the one side, reason, on the other. Stories about sages fall into the former category; all of them set forth in concrete form the right living that sages exemplify. Essays on right thinking, the role of reason, the taxonomic priority of Scripture, the power of analogy, the exemplary character of cases and precedents in the expression of general and encompassing rules – all of these intellectually coercive writings set forth rules of thought as universally applicable, in their way, as are the rules of conduct contained in stories about sages, in theirs. A great labor of generalization is contained in both kinds of non-documentary and extra-documentary writing. And the results of that labor are then given concrete expression in the documentary writings in hand; for these, after all, do say in the setting of specific passages or problems precisely what, in a highly general way, emerges from the writing that moves hither and yon, never with a home, always finding a suitable resting place.

Now, admittedly, that rather general characterization of the non-documentary writing is subject to considerable qualification and clarification. But it does provide a reason to assign temporal priority, not solely taxonomic distinction, to the non-documentary compositions I have assembled for exemplary purposes in Chapter Seven (and, again, also in Chapter Six). We can have had commentaries of a sustained and systematic sort on Chronicles, on the one side, treatises on virtue, on the second, gospels, on the third – to complete the triangle. But we do not have these kinds of books.

I wish our sages had made treatises on right action and right thought, in their own idiom to be sure, because I think these treatises will have shaped the intellect of generations to come in a more effective way than the discrete writings, submerged in collections and composites of other sorts altogether, have been able to do. Compositions on correct behavior made later on filled the gap left open by the redactional decisions made in the period under study; I do not know why no one assembled a midrash on right action in the way in which, in Leviticus Rabbah and Genesis Rabbah, treatises on the rules of society and the rules of history were compiled. And still more do I miss those intellectually remarkable treatises on right thought that our sages can have produced out of the rich resources in hand: the art of generalization, the craft of comparison and contrast, for example. In this regard the Mishnah, with its union of (some) Aristotelian modes of thought and (some) neo-Platonic propositions forms the model, if a lonely one, for what can have been achieved, even in the odd and unphilosophical idiom of our sages.[10] The compositions needed for both kinds of treatises – and, as a matter of fact, many, many of them – are fully in hand. But no one made the compilations of them.

The books we do have not only preserve the evidences of the possibility of commentaries and biographies. More than that, they also bring to rich expression the messages that such books will have set forth. And most important, they also express in fresh and unanticipated contexts those virtues and values that commentaries and biographies ("gospels") meant to bring to realization, and they do so in accord with the modes of thought that sophisticated reflection on right thinking has exemplified in its way as well. So when people went about the work of making documents, they did something fresh with something familiar. They made cogent compositions, documents, texts enjoying integrity and autonomy. But they did so in such a way as to form of their distinct documents a coherent body of writing, of books, a canon, of documents, a system. And this they did in such a way as to say, in distinctive and specific ways, things that, in former times, people had expressed in general and broadly applicable ways. We have moved beyond the wild storms of inchoate speculation, but have yet to reach the safe harbor of established fact. But the course is true, the destination in sight, the journey's end not at all in doubt.

---

[10]This is fully explained in my *Philosophical Mishnah* (Atlanta, 1989: Scholars Press for Brown Judaic Studies) I-IV, and in my *The Philosophy of Judaism: The First Principles* (in press).

Index

273

Brown Judaic Studies

Brown Studies on Jews and Their Societies

Brown Studies in Religion